PERSPECTIVES ON MUSIC

DONALD C. MEYER

Lake Forest College

Pearson
Education

PRENTICE HALL

Upper Saddle River, New Jersey 07458

Library of Congress Cataloging-in-Publication Data

Meyer, Donald Carl.
    Perspectives on music / Donald C. Meyer.
        p. cm.
    Includes index.
    ISBN 0-13-030440-9
    1. Music appreciation. I. Title.

MT90 .M49 2002
780—dc21   2002075438

Editorial Director: *Charlyce Jones Owen*
Senior Acquisitions Editor: *Christopher T. Johnson*
Editorial Assistant: *Evette Dickerson*
Art Director: *Nancy Wells*
Interior & Cover Designer: *Jill Lehan*
Cover Art: *Warhol, Andy. Beethoven, 1987.*
Screenprint on Lenox Museum Board, 40"×40".
© Copyright The Andy Warhol
Foundation for the Visual Arts/ARS, NY.
Art Resource, NY.
Marketing Manager: *Chris Ruel*

AVP, Director of Production and Manufacturing:
Barbara Kittle
Manufacturing Manager: *Nick Sklitsis*
Prepress and Manufacturing Buyer: *Benjamin D. Smith*
Production Editor: *Jean Lapidus*
Photo Researcher: *Julie Tesser*
Image Permissions Coordinator: *Valerie Gold*
Artist: *Mirella Signoretto*
Copy Editor: *Stephen C. Hopkins*
Music Permissions Specialist: *Elsa Peterson Ltd.*

This book was set in 10/15 Adobe Garamond by
Interactive Composition Corporation
and was printed and bound by Courier Companies, Inc.
The cover, end papers, & color inserts
were printed by Phoenix Color Corp.

© 2003 by Pearson Education, Inc.
Upper Saddle River, New Jersey 07458

Printed in the United States of America
10 9 8 7 6 5 4 3 2 1

ISBN 0-13-030440-9

Pearson Education Ltd.
Pearson Education Australia Pty. Ltd.
Pearson Education Singapore, Pte. Ltd.
Pearson Education North Asia Ltd.
Pearson Education Canada Ltd.
Pearson Educación de Mexico, S.A. de C.V.
Pearson Education – Tokyo, Japan
Pearson Education Malaysia, Pte. Ltd.
Pearson Education, Upper Saddle River, New Jersey

DEDICATION

To my parents, John and Norma Meyer

CONTENTS

PREFACE: *To the Instructor*

*P*erspectives on Music was created to increase the flexibility for teachers of music appreciation classes and to enhance student learning and enjoyment. These goals are pursued primarily through two significant differences between the standard music appreciation textbook and *Perspectives on Music*:

- An equal amount of time is spent on popular and classical music styles, rather than an emphasis primarily on classical music.
- The usual listening guides are replaced with more interactive Listening Activities.

The first of these changes stems from my belief that popular music is an important part of contemporary music culture, something students will enjoy learning more about while still honing their listening skills. Studying popular musical styles that are more familiar to the students can increase their confidence when they begin studying classical music, while also improving their overall satisfaction with the course.

The second of these changes, the use of Listening Activities, stems in part from the pedagogical research of Barbara E. Walvoord of Notre Dame University. Following her approach that uses more skills-oriented teaching, the Listening Activities in *Perspectives on Music* give students much more practice in listening attentively than do most music appreciation textbooks. The Listening Activities also provide greater flexibility for instructors, as is shown below. Further discussion of Walvoord's teaching principles can be found in the Instructor's Manual accompanying this book.

There are also several other features of *Perspectives on Music* that are aimed at improving the flexibility for the instructor and the experience for the student:

1. *Possibility for Modular Teaching.* The *Styles* section of the book, Chapters 7 through 15, is written so that it is easier for instructors to reorganize and cut out chapters to suit their needs. These chapters are written as self-contained units, with only occasional references to different styles or periods. This flexibility is intended both to suit the individual needs of instructors and the changing needs of an instructor from term to term. One professor might enjoy discussing classical music and jazz, and wish to focus on these styles in the class; another might want to teach only the classical material, or emphasize the popular styles more. Or it might happen that in a particular semester a fine jazz artist will be coming to an instructor's university late in the term. The instructor can simply move Chapter 8, "JAZZ," to the end of the syllabus.

2. *More Flexibility.* The Listening Activities are designed to be used in a wide variety of ways, depending on the needs and preferences of the instructor. In a small class, an instructor might assign some or all of the Listening Activities and grade them, or have them graded by a teaching assistant, if one is available. They can also be assigned, but simply checked off and not graded. The Activities can also be used simply for the students' own use, as training for the listening skills they will need to exhibit on exams or in concert reports. Finally, the Activities can be a most effective tool for in-class work. Compared with the standard prewritten listening guide, students will remain more engaged in the lecture if they are asked to fill in the answers as the instructor works out a solution in class.

3. *Pedagogical Aids.* The textbook is designed with several devices to aid student learning: Important terms are listed in the margins of the textbook; these terms are gathered together at the end of each chapter as *Key Terms,* and also defined in the on-line Glossary; and once or twice per chapter there is a concise summary of the material covered, under the heading *Checkpoints.* The companion website has extra Listening Activities and dozens of MIDI files to illustrate examples in the text.

4. *A More Graphic Look.* The textbook is aimed at students with no musical background. Many music appreciation textbooks feature musical examples, but I have found this can leave behind those students who have no training on instruments or voice. Instead, *Perspectives* makes use of graphic illustrations to represent musical lines, aiding those students who learn visually, but not unfairly favoring those with a musical background.

5. *Elimination of Early Music.* Every textbook must make some compromises. Here, because of the extra emphasis given to the blues, jazz, rock, and Latino musical styles, some classical music had to be cut. One reason for this decision has to do with the availability of concerts. Despite the Early Music revival, concerts of classical music written since 1700 are still easier to find for those instructors who use concert reports as a part of class work. This decision also stems from the difficulty of adequately explaining to beginning music students the millennium of music before the Common Practice Period.

It is my hope that *Perspectives on Music* will prove easy to adopt for those using a standard music appreciation textbook, and will be an effective tool for introducing students to the life-long habit of listening attentively to the various musical styles of Western culture.

DONALD C. MEYER
Highland Park, Illinois

ACKNOWLEDGMENTS

I am grateful to Christopher Johnson, senior acquisitions editor at Prentice Hall, for his willingness to take a chance on this new approach and for all his wisdom and encouragement as this project has come to fruition. I would also like to thank several colleagues at Lake Forest College for reading portions of the manuscript and offering invaluable suggestions: Associate Dean of the College Daniel López (who also translated some Spanish lyrics for Chapter 10) and Professors Judy Dozier, Bob Holliday, Rami Levin, and Rand Smith, in addition to my brother, Syracuse University musicologist Stephen Meyer.

The following reviewers (hired by Prentice Hall) also read this manuscript carefully and helped to improve it, in some cases through two rounds, and I am deeply indebted to them: Dr. Andra Bohnet, University of South Alabama; Dr. David Chevan, Southern Connecticut State University; Dr. John R. Dulaney, University of Mississippi; Billie Gateley, Jackson State Community College; Dr. Norma Humphreys, Ohio University; Dr. Stephen Jablonsky, The City College of New York; Kevin D. Miller, Eastern Michigan University; Dr. Joel Pugh, Heidelberg College; Dr. Douglas Rose, Albion College; Dr. Floyd Slotterback, Northern Michigan University; and Dr. Donald Williams, Marshall University.

Three students at Lake Forest College, Becky Derrico, Iwona Bielaszka, and Erin Lucido, served as assistants as I class-tested this manuscript in 2000 and 2001, providing the student perspective on the manuscript. Anjali Pai, another student, was a wonderful assistant to me as I made revisions during the summer of 2001.

I am fortunate to have started my career in higher education under a master teacher-scholar at UC Davis, D. Kern Holoman, and many of the ideas that resulted in this book first appeared as I served as his teaching assistant in the early 1990s. I also learned a great deal from my graduate student colleagues in those days, especially Matthew Daines. This book would not have been possible without the help of all these colleagues, past and present, known and unknown, and without a generous junior-faculty sabbatical program offered by Lake Forest College. Finally, I am thankful to my wife, Liz, who has supported me in all possible ways as I created *Perspectives on Music*.

Introduction:
Learning to Listen

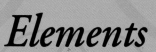

Imagine the following scenarios:

One of your newest friends is a complete jazz nut. She listens to it all the time and talks about people you've never heard of like Miles and Monk as if they were personal friends of hers. When you go to her place, she often has jazz recordings on, but you're too embarrassed to ask what on Earth she likes about this strange music. One day, however, she pins you down. "Do you like John Coltrane?" she asks, and you have to confess that, while you've heard *of* him, you've never heard his music. "Oh!" she laughs, "Have I got a treat for you!" She selects one of her favorite CD's, puts it on, then sits down with you and explains the basics of listening to jazz, and what makes Coltrane so great. By the end of the afternoon, you're converted.

You're visiting relatives in another state, where your crazy Aunt Judith has bought everyone tickets to the opera. You groan. You feign sudden illness, but she sees through it and demands that you come. You know you're going to hate it. Once you're there, in the glittering opera house, with the audience in tuxedos and evening gowns, and the orchestra beginning its scintillating introduction, and the singers starting to sing, you realize. . . you still hate it. In fact, you'll always hate it. But now you don't hate it out of ignorance; now, you can say with intelligence what qualities you like and dislike. In the end, you're glad you went.

Substitute any kind of music for *jazz* and *opera* in the scenarios above, and perhaps you've experienced something similar. At various times in our lives we receive exposure to new music, and only in rare instances does this first contact produce an immediate passion. Quite the opposite: usually our first reaction to new music is negative, or just indifferent. At best, we respect the fact that other people like it, but return to our own music as quickly as possible. We only come to like the music with repeated exposure to it, or if we are lucky enough to have a friend to help us understand it.

Teenagers hanging out at home, talking, and listening to CDs. Photo by Nancy Richmond.
Source: *The Image Works.*

This book serves a similar function: it is to be a musical friend, providing tips for making sense of new music. Some of the music discussed in *Perspectives on Music* will be familiar to you already—although different readers may be familiar with different kinds of music. Some of the music will be new. Some of this music will appeal to you, and some may not. The goal of this book is not to force you to like different music, although it would be fine if this happened. Rather, the goals of the book are these:

- To improve listening skills, no matter what the music.
- To examine familiar music in the context of historical, social, and other artistic forces.
- To expose the reader to some of the most important musical styles in currency today.
- To develop the ability to talk, think, and write about music intelligently.

ORGANIZATION

*P*erspectives on Music is organized into two parts, *Elements* and *Styles*. The *Elements* section provides a close examination of five fundamental elements of music that usually appear in all different musical styles in one form or another: rhythm, melody, harmony, timbre, and form. Along the way, we will examine other elements that are used in some musical styles but not others.

Next comes the *Styles* section, which presents detailed information about several popular and classical styles of music. We use the term *style* in the same sense as the word is used by printers and publishers: a set of rules that allows for general consistency among several works of art. When we talk about the blues,

for example, there are a specific set of rules musicians use to govern what they do, and that are used only in that style of music. A blues musician knows that the standard lyric structure for the twelve-bar blues is AAB—he or she sings a line, repeats it, then sings another line that rhymes with the first. Sometimes, a musician may choose to break the rules, but this does not mean that the rules do not exist. In some cases, musicians work with these rules instinctively; in other cases, they are very conscious of the rules of their musical style. Whatever the case, it is the flexible application of rules which makes one musical style distinct from another.

Elements Section

Styles Section

LEARNING TO LISTEN

LISTENING FOR STYLE

*I*n fact, understanding the rules of a style is one of the first steps in intelligent listening. One of the first mistakes people make when listening to new music is applying the rules of one style to another. You've probably heard people say they hate rap music for some reason—perhaps they say it's because there's no melody in rap. If you like

rap, you may have indignantly responded that, first of all, rap isn't really about melody—you listen for the rich dance grooves and the brilliant, improvised rhyming; and second, rap in fact does have some melody in it, some rather fine melodies—you just have to listen for them. Or it may be that rap is criticized for its use of sampling, a tactic considered tantamount to piracy in other styles, such as rock. Saying that rap is illegitimate for the use of sampling is as silly as saying rock is illegitimate because there's usually no dancing on stage at concerts. The two styles have different rules of operation.

Here's another example: in the early days of rock, members of the older jazz generation criticized the new music based on how it operated according to the rules of jazz. In jazz, improvisation—the ability to make up new music in solos—is very important. Many rock musicians did not improvise well, and some didn't even improvise at all. Jazz fans also criticized rock recordings. In jazz, recordings are judged by how well they capture the spirit of live performance, but in rock, recordings are generally put together layer by layer in a recording studio. Because of these two "deficiencies," among others, jazz lovers thought rock musicians had no talent. Of course, not all jazz fans hated rock, but those that did tended to assume that rock was supposed to follow the rules of jazz, rather than follow its own rules as a new musical style with different parameters. The best rock musicians are just as talented as the best jazz or classical musicians; it's just that their talent is used in a different manner, to achieve different ends.

The truth is, there is no such thing as a bad musical style. This is not to say there is no such thing as bad music—far from it. Every musical style has good and bad examples in it, based on how the musicians make use of the rules of the style. And we are certainly free to like some styles of music more than others, just as one person may prefer to watch tennis more than baseball. But in any case—be it sports or music—you can only make sense of what's happening once you understand the rules of the game.

LISTENING FOR FUNCTION

*A*nother important aspect of music is its *function,* the purpose of the music. Some music, for example, is associated with religious experiences, such as the ecstatic sounds of a gospel choir, or the trancelike Navajo chants that call on ancestral spirits. Music has also been used among workers to coordinate their physical activities, such as chopping trees or driving railroad ties, and by children to coordinate jumping rope and other games. In the

Chain gang building a road. Photo by Bettmann.
Source: CORBIS.

past, music was also used to relate stories, to pass on information and legends. Throughout history, music has provided the accompaniment for all kinds of dancing. Similarly, music has been combined with other art forms, such as drama, to create new hybrid art forms such as opera (these combinations are discussed in Chapter 15). Many people use music to set a mood or an atmosphere while they attend to other activities such as eating or studying. And then there is music to be listened to attentively, with complete concentration. This is the function we focus on in *Perspectives on Music*. Just as in the case of musical styles, knowing the intended function of a piece of music can help you know what to expect and how to enjoy it.

The music of any particular style may fall under several function categories. Partly this is just because of the free will of listeners—one person may listen closely to a baroque concerto grosso, while another may use the same music to do the dishes by. Musical styles also are intended for different functions in different settings and times. Jazz, for example, passed through a period in which everyone danced to it,

then evolved into music for listening. There is no right or wrong function to any kind of music.

Listening to music attentively, however, is probably the most challenging of these different kinds of musical function—and the most rewarding.

LISTENING VERSUS HEARING

One of the challenges to attentive listening is simply the fast pace of our lives. We live in an age of speed: fast internet connections, sound-bite political speeches, and shorter and shorter commercials. We have lost some of our ability to concentrate over long stretches. Nineteenth-century Americans would think nothing of attending a four-hour concert or reading multivolume books, but we have primed our minds for quick gratification.

We also live in a very visually oriented society. From movies to television to the internet, most of

LISTENING ACTIVITY 1.1:

Environmental Listening

Learning to listen attentively is mostly a matter of training your mind to focus on sounds for longer and longer stretches. This first Listening Activity can be done anywhere, but it should be completed in a comfortable location that you can return to later. Use a separate sheet of paper. At the top, write your name, course number, and section, if appropriate, and the date and time. Then answer the questions below in three separate paragraphs, using complete sentences.

1. As soon as you finish reading this sentence write down what you hear in your immediate environment.
2. After you finish the above, set down your pen or pencil, close your eyes for five minutes, and truly *listen.* Do not interrupt the five-minute listening session to write down new sounds; maintain your quiet pose for the full five minutes. You will hear the same sounds you heard in Question 1, but now, try to hear more. Listen *through* the sounds to the sounds farther away. Pay attention to ambient noise made by computers, lights, and other machinery. There may be birds chattering in the distance, or far-away traffic noise. Describe everything you hear.
3. Come back later today, or at a different time tomorrow, and sit in the same location for another deep-listening session. Make sure that you again close your eyes for a full five minutes. How are the sounds different at this different time? What remains the same?

our entertainment is candy for the eyes. There is nothing wrong with visual entertainment, but exclusive focus on the visual tends to dull the other senses. You may have heard that the blind often have extraordinary sensitivity to sound and touch. You need not be deprived of sight to expand your hearing ability, however. Learning to listen will deepen your awareness of your environment, enabling you to know what is going on behind closed doors, or who is walking down the hallway to your room. In addition to enriching your enjoyment of music, listening attentively will expand your awareness of the world around you.

Checkpoint

The goals of *Perspectives on Music* are to improve listening skills; to learn about music in a broad social context; to gain exposure to a variety of musical styles; and to develop skills for talking and writing about music. The book is divided into two parts: the first on elements, the second covering eight musical styles. The elements section will provide the reader with tools to analyze the styles of music; the styles section will supply the rules of operation for each kind of music, along with historical background and other information to help enjoy the music.

As we begin our journey to improved listening skills, we first need to think of the *style* of the music—the rules the composer worked with to create the music. And we need to consider the *function* of the music—what the music is used for (for dancing, to accompany a television commercial, and so forth). Most important, we need to listen attentively, focussing on the sounds around us and training our minds to think actively about the information received by our ears.

Rhythm

We begin with rhythm, arguably the most basic of musical elements. While the other basic elements of music mostly concern different aspects of pitch and tone, rhythm isolates the temporal aspect of music—how sounds and silence unfold over time. One can demonstrate rhythm by banging on a table just as easily as by playing the violin or some other instrument.

Like the other elements of music, rhythm consists of several subsidiary concepts: *beat, meter,* and *tempo.*

BEAT

Beat

Probably the most fundamental aspect of rhythm is the *beat,* a recurring pulse. These pulses are an equal distance apart. They are also sometimes *implicit,* meaning that they are implied by the structure of the music, rather than apparent on the surface. That means there may be times when there is no sound on a given beat; the notes stop, but the beat continues through the silence.

Strong and weak beats

The idea of a beat goes right to the core of our being—literally—in the form of a heartbeat. Could it be that the first music was an imitation of this elemental aspect of human existence? Beats also exist in nature, in the crashing of waves on the sand and the dripping of water into a pond, although nature rarely creates pulses of perfect regularity. We can hear more regular beats in the machinery of mankind, from the clackity-clack of a train on railway tracks to the staticky pulses of a connecting modem.

Nearly all music has a beat. That music which does not is often very striking for its lack of a recurring pulse, giving it a floating, ungrounded feeling. In music meant for dancing, the beat is usually emphasized more than in music intended for listening.

In music there also tends to be a mixture of *strong* and *weak beats.* Some of the beats seem louder, or have more emphasis than others. In fact, even when the beats are all equal in emphasis, people tend to hear the music as divided into strong and weak beats. The first step in listening attentively to rhythm is to listen for beats that are stronger than others. This will tell you something about our next rhythmic concept, *meter.*

METER

Meter
Duple meter

Meter is the organization of strong and weak beats into a regular pattern. Western listeners tend to hear the strong beat as first in the pattern. The pattern can be as simple as two beats, a strong and a weak, repeated over and over. This is called *simple duple meter,* since it has only two beats:

STRONG-weak-STRONG-weak-STRONG-weak
Example 2.1: Simple Duple Meter

```
| 1   2 | 1   2 | 1   2 | 1   2 |

| 1   2   3 | 1   2   3 | 1   2   3 |

| 1   2   3   4 | 1   2   3   4 |
```

FIGURE 2.1: *Counting Beats to Determine Meter.*

Or, the pattern could consist of three beats. In this case, we always find a strong beat followed by two weak beats, which is called *simple triple meter*:

STRONG-weak-weak-STRONG-weak-weak

Example 2.2: Simple Triple Meter

Or, the pattern could be more complex. We will look into more complex meters momentarily.

One complete unit of the beat pattern is called a *measure* or a *bar* (the two words mean the same thing, "measure" is more commonly used in classical music, while "bar" is used more often in reference to popular styles). The word *bar* comes from a feature in musical notation, where each measure is separated by a long vertical line called the *barline*. Again, in the styles studied in *Perspectives on Music,* musicians think of the strong beat as the first one of the measure, and then count the beats until they reach the next strong beat (Figure 2.1).

The first of these examples is *duple meter* because there are two beats per measure. The second is *triple meter,* and the third is *quadruple meter.* In the first example, there are four measures; in the second, three; and in the third, two measures. These are the most common meters in music. Military marches are usually in duple meter, because of their original function as music for movement (following the pattern of the soldiers' two feet—*left, right, left, right!*). Waltzes and some other kinds of dances are in triple meter, and most rock and popular music is in quadruple meter.

In any meter, the first beat of the measure is known as the *downbeat.* This comes from the hand and stick patterns used by the directors who lead musical ensembles: when the hand or stick goes down, musicians know this is the start of the measure.

OTHER CONCEPTS IN METER

Before we try our hand at determining meter, a warning: a *beat* is not the same thing as a *note.* Remember: the beat is the underlying pulse of the music. A composer can choose to cram as many notes as he or she likes into one beat—or even leave the beat empty, with no notes in it at all (this is called a *rest*). Just because the note is missing doesn't mean the beat stops or the meter changes. You must practice counting regular and continuous beats throughout the music. The best way to do this is to actually say the numbers out loud during the music, trying out one meter, then another, until one fits.

Another warning: sometimes musical pieces don't start on the downbeat. Sometimes they start in the middle of a measure. Why isn't the first beat the beginning of the measure in these cases? Because the beginning of a measure always corresponds with the first *strong* beat. In these cases, the music starts on a weak beat, and the strong beat comes in momentarily. This weak-beat beginning to a piece (or a section of a piece) is called the *pick-up.* An example of a familiar tune beginning with a pick-up is "Happy Birthday," which is in triple meter and begins on the final weak beat of an incomplete measure (Figure 2.2).

Downbeat

Triple meter

Measure or bar
Rest

Barline

Quadruple meter

Pick-up

```
Hap-py | birth-day  to | you        Hap-py | birth-day  to | you      Hap-py | birth-day dear | ....
3      | 1    2    3   | 1    2    3        | 1    2    3   | 1   2   3       | 1    2    3   |
         (Rest)                                (Rest)
```

FIGURE 2.2: *Meter in "Happy Birthday," Featuring a Pick-up.*

Oh,	Say, can you	see	By the	dawn's	ear-ly	light	What so ...
3	**1** 2 3	**1** 2 3	**1**	2 3	**1**	2 3	

FIGURE 2.3:   *Meter in "The Star-Spangled Banner," Featuring a Pick-up.*

Beat subdivision

Note the emphasis on the downbeat words "birth" and "you." Also note the *rest* on the second beat of the second and fourth complete measures, where there are no notes, but the beat continues. Another example of a familiar tune with a pick-up is the American national anthem, "The Star-Spangled Banner (Figure 2.3)."

You might be wondering how to count the beats in the second and fourth complete measures in "The Star-Spangled Banner," where the song squeezes in two notes in the last beat ("By the" and "What so"). In this case, musicians say that the beat is being *subdivided*. The basic pulse of three remains the same; there are simply more notes per beat here. In simple meters every beat can be divided into two subsidiary beats (musicians count this as "one-and two-and three-and"). These two subsidiary beats can also be split in two, and these in turn into two smaller subdivisions—really creating an infinite number of little notes per

Refer to the Appendix at the back of the book for this Listening Activity's complete worksheet. Use the following section to make notes for yourself.

LISTENING ACTIVITY 2.1:

Determining Meter

Sing through (as best you can!) these children's songs to determine their meter. (If you don't know them, you can hear examples of them on the Chapter 2 website.) For the purposes of this activity, we will consider both measures of two or four—to be *duple* meter. Remember: some beats may have more than one note in them, or no notes at all; and some songs may include a pick-up.

These are the steps to go through to determine meter:

1. Find the beat to the music, and clap along with it.
2. Find the downbeat, and clap louder on that beat.
3. Then, start saying "one" on the downbeat each time it goes by.
4. Now count the remaining beats between the downbeats, starting over at "one" when each downbeat comes around. The total number of beats is the meter. If you have trouble counting them, you may have to count the beats at a faster rate.

SONG	DUPLE OR TRIPLE?
1. "Old McDonald had a farm/Ee-eye-ee-eye-o. . . "	
2. "Hey diddle-diddle the cat and the fiddle/ The cow jumped over the moon. . . "	
3. "Peter, Peter, pumpkin eater/ Had a wife and could not keep her. . . "	
4. "Twinkle, twinkle, little star/ How I wonder what you are. . . "	
5. "Mary had a little lamb/ Little lamb, little lamb. . . "	

beat. Sometimes it can be hard to tell which "level" the beat is on. Remember that the beat is the place where the primary musical activity takes place.

MORE COMPLICATED METER

While a majority of the music heard on the radio makes use of one of the simple meters (duple, triple, or quadruple), composers in all styles of music have also experimented with more complicated forms of meter. When we talk about *complex meter,* for example, we refer to a situation where there are five, seven, eleven, or some other unusual number of beats per measure. The use of complex meters varies from culture to culture and from style to style. While fairly common in the classical music of India, for example, complex meter is almost never found in rock music (one famous exception is Pink Floyd's song "Money" on *Dark Side of the Moon,* which uses seven beats per measure).

Another kind of meter is called *compound meter,* which is different from simple meters in the way each beat is *subdivided.* You will recall that in all three simple meters (duple, triple, and quadruple), when composers want to put in more than one note per beat, the subdivision is by two's or multiples of two's (Figure 2.4).

In compound meter, however, the first subdivision is into three, not two (Figure 2.5).

Composers have also experimented with having different singers or instrumentalists playing in two

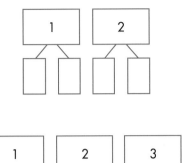

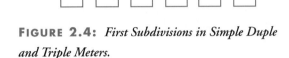

FIGURE 2.4: *First Subdivisions in Simple Duple and Triple Meters.*

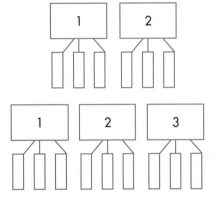

FIGURE 2.5: *First Subdivisions in Compound Duple and Triple Meters.*

Complex meter

Compound meter

different meters at once (called *polymeter*) and with changing meters rapidly during the course of the music (called *mixed meter*). All of these occur only rarely in most music.

Polymeter

Mixed meter

TEMPO

The other subsidiary concept of rhythm is *tempo,* how fast the beats go. The tempo of music is an important factor in determining its character—often, the faster the tempo, the more exciting the music. Again, there is a close analogy in the human heart rate. Our pulse averages between 70 and 90 *beats per minute* (BPM).

If we are particularly relaxed, our heart rate can slow to 60 BPM, about one beat per second. When exercising or agitated, our hearts can double that speed, pumping at over 120 BPM.

This leads us to one of the great mysteries of music: the human heart rate seems to be attracted to musical tempo. This does not mean our pulse

Tempo

Beats per minute (BPM)

matches the pulse of the music we hear (otherwise, music moving at 200 BPM or faster would probably kill us!), rather that when we hear a fast tempo, our hearts beat a little faster, and when we hear a slow tempo, our hearts slow down. You may have noticed that exciting chase scenes in movies almost always are accompanied by music with adrenaline-inducing tempos, while mournful scenes feature background music of slower tempo. If the music is well written, of course, it does more than just calibrate our hearts; it induces emotion and adds flavor. But the tempo is an important ingredient in the music's effect on us.

In classical music there are specific terms given for tempo; these are listed in Chapter 11. In other musical styles, the assignment of tempo is usually less precise.

In more folk-oriented styles, musicians decide on a tempo in conversation as they rehearse their music, sometimes trying out different tempos until they find one that seems "right." Composers of electronic music, on the other hand—whether they write for popular music, art music, or film—now have extremely fine control over tempo through their computer programs, down to a fraction of a beat per minute.

COMMON RHYTHMIC PRACTICES

Before we leave our discussion of rhythm, we must note that not all rhythm is orderly and regular. In some of the examples on

Refer to the Appendix at the back of the book for this Listening Activity's complete worksheet. Use the following section to make notes for yourself.

LISTENING ACTIVITY 2.2:

Determining Tempo

Your goal in this activity is to determine whether the tempo of each example is *fast, moderate,* or *slow*. For our purposes here, we will be approximate about these tempos: slow tempos will be those around 60 BPM; fast tempos about 120 BPM, and moderate tempos in between, at about 90 BPM. First, as you listen, figure out the beat (it helps to tap it with your hand or foot). Then, looking at a watch or clock with a second hand, count the number of beats that fall in a ten-second stretch of music, then multiply by six (or for a 15-second stretch, multiplied by four). You can then see if the number comes closest to 60, 90, or 120 BPM.

Five examples were composed specifically for this assignment. Each one is about one minute long, and can be found on the website for Chapter 2 in the form of WAV files. In some cases, you should be able to determine the tempo right away; in others, you may have to listen for a while to hear the firm establishment of tempo. In any case, you may listen to these as often as you like to determine the tempo.

EXAMPLE	TEMPO (FAST, MODERATE, SLOW)
1.	
2.	
3.	
4.	
5.	

your CD's, you may notice that the tempo is not completely steady. Musicians call this feature *rubato,* the pushing and pulling of tempo. Rubato is used to add emotion to music, or to emphasize an important moment. Another kind of rhythmic practice has to do with the placement of *accents*, or notes with extra emphasis. There is usually an accent at the start of each measure, signifying the downbeat, but sometimes composers or musicians will place accents in different parts of the measure, to add variety or rhythmic excitement. This is known as *syncopation.* And sometimes we hear music in which the meter temporarily subdivides into three rather than two (or vice-versa). This feature is called a *triplet.* There are MIDI examples of syncopation and triplets on the Web.

Rhythm is an important part of all music. The next time you listen to music of any sort, try to determine its meter, tempo, and whether there are any rhythmic peculiarities involved.

Checkpoint

Rhythm is the fundamental element of music. Rhythm consists of three main subsidiary concepts: the *beat,* or pulse of the music; the *meter,* or how the beat is organized into repeating patterns of strong and weak beats; and the *tempo,* the speed of the beats. There are three simple meters, *duple, triple,* and *quadruple;* and there are also *compound meters,* which subdivide into three rather than two; and *complex meters,* which involve measures of unusual numbers of beats. When we talk about tempo, we can refer to the number of beats per minute. We also need to listen for rhythmic devices such as *accent, syncopation, triplets,* and *rubato.*

Rubato

Accent

Syncopation

Triplet

KEY TERMS

Beat	Downbeat	Tempo
Strong and Weak Beats	Rest	Beats per Minute (BPM)
Meter	Pick-up	Rubato
Duple Meter	Beat subdivision	Accent
Barline	Complex Meter	Syncopation
Triple Meter	Compound Meter	Triplet
Quadruple Meter	Polymeter	
Measure	Mixed Meter	
Bar		

CHAPTER 3

Pitch and Melody

People make use of the terms *pitch* and *melody* in a variety of ways. You may have heard the phrase "off-pitch," meaning "out of tune." We've all heard out-of-tune singing, but what exactly is happening, in terms of acoustics (the physics of sound)? And you may also have heard people say, "That's a great melody." What makes it great? In this chapter we unlock the secrets of pitch and melody.

PITCH

To understand the nature of pitch, one must first know something about the physics of sound. When something makes a sound, what is actually happening is that it is disturbing air particles. The particles closest to the sound source are pushed out of position, knocking the next set of particles out of place, which knock the next set of particles, and so on, like dominos. If we were able to see sound, it would look like a sphere (or a series of spheres) expanding out from the source. The ear is calibrated to perceive these subtle variations in air pressure and sends this information through the auditory nerve to the brain for processing (Figure 3.1).

Sounds with *pitch* are those sounds that disturb air particles in a *periodic* fashion. In other words, when these "air spheres" emanate from the sound source at the same speed, the result is a steady tone. This does not mean periodic sounds are necessarily pleasant—the screech of car brakes also can be a periodic sound.

But without periodic sound (e.g., pitch), most of the music we love could not be created.

When the speed in which these "air spheres" emanate from a sound source varies, the pitch changes. The faster the speed, the higher the pitch. Musicians measure pitch in terms of *cycles per second,* or *Hertz* (Hz), the number of complete cycles of maximum air pressure to the lowest that occur within each second. The note A at about the mid-point of the piano keyboard, for example, has *frequency* of 440 Hz. People can hear pitches with frequencies as low as 16 or 20 Hz, and as high as 25,000 Hz. Dogs and other animals can hear sounds with even higher frequencies, as anyone who has used a dog whistle can confirm.

Hertz (Hz)

Frequency

Pitch

It can be helpful to think of sound like the waves formed when a pebble is dropped in a pool of water. The *frequency* concerns how fast the waves move. Another variable to consider is the *amplitude* of the sound signal, which in this analogy would represent the *size* of the waves: how high the peaks and how deep the troughs. The greater the amplitude, the louder the sound. The word *amplitude* is related to *amplifier*—because when an electric guitar is plugged into an amplifier, the amplitude of the sound signal is increased. If you want to increase the amplitude on an acoustic guitar, you must pluck the string harder, which makes it vibrate more widely and thus disturb the air particles more strongly.

Amplitude

In music, the word *dynamics* is used instead of amplitude. You may have heard the terms *piano* and *forte,* Italian for "soft" and "loud." These terms and others are discussed in Chapter 6.

Dynamics

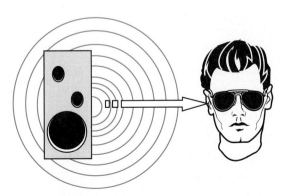

FIGURE 3.1: *Soundwaves from a Stereo Speaker Reaching a Listener.*

Photo by D. Boone.
Source: CORBIS.

SIDENOTE: MAKING MUSIC WITH BOTTLES

Many of you have probably experimented with frequency by blowing air across the tops of bottles. Instinctively, you knew that the more liquid inside the bottle, the higher the pitch. If you blow air in at just the right angle you will set the air inside the bottle into vibration, creating pitch. The less room there is for air to vibrate, the faster the air vibrates, increasing the frequency and the pitch:

air in: air in:

Higher pitch   Lower pitch

PITCH NAMES

We call the range of possible frequencies the *frequency spectrum*. All musical cultures divide the frequency spectrum up into discrete units called *notes*. The number of notes varies from culture to culture. One nearly universal feature of the way cultures deal with the frequency spectrum, however, concerns the doubling of frequencies. When a frequency is exactly doubled, it sounds like the same note. We can tell the second pitch is higher, but it sounds so similar to the first pitch, we *treat* the two pitches as though they were the same. In fact, when men and

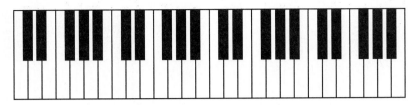

FIGURE 3.2: *Part of the Piano Keyboard.*

women sing a melody together, men usually sing their notes at exactly half the frequency as the women sing their notes, because their voices are naturally lower. In Western music (for example, the music of Europe, the Americas, and other places with European heritage), this doubling of pitch is called an *octave*.

Western musicians divide this octave into twelve notes. The piano keyboard provides a graphic representation of this division, through the pattern of white and black notes. Where the pattern of black and white notes repeats, a new octave begins (Figure 3.2).

Of these twelve notes in the octave, Western musicians use *seven primary notes,* and they designate these by letters of the alphabet, A, B, C, etc. After G, musicians call the next pitch A again, a sign of how they think of the octave as a repeating of a note at a doubling of the pitch. The seven primary notes correspond to the white keys on a piano keyboard (Figure 3.3).

You might have noticed that these seven pitches are not exactly the same distance apart: some have black notes (the black keys on the piano) between them and some do not. The white notes with a black note between them are considered to be a *whole step* apart, and these are the majority of the notes. But some notes—B and C, and E and F—are half that

distance, a *half step* apart. If you look at the diagram above, you can see that between B and C and E and F there are no black notes (black keys). This particular combination of notes a whole step and half step apart creates a pattern of pitches that is pleasing to the Western ear.

If the white notes are given alphabetical names, what about the black notes on the piano? Western musicians refer to these notes as an altered form of the neighboring primary note: if above the white key, it is known as a *sharp* (represented by the symbol, ♯); if below, it is known as a *flat* (represented by the symbol ♭). The black note just to the right of the note A, for example, is called A-sharp; the note to the left, or lower, is called A-flat (Figure 3.4). This means that any note could be given at least two names: G-sharp is the same note as A-flat; and the note B could be called C-flat, even though B is a white note (key). These different names for the same frequency are called *enharmonic equivalents*. The name musicians assign a particular note depends on the context of the music.

This division of the octave into seven primary notes and five sharp or flat notes is mostly a Western phenomenon; and even in the West, it is not entirely universal. In other cultures, the octave is often divided differently, either having more notes or fewer.

Half step

Octave

Sharp
Flat

Enharmonic equivalents

Whole step

FIGURE 3.3: *The Seven Primary Notes in Western Music.*

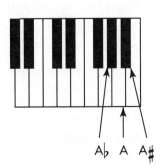

FIGURE 3.4: *Half Steps Around the Note A.*

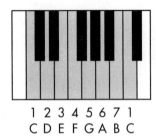

1 2 3 4 5 6 7 1
C D E F G A B C

FIGURE 3.5: *How to Play the C Major Scale on the Piano.*

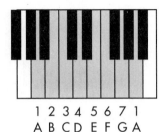

1 2 3 4 5 6 7 1
A B C D E F G A

FIGURE 3.6: *How to Play the A Natural Minor Scale on the Piano.*

Minor scale

SCALE

Scale

Any time we talk about a collection of notes in this way, we are really talking about a *scale,* from the Italian word *scala,* or stairs. If you've spent any time around musicians, you've probably heard them practicing scales, running up and down the notes over several octaves. Scales aren't really music, rather just the source material for music. Think of a scale as an artist's palette, each note representing a different color. Just as an artist places colors on the canvas in a certain pattern, so too do musicians choose from their palette of notes to create patterns in sound.

Blues scale
Blue notes

Major scale

The most common scale in western music, the *major scale,* is a seven-note scale consisting of the white notes on the piano between C and the following C (eight notes if you count the second C). You can try it out yourself on a piano or keyboard following the illustration below, or hear an example on the web page for this chapter (Figure 3.5).

Another scale, the *natural minor scale,* can be made by playing all the white notes within an octave starting on A (Figure 3.6).

It is important to start on these notes (C or A), because if you don't, you will play a different ordering of whole steps and half steps, and thus create a different scale. In order to create a major or minor scale starting on a different note, musicians must substitute sharps or flats for some of the white notes.

Major and minor scales are the most common in the musical styles discussed in this book, but they are not the only ones. An important scale in the blues, jazz, and rock is the *blues scale*. This is essentially a major scale with *blue notes,* occurring on the third, seventh, and sometimes the fifth scale degrees, where the pitch may be flattened. This is one way in which these popular styles differ from classical styles, in that the performer has the option to bend certain notes; in classical music, pitches are more or less fixed.

It is hard to indicate the notes of a blues scale on a piano since the notes cannot be bent (unlike a guitar

---

SIDENOTE: MAKING MAJOR AND MINOR SCALES

For those who are interested, you can create major and minor scales on any Western instrument by using the following pattern of whole steps and half steps. Start on any pitch, then use the following formulas to determine the note to go up to next (W represents a whole step—two notes apart on the keyboard; while H represents a half step, using notes adjacent to one another):

Major Scale: W-W-H-W-W-W-H
Natural Minor Scale: W-H-W-W-H-W-W

Your instructor can provide further information about creating scales.

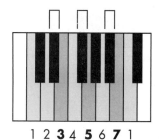

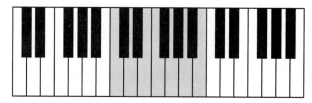

FIGURE 3.8: *The Chromatic Scale.*

1 2 **3** 4 **5** 6 **7** 1

FIGURE 3.7: *The Blues Scale. The "Blue Notes" are Bracketed and Numbered in Bold.*

possible pitches in the octave are used. Here, all the pitches are a half-step apart (Figure 3.8).

or the human voice). In the diagram below, we will show all the possible notes; keep in mind, however, that there are not ten notes to this scale, but rather seven—three of which can bent or not at the whim of the performer or composer (Figure 3.7).

Yet another scale used sometimes in Western music is the *chromatic scale,* one in which all twelve

There are many different scales to choose from; some composers have even invented their own scales. The important thing, however, is not so much the scale a composer chooses but what he or she *does* with that particular collection of notes. One of the most important things, of course, is to place those notes in a particular order to create a *melody.*

Melody
Chromatic scale

MELODY

A melody is a coherent sequence of pitches. Notice that a melody is not necessarily a *pleasant* sequence of pitches, just any sequence that makes some kind of sense. Melodies usually make use of a single scale, although they often travel between several octaves in that scale. On occasion, however, melodies make use of pitches outside of the chosen scale, or they change scales in the middle.

In one respect, creating a melody is as simple as selecting one pitch to follow another. The reality, of course, is usually more complicated than this. Still, on its most basic level, a melody is a linear sequence of pitches. One way of talking about this sequence of pitches is in terms of its *contour.* Does the melody shoot up in jagged peaks? Or does it undulate like rolling hills? Or is it rather static, a *monotone* (that is, "one pitch"), flat line of a melody? On a more detailed level, the contour of the melody can be *conjunct* or *disjunct.* A conjunct melody is one where the notes are generally close together; a disjunct melody features angular leaps—which can be hard to

sing—and yet be very striking. One example of a disjunct melody is "The Star-Spangled Banner," a disjunct melody that has perplexed the average singer for several generations (Figure 3.9).

Another interesting trait of melodies is their tendency to orient around a single note, typically the bottom note of a scale. This note is called the *tonic* or *key.* You may have heard musicians talk about a piece

Tonic
Key

Monotone

Conjunct disjunct

FIGURE 3.9: *Samples of Melodic Contour.*

Melodic contour

Motive

Riff

Phrase
Phrase segments

Cadence

"in the key of G." This means that G serves as a kind of center of gravity for the melody and harmony. Melodies drift away, but seem to have a innate desire to return to this central note. When it finally reaches the tonic, the melody sounds satisfying and complete.

PHRASES AND PHRASE SEGMENTS

Another important way to look at melodies is how they are constructed over time. Just as the words of a paragraph are broken up into grammatical phrases and sentences, so too are the notes of a melody broken up into musical *phrases* and *phrase segments*. For those instruments such as the human voice that require breath to make music, the musician can go only so long before requiring another breath. One of these chunks of melody is called a phrase—not the whole melody, just a part of it. As it turns out, even for instruments that are not breath-oriented, such as the piano, melodies still tend to be broken down into phrases. The phrases can be of different lengths, just as sentences can be of different lengths. One can extend the grammar metaphor even farther and say that some musical phrases sound like they end in a comma, some in a period, some in a question mark, some in an exclamation point, and some seem to trail off inconclusively, corresponding to ellipses (. . .). This ending "punctuation" part of a phrase is called a *cadence*.

Sometimes, there seems to be a division within a phrase of some length, which we call a *phrase segment*. It may be that in a phrase of four measures, there is a little rest in the middle, so that the phrase seems to be constructed of two two-measure sections. Unlike a

phrase, a phrase segment usually does not end in a cadence; a phrase segment, in other words, is not as complete a musical idea as is a phrase.

MOTIVES AND RIFFS

The smallest segment of a melody is called a *motive* or a *riff*. The terms mean essentially the same thing, although *motive* is more commonly used in classical music, and *riff* in popular music. Either one is a short musical idea—often just a few notes long—which is used to build up phrases and melodies. Usually motives and riffs are catchy and have a defining rhythmic element. In fact, motives and riffs often have more to do with rhythm than melody in character. But their *function* is melodic, because they are used as a melodic seed.

The most famous motive in classical music is heard at the beginning of Beethoven's Fifth Symphony: *short-short-short-LONG*. Listen to the beginning of Beethoven's Fifth Symphony as to how Beethoven presents the motive twice, then uses it to build up the melody (Figure 3.10).

In rock, jazz, and other kinds of popular music, we think of riffs as used to generate instrumental solos, although they can also be used as the basis for the main melodies of the songs. One difference between a motive and a riff is that a riff often stands alone, while a motive is used to build up longer musical ideas.

A motive or riff is not a mandatory ingredient in the creation of a melody. Some composers like to build up their melodies out of memorable, short ideas; others prefer melodies with no perceivable motivic construction; and others still use a mixture of

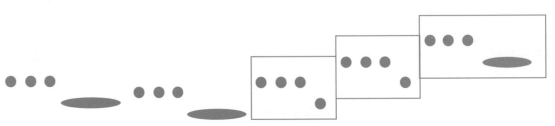

FIGURE 3.10: *Graphic Representation of the Use of Motive at the Beginning of Beethoven's Fifth Symphony.*

motivic and nonmotivic construction. No one way is better or worse—just different.

TUNEFULNESS

One final parameter for us to consider is a melody's *tunefulness*. To say that a melody is *tuneful* means that it is catchy and easy to repeat. Tuneful melodies stick in a listener's head long after the song or piece is over. This is, to some degree, a subjective assessment, since what sticks in the mind of one person may not stick in the mind of another. There is also a nonsubjective element to this as well, since tuneful melodies have several qualities in common:

- They tend to repeat phrases or phrase segments, helping the listener to remember them;
- Within phrases and phrase segments, they tend to use repeating rhythmic ideas, with perhaps a single rhythmic motive running through the whole melody;
- They have a memorable contour, usually with one single high point;
- They tend to be *conjunct* rather than *disjunct*.

It may seem that tunefulness is a qualitative assessment of music; in other words, that the more tuneful a melody is, the better. This is not really the case. Television jingles can be extraordinarily tuneful—what would be better for an advertiser than to have the product name buzzing in the listener's head all day? Yet very few of us would consider television jingles great music. Instead, think of tunefulness simply as a characteristic of melodies. Some great music does, in fact, feature tuneful melodies; some equally great music does not.

The desire for tunefulness seems to come in waves. In the history of classical music, the late eighteenth century was a time of great tunefulness, but the early twentieth century was a time when hardly a tuneful melody was written. In jazz, the swing era was relatively tuneful, but later jazz often was not. The most tune-oriented style we will study is rock, but even in rock there are substyles (think of punk and heavy metal) where tunefulness is definitely uncool.

Tunefulness

Checkpoint

Sounds are made through the disturbance of air particles, a series of invisible spheres rapidly emanating from the sound source. When these spheres are emitted regularly, the result is a steady pitch, or tone. The higher the periodic frequency, the higher the pitch, and the greater the amplitude, the greater the volume.

A police siren slides up and down through the frequency spectrum, but in music, we tend to divide the spectrum up into distinct units called *notes*. When the frequency is doubled, the notes seem to sound the same; in the styles of music covered in this book, this is called an *octave*. In these styles, an octave is

LISTENING ACTIVITY 3.1:

Assessing Melody

Compare and contrast the melodies in the following two listening excerpts from your CD's, considering the nature of their phrase structures; their melodic contours; and the ways in which the composers make their melodies memorable. Type your essay on a separate sheet of paper.

1. Mozart, *Eine kleine Nachtmusik*, movement 1, from the beginning through about CD time :15.
2. Smetana, *The Moldau*, CD time 1:07 through 2:05.

divided into seven main notes (labeled A through G), and five other notes (making a total of twelve divisions), referred to as *sharps* and *flats*. The collection of notes within an octave is called a *scale,* which is the source material to create melodies.

A melody is any coherent sequence of pitches. Melodies can be analyzed by their *contour* (how they go up and down in pitch); whether they are *conjunct* or *disjunct;* their sense of the *tonic,* or orientation around a single pitch; and how they are divided into smaller units such as phrases, phrase segments, motives, and riffs. Melodies can also be assessed in terms of *tunefulness,* based on their "catchiness" and memorability.

KEY TERMS

Pitch	Sharp	Monotone
Frequency	Flat	Conjunct
Hertz (Hz)	Enharmonic equivalent	Disjunct
Cycles per second	Scale	Tonic
Amplitude	Major Scale	Key
Dynamics	Minor Scale	Phrase
Notes	Blue Notes	Phrase Segment
Interval	Blues Scale	Cadence
Octave	Chromatic Scale	Motive
Whole Step	Melody	Riff
Half Step	Melodic Contour	Tunefulness

Harmony and Texture

In the previous two chapters, the primary concern has been with the linear aspects of music. But in music, there are usually several sounds occurring at the same time. Chapter 4 explores how those simultaneous sounds are organized through harmony and texture.

HARMONY

Harmony

When two or more notes are sounding at the same time, this creates *harmony.* Like the term *melody,* musicians use the word *harmony* in a neutral sense, referring to any combination of notes whether or not they are pleasing to the ear. One way of putting it is that *harmony* does not have to be *harmonious.* When two or more notes sound sweet together, they are considered to be *consonant;* and when the notes clash, they are said to be *dissonant.*

Consonant
Dissonant

To some degree, these are relative terms. What sounds pleasant to one listener may sound ugly to another. But there is also a physical quality to pitches that makes them blend more readily with some notes than others. This quality has to do with a pitch's *overtones.* When a musician plays a note on an instrument, there are actually several, higher notes that are sounding, usually so faintly that you can't hear them, and each successive overtone going up from the *fundamental* pitch generally gets fainter and fainter. Even though imperceptible, the overtone series adds a great deal to the quality of the sound made by instruments. If you were to play the note C on the piano, the following shaded pitches would be the approximate position of the first seven overtones (Figure 4.1).

Overtones

Fundamental

Chord

Triad

When you play two notes together, if the second note is related to the first through the overtone series,

they are more likely to sound consonant. The lower down on the overtone series this second note is (that is, the closer it is to the fundamental pitch), the more consonant the harmony, in general. If you try this out on a piano, it should be clear to you: play the note C (as illustrated above) against any one of the overtones. All the notes except perhaps the next-to-last overtone in this illustration (B-flat) will probably sound consonant to your ears.

Despite this physical property, consonance and dissonance are also a product of cultural conditioning; some cultures find dissonant what others find consonant. Even within Western culture there is wide disagreement as to what combination of notes is consonant or dissonant.

CHORDS

Three or more notes sounded simultaneously are called *chords* (pronounced "cords"). The most important kind of chord in Western music is a *triad,* a three-note chord built in a specific way. Starting on any of the notes within a seven-note scale, you play the bottom note of the triad, skip the second scale degree, then play the third note, skip the fourth, and play the fifth (for example, C-E-G). If you try to play a triad on a

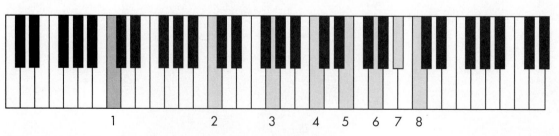

1   2   3   4 5 6 7 8

FIGURE 4.1: *First Seven Overtones Above C.*

keyboard, you will understand why they are so common: they seem to fit comfortably in a pianist's hand, using the thumb, middle finger, and pinkie.

Like any other combination of notes, chords can be consonant or dissonant, depending on whether the notes are considered to clash with one another. Triads and cerain other chords can also be referred to by their *mode*. The two main modes are *major* and *minor,* terms we have already encountered when discussing scales. Try playing the following notes on a piano (or listening to them via the class website), first successively then all together (Figure 4.2).

This is a major triad, which to most listeners sounds bright and cheerful, while a minor triad sounds more melancholy (Figure 4.3).

The quality of major and minor is not just relegated to isolated chords. In fact, we also think of entire pieces of music as being in the major or minor mode, even though an occasional chord of the opposite mode may appear now and then. When we talk about this overall mode, we are talking about harmony in a more global sense. What determines the global harmony is the scale the composer chooses as he or she begins the piece.

In much of popular music, chords appear in a repeating sequence. Sometimes this *chord progression*

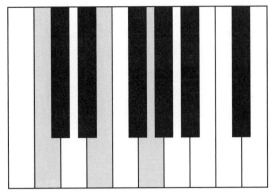

Mode
Major
Minor

FIGURE 4.2: *How to Play a Major Triad on the Piano.*

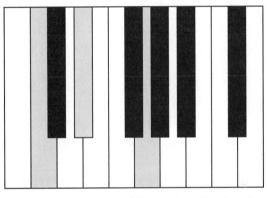

FIGURE 4.3: *How to Play a Minor Triad on the Piano.*

Chord Progression

Refer to the Appendix at the back of the book for this Listening Activity's complete worksheet. Use the following section to make notes for yourself.

LISTENING ACTIVITY 4.1:

Major versus Minor

You will hear five triads (available on the website for this chapter). Label them major or minor.

Triad No. 1

Triad No. 2

Triad No. 3

Triad No. 4

Triad No. 5

Tonic

consists of just two or three chords, sometimes more. Just as melodies tend to orient around a single pitch, the *tonic*—which is the first (or bottom) note of a scale—so too does harmony tend to orient around the first triad of a scale, the "I" chord (that is, if you are using the C Major scale, the "I" chord will be the triad built on C—C-E-G). The harmony of a piece of music or a song often begins with the "I" chord, drifts away from it, then eventually returns to it. As you become a more attuned listener you will become more adept at hearing the "I" chord, and the satisfying feeling when it returns after a long absence.

TEXTURE

Texture

Another way of looking at the vertical aspect of music is through *texture,* the way in which different musical lines are put together. We categorize music into four different kinds of texture:

Monophonic

Monophonic   (from the Greek for "one sound") texture: all the instruments or singers are playing the same melody. (Noun: *monophony).* The idea of *monophony* is essentially the same as *unison.*

Homophonic

Homophonic   ("the same sound") texture: there is one important melody, and the other instruments or singers are accompanying it. (Noun: *homophony*)

Polyphonic
Imitative Polyphony

Polyphonic   ("many sounds") texture: there are two or more melodies of roughly equal importance. (Noun: *polyphony*)

Heterophonic
Round

Heterophonic   ("different sounds") texture: there is one important melody, but while this is heard, the musicians are improvising ornaments and sometimes independent lines around the main melody in a freewheeling manner. In other words, there are several simultaneous versions of the same melody heard at the same time. This kind of texture is

most commonly applied to Dixieland jazz (see Chapter 8). (Noun: *heterophony*)

It is important to know that texture does not concern *how many* musicians are playing at the same time, only the ways in which their melodies interact. A monophonic texture could be produced by a hundred singers (if you could convince them to all sing the same melody together), while polyphony is often created by a single musician at an organ, weaving together several lines. The most common of these four textures, across the musical styles, is the homophonic texture: a single important melody with accompaniment. Most popular music features a sung melody with supporting instruments like bass, guitar, and drums.

One special kind of polyphony is *imitative polyphony,* in which the separate lines present the same melody, but with staggered entrances. A genre that uses imitative polyphony is the *round,* for example, the song "Row, Row, Row Your Boat."

On your CD's and on the website for this chapter is the hymn "Simple Gifts" presented with different textures. The first version is in monophonic texture, a single melody line with no accompaniment (Figure 4.4).

FIGURE 4.4:   *Monophonic Texture.*

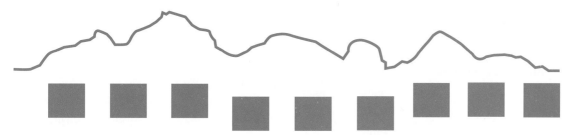

FIGURE 4.5:   *Homophonic Texture.*

FIGURE 4.6:   *Polyphonic Texture.*

The second example is homophonic, a clearly dominant melody with accompaniment (Figure 4.5).

We can also present this music in a polyphonic texture, with two independent melodies interweaving together (Figure 4.6).

Or even a heterophonic texture (Figure 4.7).

Sometimes, hearing different textures is very easy and obvious. At other times, it can be challenging. Imagine a rock song in which the electric guitar begins with a catchy riff that seems to be the main melody; a moment later, however, the lead vocalist comes in with a new tune that takes primary importance in the texture, and the guitar line then recedes into the background. Is this homophonic or polyphonic texture?

On one hand, this is the blending together of two independent melodies, which would suggest polyphony. On the other hand, the vocal melody is clearly dominant, suggesting homophony. The best way to think about these two kinds of textures is in the form of a continuum. At one end is pure homophony, music where there is little doubt that one melody dominates and other sounds are accompanimental. On the other end is pure polyphony, in which the melodies are so independent you cannot determine which one is the main melody. In the middle of this continuum are mixed textures, where the accompaniment has some degree of independence, but not to the level of true polyphony (Figure 4.8).

FIGURE 4.7:   *Heterophonic Texture.*

Pure Homophony   *(some degree of independence in accompanying lines)*   *Pure Polyphony*

FIGURE 4.8:   *Homophony-Polyphony Continuum.*

Checkpoint

In this chapter the vertical aspects of music have been discussed, first in terms of *harmony,* then in terms of *texture*. Harmony concerns the way individual notes are combined into *chords* (such as *triads),* while texture concerns the way melodies are combined.

Because of the physics of each note's *overtone series,* certain kinds of harmony sound *consonant,* and others sound *dissonant*. In part these assesments are also culturally determined. In assessing harmony we also listen for the *mode* (*major* or *minor*). The concept of *scale* appeared in Chapter 3, "Pitch and Melody," as well as in this chapter. In both cases, scale describes an ascending collection of notes used as source material for music.

There are four different kinds of *textures: monophonic* (everybody producing one melody line, in *unison*); *homophonic* (one melody line with accompaniment); *polyphonic* (several equally important melody lines woven together); and *heterophonic* (one melody line with improvised ornaments). Homophony is the most common of these in the musical styles we will be studying.

Listening Activity 12.2 will provide further training on distinguishing between monophonic, homophonic, and polyphonic textures.

KEY TERMS

Harmony
Consonant
Dissonant
Overtones
Fundamental
Chord

Triad
Mode
Major
Minor
Chord Progression
Tonic

Texture:
   Monophonic
   Homophonic
   Polyphonic
   Heterophonic
Imitative Polyphony
Round

Timbre and Instrumentation

CHAPTER 5

Vanessa Mae playing the violin. Photo by Rune Hellestad.
Source: CORBIS.

If you were to hear a recording of a trumpet and a flute playing the same note, how would you be able to tell which was which? Your first answer might be that the trumpet is louder than the flute, but this isn't really how you can tell the difference between them. It has more to do with the quality of their sound, what some people call *tone color,* or *timbre* (pronounced "TAM-ber"). The different timbres of the various instruments and voices around the world add much to the character and meaning of music.

TIMBRE

Timbre

T imbre is a critical element of music, yet surprisingly difficult to pin down. How would you describe the timbre of your favorite singer's voice? Analogies such as "raspy," "buttery," "sweet," or "pure" are usually utilized to describe timbre. This is even more challenging when talking about jazz singers, many of whom pride themselves on their ability to change the timbre of their voices for expressive purposes.

The physics of timbre

Timbre is created through the physics of the overtone series, discussed in Chapter 4. When different overtones are emphasized, different timbres result. The classical *flute,* for example has a relatively "pure" timbre because it has a strong fundamental pitch and only a few, faint overtones. The clarinet, on the other hand, has a more complex timbre, one in which the odd-numbered overtones are louder than the even-numbered ones. The oboe produces a timbre in which the higher overtones are emphasized. The exact presence of particular overtones cannot be heard by the human ear—this information can only be gathered by a machine—but it is clear that these instruments have different tone qualities. It is the timbre of the instruments that makes them different from one another and gives them their flavor.

Different musical styles and cultures have different attitudes about timbre. Classical music generally favors pure or rich timbres. Most world musical cultures, on the other hand, prefer timbres with some buzz to them. The East African instrument called the *mbira,* or thumb-piano, is a gourd or wooden box with little metal bars of different pitches to be played by the thumbs; included on each bar is a bead that rattles when the bar is played. A classical flute player strives for a pure pitch, but a musician playing the Japanese flute, the *shakuhachi,* intentionally leaves breath in the tone to add to the color. In rock music, timbre is one of the most important ingredients in distinguishing substyles. It is the angry distortion of the electric guitar in heavy metal and alternative rock that helps mark this music as different from the sweeter Top-40 fare.

Girl playing the clarinet in a band in Rome, Italy.
Photo by James L. Amos.
Source: CORBIS.

INSTRUMENTS

All sound is produced through three stages: *energy source, vibrating element,* and *resonating chamber.* Most instruments can be identified by how they operate in these three stages. The flute, for example, uses the human breath as an energy source; the air then vibrates as it is blown across the opening; and the tubular body of the flute serves as the resonating chamber. The *clarinet* is similar to the flute, but differs in its second stage; instead of the air blowing across an opening, the clarinet's vibrating element is a little strip of wood called a *reed* (see table below). The *trumpet,* on the other hand, uses the vibration of the player's lips against a metal cup called the *mouthpiece* to start the vibration. We can summarize these differences (shown in Table 5.1).

Energy source
Vibrating element
Resonating chamber

The stages of sound production

Reed
Mouthpiece

TABLE 5.1: DIFFERENCES IN SOUND PRODUCTION AMONG SAMPLE INSTRUMENTS.

INSTRUMENT	ENERGY SOURCE	VIBRATING ELEMENT	RESONATING CHAMBER
Flute	Air	Air across opening	The body of the instrument
Clarinet	Air	Reed	The body of the instrument
Trumpet	Air	Lips	The body of the instrument

All three of these instruments are broadly categorized as *wind* instruments, because of their similarity in the first stage of sound production. Wind instruments are subdivided into two *instrument families,* known as *woodwinds* and *brass*. The flute and the clarinet are woodwind instruments, while the trumpet is a brass instrument. Note that not all woodwinds are made out of wood, nor all brass instruments out of brass; these names come from the primary materials use to make them in earlier years.

INSTRUMENT FAMILIES

*I*n Western music there are seven instrument families. We can make general observations about these families through the same three-step process of sound production (shown in Table 5.2).

Keyboard instruments represent a diverse family that includes pianos, harpsichords, and organs, with a variety of constructions. What groups them together is the use of the keyboard.

Electronic instruments are interesting in that there are usually two energy sources, and sometimes two vibrating elements, working simultaneously. In the case of the *electric guitar,* for example, the strings must be plucked to induce vibration, but what is really setting the air particles in motion is the vibration of the speaker cone in the amplifier. This category is also unique in that the body of the instruments do not

Wynton Marsalis playing the trumpet. Photo by Lynn Goldsmith.
Source: CORBIS.

serve as resonating chambers (except in unusual cases, such as the hollow-body electric, in which there is a partial resonance in the body of the instrument).

Many people do not think of the human voice as an instrument, but it certainly is—the oldest and most basic instrument to all human cultures.

Here are some of the most common instruments in Western music, generally organized from highest to lowest in pitch in each family (shown in Table 5.3 on the next page).

Woodwind

Brass

Keyboard

Electronic

String

TABLE 5.2: THE SEVEN INSTRUMENT FAMILIES.

FAMILY	ENERGY SOURCE	VIBRATING ELEMENT	RESONATING CHAMBER
Woodwind	Air	Air or Reed	The body of the instrument
Brass	Air	Lips	The body of the instrument
String	Hand muscle	Strings	The body of the instrument
Percussion	Hand muscle	Skin of drum, or metal or wood	The body of the instrument
Keyboard	Hand muscle and keyboard mechanism	Strings or pipes (in the case of the organ)	The body of the instrument or the inside of a church (in the case of the organ)
Electronic	Hand muscle and Electricity	The cone of a loudspeaker	The cabinet of the loudspeaker
Voice	Air	Vocal cords	The singer's head

TABLE 5.3: COMMON INSTRUMENTS.

WOODWINDS	BRASS	STRINGS	PERCUSSION	KEYBOARD	VOICE	ELECTRONIC
Piccolo	Trumpet	Harp	Timpani	Piano	Soprano	Electric Guitar
Flute	French Horn	Violin	Snare Drum	Harpsichord	Mezzo-Soprano	Electric Bass
Oboe	Trombone	Viola	Bass Drum	Organ	Alto	Synthesizer
Clarinet	Baritone Horn	Cello	Cymbals		Tenor	Computer
Saxophone	Tuba	Double Bass	Xylophone		Baritone	
Recorder	Sousaphone	Acoustic Guitar	Marimba		Bass	
Bassoon		Banjo	Miscellaneous noise makers			

FAMILIES WITHIN FAMILIES

Within these instrument families there are often subcategories. Some of these instruments come in several sizes. Often, they borrow the names from the voice family to indicate versions of an instrument in different *ranges* (indicating how high or low they can play). The saxophone, for example, commonly appears in one of five different sizes:

> Soprano Saxophone
> Alto Saxophone
> Tenor Saxophone
> Baritone Saxophone
> Bass Saxophone

We find similar subdivisions among flutes (where the highest instrument is called the *piccolo*), clarinets, recorders, and other instruments. Sometimes, the names for different versions of an instrument have different names, however. An alto oboe, for example, is called an *English horn*. There is no commonly used tenor oboe, but the baritone range is taken by the bassoon. A bass bassoon is called a *contrabassoon*.

Another distinction within the woodwind family has to do with the mechanics of the instrument. Clarinets and saxophones are sometimes referred to collectively as *single reed* instruments, since they feature a single reed strapped into a plastic *mouthpiece*. Oboes, English horns, bassoons, and contrabassoons are known as *double reed* instruments, because their

sound is made by the vibration of two identical reeds in the player's mouth. Once you train your ears, the difference between single reed and double reed instruments becomes obvious: double reed instruments have a more sinewy, piercing sound than single reed instruments.

In the percussion family, we can separate the *pitched* from the *unpitched* instruments. Chapter 3 discusses how pitch is created through periodic waveforms. Many percussion instruments, such as the cymbals, the bass drum, and the snare drum, do not produce sounds with periodic waveforms, and thus no specific pitch can be discerned. Other percussion instruments, such as the xylophone and the marimba, are definitely pitched, and are even laid out like a piano keyboard. The timpani drums feature pedals for tuning them up to the right pitch.

Within the string family, there is a distinction between *bowed* and *nonbowed* instruments. The violin, its alto and tenor versions the viola and cello, as well as the double bass, all make their sound by drawing a *bow* made of wood and horse hair across their strings, creating a continuous sound. These instruments can also be plucked, too (called *pizzicato*). Other string instruments, such as the guitar, the mandolin, and the banjo, cannot be bowed. These are meant to be plucked by the finger or pick. These three also are different from the bowed instruments because they have *frets*, little ridges on the fingerboard that help the player land exactly on pitch. The bowed instruments all have smooth fingerboards, allowing

Percussion Range

Pitched and unpitched percussion

Bowed and nonbowed strings

Bow

Pizzicato

Single-reed and double-reed woodwinds

Fret

John Bonham of the band Led Zeppelin playing the drums. Photo by Neal Preston.
Source: CORBIS.

Vibrato

Orchestra

the player to slide between pitches and produce other effects, such as *vibrato*, a gentle wavering of pitch.

DIFFERENCES BY ENSEMBLE

Another way in which these families are subdivided is by the setting in which they usually appear. The bowed string instruments mentioned above commonly appear in an *orchestra*, but the nonbowed strings do not, with the exception of the harp. A clarinet is common to an orchestra, but its cousin, the saxophone, is not. Composers like to experiment with nontraditional instruments, and so exceptions to these rules are common, but we can still categorize these instruments by their presence in the following large ensembles (shown in Table 5.4–5.6).

TABLE 5.4: COMMON ORCHESTRAL INSTRUMENTS.

WOODWINDS	BRASS	STRINGS	PERCUSSION	VOICE	ELECTRONIC
Piccolo	Trumpet	Harp	Timpani	Possibly a chorus or one or more soloists	Sometimes synthesizer, especially in films
Flute	French Horn	Violin	Snare Drum		
Oboe	Trombone	Viola	Bass Drum		
Clarinet	Tuba	Cello	Cymbals		
Bassoon		Double Bass	Miscellaneous noise makers		

Ye Zhu playing the piano. Photo by David H. Wells.
Source: CORBIS.

TABLE 5.5: COMMON INSTRUMENTS IN A CONCERT BAND.

WOODWINDS	BRASS	STRINGS	PERCUSSION	VOICE	ELECTRONIC
Piccolo	Trumpet	none	Snare Drum	none	none
Flute	French Horn		Bass Drum		
Oboe	Trombone		Cymbals		
Clarinet	Baritone Horn		Glockenspiel		
Bassoon					
Saxophones	Tuba or Sousaphone		Miscellaneous noise makers		

TABLE 5.6: COMMON INSTRUMENTS IN A LARGE JAZZ ENSEMBLE.

WOODWINDS	BRASS	STRINGS	PERCUSSION	VOICE	ELECTRONIC
Saxophones	Trumpet	none	Drum set (kick drum, snare, toms, cymbals)	None, although occasional soprano or baritone singer	Electric Guitar
Sometimes a clarinet or flute	Trombone		Sometimes a vibraphone		Electric Bass (or Double bass)
			Sometimes other percussion		Electric Piano (or Acoustic)

Refer to the Appendix at the back of the book for this Listening Activity's complete worksheet. Use the following section to make notes for yourself.

LISTENING ACTIVITY 5.1:

Identifying Instruments

*I*n the list below are several excerpts from your recordings. Listen to the specified segment on the CD track, then determine the *predominant instrument* in the excerpt (usually the one carrying the melody). List the instrument's *family* (voice, woodwinds, brass, etc.) and the *range*—whether it's a *high, medium,* or *low* member of that family. (If none of the choices applies, write in *n/a*.)

EXCERPT	FAMILY	RANGE
1. Smetana, "The Moldau," (CD 2/6) 0:00–0:30		
2. Smetana, "The Moldau," (CD 2/6) 1:00–1:30		
3. Puccini, "*Che Gelida Manina,*" (CD 2/15) 0:00–0:30		
4. Copland, *Appalachian Spring,* (CD 2/10) 1:53–2:15		
5. Meyer, Listening Activity 2.2, track 2		
6. Parker, "Mohawk," (CD 1/8) 0:40–1:40		
7. Puente, "*Mambo Guzon,*" (CD 1/11) 1:56–2:00		
8. Berry, "Johnny B. Goode," (CD 1/10) 0:00–0:15		
9. Vivaldi, "Spring," I, (CD 1/13) 0:30–1:00		
10. Brahms, Intermezzo, (CD 2/5) 0:00–0:30		

IDENTIFYING INSTRUMENTS

*L*earning to identify instruments by their timbre is an important part of enjoying music. Unfortunately, there are no short-cuts to developing this skill. Those who attend concerts regularly have an advantage over those who do not, simply because they can see the instruments in action. Over time, you'll become increasingly familiar with the timbre of different instruments, and will even be able to determine the instrumentation of recordings.

Checkpoint

Timbre is the quality of sound which helps us distinguish between different instruments and voices. Different instruments produce different timbres because of the differences in emphasis in the overtone series.

The various musical styles and musical cultures have different values regarding timbre; some prefer pure timbres, while others prefer timbres with other noise elements.

Timbre is determined in part by the way the sound is produced through the energy source, vibrating element, and resonating chamber. These differences help distinguish between the seven instrument families: woodwinds, brass, strings, percussion, voice, and electronic. Some instruments are members of families within families, such as the saxophone, which comes in five different sizes. Within families, there are also other categories, such as the single *reed* and *double reed* groups (woodwinds); the *pitched* and *unpitched* group (percussion); and the *bowed* and *nonbowed group* (strings). In addition, instruments can be organized based on the kinds of large ensembles in which they typically are used, *orchestra, concert band,* or *jazz ensemble.*

KEY TERMS

Timbre

The physics of timbre

Energy source

Vibrating element

Resonating chamber

The stages of sound production

Reed

Mouthpiece

Woodwind

Brass

String

Percussion

Keyboard

Electronic

Voice

Range

Single-reed and double-reed
    woodwinds

Pitched and unpitched percussion

Bowed and nonbowed strings

Bow

Pizzicato

Fret

Vibrato

Orchestra

CHAPTER
6

Form and Other Elements

We will now discuss musical form, and we will survey other aspects of music.

FORM

*F*orm is the way in which composers structure the musical elements to give their music unity and coherence. Form is revealed through the repetition of musical elements such as melody, rhythm, and so forth. Form is something that is generally not in the foreground, that calls attention to itself. But this does not mean it is unimportant. Even when listeners are not concious of the structure, they still have expectations about it. When a composer fulfills these expectations, the listener feels satisfied; when the composer does not, the listener may feel unsettled. Form can be a powerful tool in the effectiveness of music.

The construction of music can be compared to the construction of a house. Form in music is like the frame of a house, providing important internal structure and yet not determining the final appearance of the building. Indeed, houses built using the same floorplan and framing can end up looking quite different, depending on the materials used in the final stages of construction. In music, this is even more true: the same form can be used to produce hundreds, even thousands of distinct musical end results. Of course, some subdivisions are filled with "cookie-cutter" houses, replicated buildings with no individual character. Likewise, some music can be criticized as being too "formulaic."

The fundamental concern of musical structure is *repetition* and *contrast.* Music with pleasing form has a fair amount of both—the music changes enough to be interesting, but also provides the satisfaction of returning to the familiar. Too much of either repetition or contrast creates problems in form. Too much repetition makes for dull music, but too much contrast makes for aimless, drifting music without anchor.

It is important to understand that repetition and contrast are not absolutes, but rather represent the opposite ends of a continuum (see Figure 6.1). Sometimes a segment of music is repeated verbatim; at other times, when the segment is repeated there are slight changes. Likewise, a segment of music may be followed by contrasting music that is totally different, or—more often—this contrasting segment may have some elements that can be traced to the original music. To some degree, analyzing form is a matter of assessing when the next segment of music has changed enough to be considered new.

Different periods in music history have different relationships to form. At certain times, such as in the late eighteenth century, as well as the current phase in popular music, form is fairly regular. At other times, such as in the late nineteenth century, and in much of the rock music of the late 1960s and early 1970s, regularity in form is studiously avoided. This does not mean these styles of music are *formless,* rather that the form is idiosyncratic, changing from composer to composer and even piece to piece.

Form

LISTENING FOR FORM

*I*n different musical eras, musicians and listeners have also used different terms to describe their forms. Early nineteenth century

Repetition and contrast

The musical segment repeats exactly.	The repetition is somewhat varied from the original.	The next bit of music bears some degree of resemblance to the first segment.	The next musical segment is entirely different.

FIGURE 6.1: *Repetition and Contrast as a Continuum.*

music critics used words like *exposition, development,* and *recapitulation;* jazz musicians speak of a *head,* a *refrain,* and a *tag;* rock musicians refer to *verses, choruses,* and *bridges.* In the chapters on musical styles that follow, terms appropriate for each style are used.

One system for analyzing form that applies to all styles is simply to use letters of the alphabet to represent different musical segments. When a segment repeats, the same letter of the alphabet can appear twice; if it changes, the next letter should be used. If the next segment is *almost* identical to the first, but with noticeable changes (moving from the "left" toward the "middle" of the continuum discussed above in Figure 6.1), this is indicated by adding a prime symbol (′) to the repeated letter (for example, A A ′).

Listen to the musical example familiar to us from Chapter 4, "Simple Gifts" (on the website for Chapter 6), all the way through. The first step in analyzing the form is to determine what constitutes a *segment* of music. To do this, it is helpful to review the structure of melodies discussed in Chapter 3: how melodies have natural pauses every so often called *cadences,* corresponding to punctuation in grammar. The stretch of melody between the cadences is called a *phrase,* which can be made up of smaller chunks called *phrase segments.*

Here are the words to "Simple Gifts." If you can, sing along with the melody, or at least follow along with the words in your head. The lyrics will be used as referents in the discussion of form that follows:

'Tis a gift to be simple, 'tis a gift to be free
'Tis a gift to come down where we ought to be
And when you find yourself in a place just right
'Twill be in the valley of love and delight

When true simplicity is gained
To bow and to bend we shan't be ashamed
But to turn, turn, 'twill be our delight
And by turning, turning, we come 'round right

Notice that in the first line of "Simple Gifts," there is a little break after the word "free." But after the word "be," there seems to be a more pronounced break. Most musicians would probably breathe at this point, making the first two lines of text into a single phrase, one which consists of two phrase segments. These two lines can be considered one chunk of music and labeled "A."

How does one decide what constitutes the next chunk? In music, as in other fields, the simplest solution is often the best. In this case, that the music continues in the same phrase structure indicates the next chunk. The next phrase of the tune ("And when you find yourself . . . ") does, in fact, naturally divide in a similar fashion to the beginning, with two lines of text making up the next phrase. This tendency for music to divide into equal parts is especially common in folk songs like "Simple Gifts"; when this happens, a piece of music is said to possess a *regular phrase structure.*

What letter would best represent this second phrase, "A" (the music is repeated exactly), "A′" (repeated with alterations), or "B" (significantly different)? The best way to decide this is to listen to the two phrases several times, back to back. In this case, the second phrase starts off very similarly to the first phrase, but ends differently. When this happens, the second phrase is really a variant of the first, and should be assigned the letter "A′."

It is in the third phrase that a difference worth noticing can be found, at last. The first two phrases had started off with lower notes, then moved generally upwards (Figure 6.2).

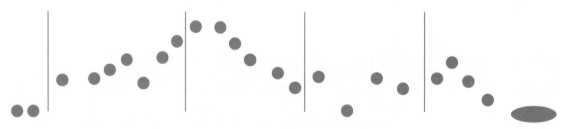

FIGURE 6.2: *Graphic Representation of the First Phrase of "Simple Gifts."*

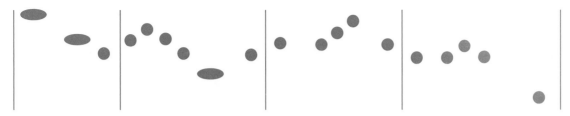

FIGURE 6.3: *Graphic Representation of the Third Phrase of "Simple Gifts."*

A A' B A''

FIGURE 6.4: *The Form of "Simple Gifts."*

But the third phrase starts with the highest note of the song and generally works its way downward (Figure 6.3).

This makes the third phrase different enough to be labeled "B." The fourth and final phrase returns to something more similar to the first and second phrases. If this phrase represents a significant modification of either of the first two phrases, two prime symbols ("A''") can be used. Thus, the form of the whole tune can be represented as shown in Figure 6.4.

SUBSIDIARY FORM

*I*n "Simple Gifts," the structure of the music happens to correspond to the phrase structure, but this is not always the case. In many pieces, a chunk of music consists of several phrases put together, or even a longer passage of music. You will find that you will have to make adjustments in the size of the musical chunks you analyze in order for your analysis to make sense for a particular piece of music. You will need to specify, in writing, what span of music your "A" encompasses.

Sometimes, analyzing form can only make sense if you take into account more than one formal level. Your "A" might consist of several smaller sections, which you can indicate with lower-case letters. This is called *subsidiary form,* meaning it describes the structure of only *part* of a piece of music. Very elaborate music can have levels within levels within levels, like Russian *babushka* dolls. Remember the axiom, however, that sometimes the simplest explanation is clearest. Usually, there is a single most important level that form operates on, containing the most important musical events. You must make sure the details do not cloud the big picture.

Subsidiary form

LISTENING PREPARATION

In popular music, the following terms are used to describe musical form:

Introduction	The beginning, instrumental part of the song.
Verse	Verses present the narrative of the song, if there is one; usually the music repeats but the words change each time. We can indicate successive verses with numbers: Verse 1, Verse 2, etc.
Chorus	Choruses are usually the musical climaxes of the song, often featuring the song's title. Unlike verses, both words and music usually repeat in choruses.
Bridge	Neither verse nor chorus, a bridge is usually just past the midway point of a song, presenting new music and lyrics.

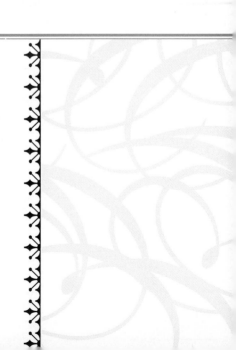

Intro	Verse 1	Chorus	Verse 2	Chorus	Bridge	Chorus	Chorus

FIGURE 6.5: *Typical Form of Popular Music, ca. 1975–2000.*

Intro	Verse 1	Chorus	Verse 2	Chorus	Solo	Verse 3	Chorus	Chorus

FIGURE 6.6: *One Variant on the Typical Pop-Song Form.*

Intro	Verse 1 (A)	Chorus1 (B)	Chorus 2 (C)	Verse 2 (A)	Chorus 1 (B)	Chorus 2 (C)	Bridge	Chorus 1 (B)	Chorus 2 (C)

FIGURE 6.7: *Another Variant on the Typical Pop-Song Form, the "ABC" form.*

Solo	Sometimes in place of a bridge, or in addition to it, there is an instrumental solo.
Tag or Coda	The ending music. This can be instrumental, or, more often, it features repeating elements of the chorus, which slowly fade out.

Possibly the most common layout of a popular song can be diagramed as shown in Figure 6.5.

Exceptions to this, however, are probably just as common. The song you listen to may feature a guitar solo rather than a bridge, and a third verse after the solo (Figure 6.6).

Another variant, which can be called the "ABC Form," features a two-part chorus (Figure 6.7).

In the Listening Activity that follows, you will be making your own formal diagram. Whatever the form your song takes, remember that it is what the artists *do* with the form that counts.

LISTENING ACTIVITY 6.1:

Hearing Form

On a separate sheet of paper, diagram the form of a popular song of your choice. Using the terms above, plus any other terms or symbols you think might help in your explanation (such as letters of the alphabet), create the clearest diagram you can for your music. Include both a diagram and a paragraph or two explaining in words what happens.

OTHER MUSICAL ELEMENTS

The five main musical elements have now been discussed: rhythm, melody, harmony, timbre, and form. There are a few other matters to address before beginning a detailed look at several musical styles, other elements such as dynamics and lyrics, as well as how to write about concerts and recordings.

DYNAMICS

In classical music, the term *dynamics* refers to volume. Just like other aspects of classical music such as rhythm, there are Italian words used in the music to indicate how loudly or softly the musicians are supposed to play:

DYNAMIC TERM	ABBREVIATION	MEANING
pianissimo	*pp*	very soft
piano	*p*	soft
mezzo-piano	*mp*	somewhat soft
mezzo-forte	*mf*	somewhat loud
forte	*f*	loud
fortissimo	*ff*	very loud

And there are terms for gradual changes in dynamics as well:

DYNAMIC TERM	ABBREVIATION	MEANING
crescendo	*cresc.*	gradually getting louder
decrescendo	*decresc.*	gradually getting softer
diminuendo	*dim.*	gradually getting softer

Dynamics are an important ingredient in classical music, creating echo effects and adding to the music's expressiveness. Indeed, one of the signs of an excellent classical musician is his or her attentiveness to subtle shades of dynamics, making a *mezzo-forte* truly different from a *forte,* for example.

Of course, volume is not just important in classical music. Some rock musicians have even given instructions on the proper volume at which an album is to be played (usually *very loudly!*). For a time in the 1970s, rock bands had an unspoken contest to see who could play the loudest concert (which The Who won), eventually compelling cities to enforce noise ordinances for the sake of the neighbors of the concert stadiums.

Most musicians, even rock musicians, try to avoid such extremes. If music is too loud, our ears can be permanently damaged. Of course, if music is too soft, it becomes too easy to ignore, such as the ambient music played as background in stores. In between these extremes, the volume of music has the potential to move us greatly, from the soothing softness of a

Dynamics

Photo by Randi Anglin.
Source: The Image Works.

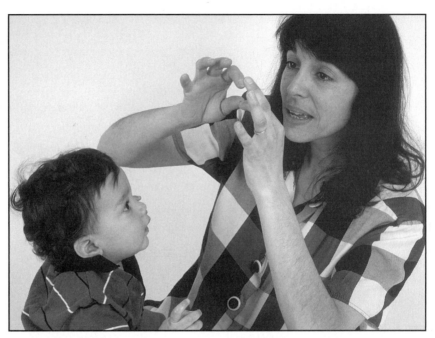

Photo by Laura Dwight.
Source: CORBIS.

lullaby to the stirring excitement of a loud marching band in a parade. As you listen to music, think of how the dynamic level is changing, and what effect this has on you at any given moment.

LYRICS

Lyrics

The words that are set to music, *lyrics,* can also be an important element. Not all music features words, of course, but most popular music does. Lyrics provide extra insight into the meaning of a song. Words carry emotional weight that can add to the overall effect of the music, and the emotional power of music, in turn, can amplify the meaning of the text.

There can be a great variety in the ways a composer deals with lyrics. Some composers deliberately send mixed messages, setting sad lyrics with happy music or vice versa, giving the song a kind of irony. Or, they might set different parts of the lyrics differently, highlighting a sense of transformation in the text. On a more detailed level, sometimes it can be interesting how a composer sets particular words, providing an emphasis through dynamics or rhythm

that may not be present in the original text. Some music scholars have looked at how several different composers set the same poem to music.

In classical music, the lyrics often have had an independent life as poetry before becoming co-opted by a composer, but this is not always the case with popular music. Songwriters have a variety of working methods: some work in teams, where one musician provides the words for another to set to music; sometimes a band will improvise music to which one or more members then apply lyrics; and for other songwriters, the lyrics and music are really created simultaneously, inextricably wedded together. There is no one best way of working; the important thing is how the lyrics and music complement each other in the final song.

Have you ever heard songs where the lyrics seem awkward or ungainly? Many novice songwriters produce songs where the natural emphasis of the words and music do not quite line up. Songwriting is harder than it seems. As you explore the many styles of music ahead—and in your own listening—think about how the music and text interrelate, whether they support each other or fall into deliberate or accidental conflict with each other.

INTONATION

*T*he term *intonation* refers to how in tune an instrument or singer is. How in tune a musician is—with other musicians or just by himself or herself—can be a major factor in how good the musician sounds. In Western music, especially classical music, professional musicians are expected to play exactly in tune, and a musican who plays well but has not tuned his instrument properly can ruin an otherwise fine performance.

Intonation

WRITING ABOUT MUSIC

*T*he ability to put all these elements together into words that describe music can be difficult. Even professional music critics complain about how difficult it can be to capture the essence of music on paper. With a little practice, however, and some guidelines, you might find that the writing process enhances your enjoyment of music, enabling you to formulate concrete statements about musical events that clarifies what is happening. Here are some things to think about as you begin to write about music:

The Quality of Writing Still Counts: Beginning students of music often get so caught up in the magic of the music they are describing, they let their writing style degenerate. All the rules of good writing are just as applicable when writing about music as they are when writing about anything else.

When in Doubt, Be Specific: Another temptation in writing about music is to use vague terms (for example, "the music was very flowing"). The more specific you can be, the better. Use the terms discussed in these chapters to describe exactly what is happening (for example, "the melody was very tuneful"). Your goal is to give the reader a clear understanding of the music.

Make Your Observations Add Up to Something: Musical writing with *too many* specifics can be just as bad as writing with too few specifics, however. Many beginning students pile on detail after detail,

exhausting the reader with too much information. It is not necessary to run through a checklist of musical elements, since not every element will be important or even present at any given time in the music. Instead, focus on the most important features, describe them precisely, and then show how they contribute to the broader picture—the beauty and meaning of the music. Having a thesis for your report can help, a single point you found most important about the performance that you want to convey. With this strategy all your musical observations can support your thesis.

Common Musical Misspellings: Here are some musical terms that music students often misspell. When in doubt, look up the word in a music dictionary:

MISSPELLED WORD	CORRECT SPELLING
Base	Bass
Chello	Cello
Creshendo	Crescendo
Symbol	Cymbal
Rythem	Rhythm
Saxaphone	Saxophone
Tympany	Timpani
Virtuous	Virtuosic

Different Rules for Different Styles: Remember, different musical styles have different modes of operation. At a classical concert, it is considered inappropriate to make any noise while the music is being played. At a rock concert, on the other hand, the musicians would probably be very concerned if the crowd was not cheering, clapping, singing, or at least holding up a burning cigarette lighter all throughout the music. Make sure you write about the music according to the rules and terminology appropriate to that style.

Enjoy your musical journey!

Checkpoint

Form is the last of the five main musical elements. When listening to form, attention is drawn to the repetition and contrast of "chunks" of a musical composition. Repetition and contrast can be considered to be two ends of a continuum; usually in repetition there is some contrast, and vice versa. Different musical styles use different terms for their formal units, but one method of analysis, which can be used with any musical style, is an alphabetical notation (A, B, A′, etc.). Form can operate on several layers at once.

Other musical elements include dynamics (how loud or soft the music is) and lyrics—more specifically, how the lyrics are set to music.

The final challenge is putting all these tools together in order to write elegantly about music.

KEY TERMS

Form	Subsidiary form	Lyric
Repetition and contrast	Dynamics	Intonation

The Blues

Virtually every substyle of American popular music in the twentieth century—among them jazz, country, rap and rock—can claim origins in the blues. While the blues has never been the most popular form of music across the country, it has left an indelible mark on popular music in the United States and around the world. What was once played by and for a small group of poor black sharecroppers has circled the globe and continues to influence popular and art music today.

BLUES BACKGROUND

The phrase "having the blues" can be traced to Elizabethan England. When one felt sad, one was supposedly being attacked by "blue devils." The term was not applied to music until the first decade of the twentieth century, but as a description of emotion it was in common use throughout the South for centuries. And the emotion itself was in plentiful supply as well.

Sharecroppers

After the slaves were freed during the American Civil War, there was some uncertainty about their future. Despite the aims of the Reconstruction period after the war to transform the South, a system of sharecropping eventually emerged that was not too different from slavery. The landowners of the former Confederacy had no money, but they did have land. Most former slaves had neither wealth nor land. So they returned to the lives they had known before Emancipation, planting crops and picking cotton from sun up to sun down. The landowners fed and housed the sharecroppers in a minimal fashion, then deducted the cost of room, board, and the use of their equipment from the workers' compensation.

Field holler
Call and response

Having been denied education for the most part, the black workers had little knowledge of numbers, so at the end of a harvest season they might learn that the cost of room and board had exceeded their earnings by $400, and thus they were bound to continue working on the plantation to pay off their "debt." Many plantations did not pay the sharecroppers at all, at least not in the traditional sense; the workers may have been paid in a currency minted on the plantation, and thus only good at the plantation store, owned by the landowner; or the workers may have been paid in the form of a "share" of the crops (thus the name "sharecropper"). Those sharecroppers who found a way to get out of this system and leave a plantation would often be arrested for vagrancy and sent to prison, where they would typically be sentenced to hard labor in chain gangs. Plantation owners varied greatly in how they treated their former slaves, but in general the South was dependent on cheap black labor and treated its sharecroppers in an exploitive fashion.

WORK MUSIC

As they worked in these miserable conditions, black sharecroppers created beautiful music. When the work involved a regular pace—such as hammering railroad ties and chopping trees—their songs emphasized the rhythm and helped coordinate the work. For work that demanded an individual pace among the workers, such as picking cotton, a different kind of song emerged: the *field holler*, more languid and mournful. Both kinds of work songs featured a *call-and-response* format, where a leader would call out the beginning of a musical phrase and the other workers would join in as they wished. The texture of black work songs was *heterophonic* (see Chapter 4). This work music strongly influenced the character of the blues.

Although they were influenced by work music, the blues were not typically sung at work. The blues—along with other kinds of popular songs—were heard after hours, for entertainment. On a

Saturday night, one of the workers' shotgun shacks would be converted into a makeshift bar for what was called a house party. Drinking bootleg liquor, the workers would dance to the blues. The blues was not strictly a country phenomenon found among share-croppers; many musicians, especially blind ones, who could not otherwise work, made their living playing the blues on street corners of cities.

SUBSTYLES OF THE BLUES

The blues can be grouped into four sub-styles that roughly correspond to a chronology of the style development. The oldest substyle is called country blues, an acoustic style which emerged in the last decades of the nineteenth century. In the teens and twenties, an urbanized version of the blues developed that is now called classic blues, usually featuring a prominent female lead singer backed by various instruments. Starting in the 1930s, country blues musicians who had relocated to Chicago and other northern cities began to use amplified instruments; this substyle is now generally referred to as Chicago blues. The final substyle to be discussed in this chapter will be loosely referred to as contemporary blues, encompassing all the different ways in which the blues is manifest today.

MUSICAL ELEMENTS OF THE BLUES

The musical elements of the blues are particularly difficult to pin down. Not only are there vast differences between the different substyles of the blues listed above, there are also enormous differences from performer to performer and even between different performances of the same piece. There are, however, certain tendencies that characterize the blues:

Rhythm: The meter in the blues is almost always quadruple. Sometimes there is a suggestion of a *triplet* (meaning the four beats of the measure get subdivided into three rather than two)—so much so that sometimes there seem to be measures of twelve quicker beats rather than four. Many blues fall into two tempo categories: fast and danceable, and slow and melancholy. There are, however, many blues with tempos somewhere in the middle. Some blues are notable for their rhythmic complexity, featuring syncopation and cross-rhythms.

Melody: The blues features a call-and-response format borrowed from the field holler. In most cases, a singer makes the "call" and an instrument, most typically a guitar, gives a "response." In the early days of the blues, melodies were not particularly tuneful, but the tunefulness increased as it became an increasingly commercial product through the classic blues and Chicago blues eras. Likewise, the melodic contour, which was jagged and unpredictable in country blues, gradually smoothed out in the later commercial eras. One of the most important features of blues melodies is the use of *blue notes,* the downward bending of certain pitches (especially the third, fifth, and seventh scale degrees) for expressive effect (see Chapter 3 on the *blues scale*). Blues melodies also feature a lot of sliding between notes, sometimes landing on *microtones,* notes "between the cracks of the piano" keyboard. The more you listen to the blues, the more you can hear the beautiful melodic subtleties.

Harmony: Because of the blue notes, sometimes it can be difficult to determine exactly what is happening harmonically, since bending the third of a major chord downward will eventually make it sound minor. But in general, blues harmony is among the simplest of all styles of music discussed in this book. Usually a blues song will feature three chords, and some older blues numbers just use a single chord throughout.

Texture: The blues is usually homophonic, featuring a single melody line with accompaniment, either by solo guitar or a full band. In some cases, however, a kind of countermelody played by an instrument

House party

Country blues

Classic blues

Blue notes

Chicago blues

Microtones

Contemporary blues

weaves a sinuous line through the vocal melody, creating a heterophony reminiscent of the black work song.

Timbre and Instrumentation: The most important instrument for the blues is the guitar, originally acoustic, then electric. One of the most distinguishing characteristics of the blues is the use of a slide on the left hand, allowing the guitarist to slide between notes and providing a unique metallic timbre. Today, guitar stores sell glass and metal slides, but in the early days guitarists used broken bottle necks or knife blades. Another distinctive blues instrument is the harmonica, known in this context as a *blues harp,* which was amplified starting in the Chicago blues era. The classic blues era saw a variety of instruments not unlike those found in the typical jazz ensemble of the day, but since then the instrumentation of the blues has been mostly similar to a rock band (and in fact it has served as the model for the modern rock ensemble): one or two electric guitars, vocalist, electric bass, drums, and the addition of a harmonica and perhaps a few horns (meaning saxophones and trumpets).

Blues harp

Just as important as the kind of instrument is the way it is played. Blues musicians favor a particularly raspy timbre that cuts across all the instruments to some degree. The singers' voices often sound hoarse or strained, and guitars and blues harps may be amplified to the point of distortion. Scholars have traced this aesthetic back to certain regions of Africa, where musicians place beads and other objects on drums, xylophones, and other instruments to create buzzing sound whenever they are played.

Form: The blues have always been created in a variety of forms, but especially since the advent of recordings in the 1920s a certain degree of standardization has become evident. The blues is a *strophic* form (that is, a song made up of several verses, but no other sections), and in the standardized version, each verse is twelve bars long. These twelve bars are divided into three groups of four measures each. The first two groups feature the same line of lyrics, and the last group presents an answer, usually rhymed. Within each four-bar group, the singer sings for

Blues guitarist Furry Lewis (1964). Photo by Ray Flerlage.
Source: Chansley Entertainment Archives.

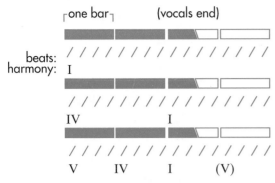

beats:
harmony:

FIGURE 7.1: *Standard Blues Format, One Verse. The Shaded Areas Are the Approximate Extent of the Singing in Each Line.*

about two and a half bars, then the guitar or another instrument responds to fill out the remainder of the four bars.

In addition, the blues format is known for a particular harmonic progression, marching through its three chords in a similar way each time. A diagram of the standardized blues form would thus look like Figure 7.1.

Lyrics: The words of the blues are among the most intriguing aspect of the music. Blues lyrics, like much else in the music, were originally improvised. Singers did not make everything up, however. There were a number of stock phrases that all blues singers knew and could pull up on the spot, such as "Don't you hear me weep and moan?" or "I got a handful of nickels, a pocketful of dimes." In the early days, therefore, a blues song would never be performed the same way twice; the general mood and several key phrases would be maintained, but other phrases would be called up on the spot by the singer. In fact, this may be the reason for the unusual lyric pattern of the blues: repeating the first line gave the singer an opportunity to make up a witty line that rhymed.

In content, blues lyrics cover a wide range from the profound to the obscene, from poetic metaphor to utter nonsense. Especially before the blues became a national phenomenon, the lyrics tended to relate to matters close to the singer. Many of these songs featured the names of actual people, places, and situations drawn directly from the singer's life. After the blues became more widely distributed through records, some of the personal nature of the lyrics disappeared.

Blues form

COUNTRY BLUES

The Mississippi Delta is a 200-mile swath of land stretching from just south of Memphis, Tennessee, down to Vicksburg, Mississippi, about thirty miles wide with the Mississippi River forming its western boundary. A former floodplain, the Delta was cleared for farming beginning at the end of the nineteenth century. This involved building massive levees to discourage the mighty river from escaping its banks, and clearing the land of trees and undergrowth. The land underneath that growth was rich with dark alluvial soil, perfect for cotton and other crops.

African-Americans came from miles around to the Delta for work, attracted by the higher pay and the nature of the work. Instead of being tied to a single plantation, many black workers in the Delta had the opportunity to move from job to job, and thus slip away from a potentially bad situation. In the first three decades of the twentieth century there were still forests to be cleared in the Delta, as well as railroad tracks to be laid and highways to be built, in addition to the traditional farm work. Yet despite this freedom, or perhaps because of it, life was hard in the Delta for most blacks. A frontier mentality prevailed,

Charley Patton
(1891–1934)

where a worker could be killed if he or she stepped out of line. Because the men, especially, were constantly moving from job to job, their lives became rootless and nuclear families rarely remained intact. A common saying in the Delta was that a mule was worth more than a black man.

THE MUSIC OF THE DELTA

*I*n the Delta, at the bottom of the black social scale stood the musician. Religious folk associated music with illegal alcohol and prostitution, and the professional musician, who did not put in his hours behind the plow or hunched over in the field picking cotton, was often seen as lazy and useless by other blacks. Some of the early blues singers were itinerant workers who sang as they moved from job to job. Nevertheless a small group of professional musicians slowly emerged in the 1910s and 1920s, those who made some or most of their living off their music. Some played at house parties; some at more established places called *juke joints;* some played at the docks and street corners for whatever coins the passersby would toss them. Most musicians led an even more rootless life than the average worker, staying in one place for only a night or two before moving on. Because of the rootlessness of blues musicians, the music quickly spread out of the Delta to other regions of the South.

Although ancestors of the blues began to develop after the Civil War, the blues did not really exist before around 1900. The original traveling blues musicians played a wide variety of music: long storytelling ballads, versions of work songs sung in the fields, old-time fiddle tunes, and music for dancing called *jump-up tunes.* The guitar was just one of the instruments heard: musicians also played fiddles (violins), various brass and woodwind instruments, even homemade instruments such as the one-string *diddley-bow* and the jug, which musicians blew over the top to create a deep, resonant bass sound.

CHARLEY PATTON (1891–1934)

*S*tarting with the career of Charley Patton, both the guitar and the blues began to take leading roles in the music of the Delta. Patton learned the guitar from a fellow worker on the large Dockery plantation in the northern part of the Delta when he was a teenager, and this is where he gave most of his performances, at the dances held by sharecroppers. He was a consummate entertainer, stomping out rhythms with his feet and throwing his guitar up in the air for effect. Patton made some of the earliest recordings of any Delta blues artist, starting in 1929, and became the first celebrity from that region. Musicians who passed through the Dockery farm sought him out, and he happily taught them his technique and songs. Virtually every Delta blues musician of that time—including Willie Brown, Son House, Tommy Johnson, and Louise Johnson (no relation to Tommy)—learned from Patton and later became recording artists through his influence. Son House and Willie Brown, in turn, were the primary mentors of Robert Johnson (see Biography 7.1), who was the star of the next generation of blues musicians.

In the late 1930s and early 1940s, the great migration of African-Americans to northern cities began to alter the nature of the Delta blues. Most of the great musicians spent increasing time in the big cities of the so-called Blues Highway—Memphis, St. Louis, and ultimately, Chicago—and eventually moved away permanently from the Delta. In the cities, the character of the blues changed radically. Only in the 1950s and 1960s, when white listeners were becoming interested in folk music, did the original acoustic blues get the nationwide attention it deserved, and by that time most of the great performers were dead or had changed their style.

MUSICIAN BIOGRAPHY 7.1:

ROBERT JOHNSON *(1911–1938)*

Robert Johnson was born out of wedlock in Hazlehurst, Mississippi, a small town southeast of the Delta, and spent most of his childhood in a different small town in the north of the state, Robinsonville. In his early teens he taught himself to play the blues harp, turning to the guitar in the late 1920s. His first mentor was the local musician Willie Brown, a friend of Charley Patton, and Johnson followed the two of them around when they played in Robinsonville. At this point, music was just for fun, and at the age of eighteen Johnson got married and moved to a large plantation nearby to begin his life as a sharecropper.

All this was shattered in April 1930 when his sixteen-year-old wife and the child she was carrying both died in childbirth. After this Johnson turned toward his music more actively, apprenticing himself to another colleague of Patton's, Eddie "Son" House (1902–1988). Johnson was apparently not very good at this point, and Patton, Brown, and House would often make fun of his playing. Later in 1930 he decided to leave home and travel to Hazlehurst in an unsuccessful search for his biological father. When he returned several years later and played for his former mentors, they could only stare in disbelief. Johnson was now playing better than any of them, making his guitar sound like an entire band.

The rest of his short life was spent on the road, moving quickly from town to town, woman to woman. His travels took him to Chicago, New York, even Ontario, but he always returned to the Delta region. He was recorded only in two Texas recording sessions in 1936, totaling 29 songs, and saw only moderate success as a recording artist in his lifetime. But his talent was legendary. If he heard a song once—even while in the middle of a conversation—he could immediately play it perfectly. The sound of his guitar, according to one fellow musician, "affected most women in a way that I could never understand"—and this magnetism may have been his downfall. In the summer of 1938, Robert had an affair with the wife of the bar owner where he had been performing. The owner reportedly put poison in Johnson's whiskey, and by August 16, 1938, he was dead.

SIDENOTE: VOODOO BLUES?

One of the most famous stories about Robert Johnson was that he sold his soul to the devil in order to learn to play the blues so well. This is a well-traveled story, applied to many blues musicians: a young man walks out to a crossroads at midnight with his guitar, and a mysterious large black man appears out of nowhere and strikes the deal. The popularity of the story says something about the mystique of the blues, and the fact that many proper church-going black folk considered the music evil. Versions of this tale can be found in ancient Voodoo lore, the African religion found in the Caribbean, where the trickster god Legba materialized at crossroads to offer men secret powers—for a price. Although the voodoo religion has largely disappeared, certain myths and superstitions in African-American culture can be traced to it, and these occasionally crop up in both lyrics and stories about the blues.

LISTENING PREPARATION

Robert Johnson, "Cross Road Blues" (Recorded 1936).

This is probably the most famous of Robert Johnson's blues recordings, in part due to various re-make versions of it by Eric Clapton and others, and in part due to the extramusical associations given to crossroads in Voodoo lore (see the Sidenote box). You will find in these lyrics no mention of the devil, but that has not prevented fans from reading a subtext into the song. This is perfectly fair, since one of the best features of the blues is its use of *double entendre*.

For those who have heard more recent samples of the blues, these early recordings can seem quite foreign. There is a homespun quality to this recording, with various room noises creeping in and a buzzy quality to the slide guitar work. Johnson's vocal timbre is pinched and variable, and the melody he sings seems to leap almost randomly across the scale. Perhaps most striking is the way he treats the blues form. While he maintains the AAB lyric profile, the measure-count—like the melody—varies widely. One line may have the standard four bars, then the next may have five, or three and a half. The length seems to have been governed entirely by what Johnson felt he needed to say with his guitar. Just like any other kind of music, however, the more you listen to it, the more it grows on you, and what at first seem to be anomalies later become integral elements of the music's expression and power. Note especially how Johnson seems to play rhythm and lead guitar parts simultaneously. When Johnson's music was rediscovered long after his death, some listeners thought there was more than one guitar playing on his recordings.

LISTENING ACTIVITY 7.1:

Robert Johnson, "Cross Road Blues" (CD 1/1)

1. On your first listening, mark the CD times for the start of each line:

0.00	Introduction
0.09	I went to the cross road, fell down on my knees
_____	I went to the cross road, fell down on my knees
_____	Asked the Lord above, "Have mercy, save poor Bob, if you please."
_____	Mmm, standin' at the cross road, I tried to flag a ride
_____	Standin' at the cross road, I tried to flag a ride
_____	Ain't nobody seem to know me, everybody pass me by
_____	Mmm, the sun goin' down, boy, dark gonna catch me here
_____	ooh eee, boy, dark gonna catch me here
_____	I haven't got no lovin' sweet woman that love and feel my care
_____	You can run, you can run, tell my friend-boy Willie Brown
_____	You can run, tell my friend-boy Willie Brown
_____	Lord, that I'm standin' at the crossroad, babe, I believe I'm sinkin' down

2. Describe the lyrical content of each of the four stanzas of text. (As a point of reference, the slang phrase "friend-boy" in Stanza 4 simply means a male friend.)

   Stanza 1:

   Stanza 2:

   Stanza 3:

   Stanza 4:

3. Based on what you wrote above, construct a narrative of the events Robert Johnson describes.

4. How does the music—both the guitar work and the vocal delivery—correspond to the meaning of the words? Refer to specific lines of the text in your answer.

BLUES WOMEN

*E*ven though country blues is now considered the basis for most of the popular music that followed, what is now called "classic" blues was the most popular music in the black community at this time. In the 1920s, women blues singers were not only the most important performers of the community, they were symbols of pride for other black women across the nation, and they seemed to speak with the voice of their people.

The origins of classic blues can be found in black vaudeville. Vaudeville, both black and white, was a very popular form of entertainment in the United States starting in the 1880s, featuring a long evening of widely varying acts: comedy, drama, juggling, singing, dancing, acrobatics, magic, hypnotism, dog tricks, etc. There were several circuits of vaudeville theaters strung across the country, one of which—the Theater Owners' Booking Association (T.O.B.A., established 1909)—was reserved for black entertainers and audiences. At this time in both the North and the South, most theaters and other institutions, such as schools and hospitals, were strictly segregated, and the African-American community had its own entertainment industry.

On the black vaudeville circuit it soon became clear that among the most popular acts were women blues singers. At first, there was a certain falsity to this: the songs were usually not actually the blues, but rather Tin Pan Alley tunes written by professional black songwriters, sprinkled with blues elements. Even so, these numbers stopped the show, especially in the South. Their popularity encouraged two of these songwriters, Perry Bradford and W. C. Handy, to make a recording. They found great resistance at the white-owned record companies, where executives grossly underestimated the strength of the black market. Bradford, who was a noted songwriter, decided to join forces with the popular black singer Mamie Smith, star of a Broadway show called *Maid*

of Harlem. After several rejections, the team was finally accepted at Okeh records, recording "That Thing Called Love" with "You Can't Keep a Good Man Down" for the "B" side. (Note: records in those days held about three minutes on each side; each release would feature one main song and a second song for the reverse, or "B" side.) Recorded in February 1920, it was released that summer to much fanfare in the black press, but little promotion on the part of the record company. Still, it became a hit, with sales exceeding 100,000, a very large number in those days, revealing the extent of the African-American market. The Okeh recording manager called this the "race market," and thus the unfortunate term "race records" was born. This first recording session had featured vaudeville songs, but in the next session in August 1920, Smith recorded a song of Bradford's called "Crazy Blues," which was a smashing success. Soon, every record label in the country rushed to record new blues artists, announcing their discovery of the latest "blues queen." As an interesting side note, it was the popularity of these "blues queen" records that encouraged record companies to send out field recording units to record the male country blues singers of the Mississippi Delta and elsewhere.

THE NATURE OF CLASSIC BLUES

*D*ozens of black women were recorded during the 1920s, but two in particular stand out: Gertrude "Ma" Rainey (1886–1934) and Bessie Smith (see Biography 7.2). Rainey was one of the original classic blues singers, and maintained a country quality in her act throughout her long career. Her protégé, Bessie Smith (no relation to Mamie Smith), was somewhat more sophisticated in

Vaudeville

Vaudeville circuits

T.O.B.A.

W. C. Handy (1873–1958)

Ma Rainey (1886–1934)

Mamie Smith (1883?–1946)

her style, creating what was probably the most lasting legacy of any of these blues women. Because of the connection to vaudeville, none of these women sang the blues exclusively, but rather presented a varied program, which included pop hits and even versions of white songs. The blues, however, are what they are remembered for.

The topics of these blues were wide-ranging, although a large proportion spoke of love lost. Even when "weeping and moaning" over the disappearance of her man, however, the blues queen displayed her strength and resiliency. Some of the blues they sang were about alcohol, gambling, or other vices of the day; others were replete with violent images, the narrator bent on vengeance. Many of these songs took the form of advice to other women; Ida Cox, in "Wild Women Don't Have the Blues," urged her fellow women to kick out that "mistreatin' man." Clara Smith (no relation to Bessie or Mamie) recommended women keep four or five lovers in order to lessen their dependence on just one man. On the other hand, some of the blues tapped into the ancient African-American tradition of *signifying,* a kind of verbal competition where two or more people vie to think up the most creative insults for each other. An example is Clara Smith's "Every Woman's Blues":

> Women talk about me, they lies on me, calls me
> > out of my name
> They talks about me, they lies on me, calls me
> > out of my name
> All their men comes to see me just the same

An important element of the blues in concert was the improvisation of new words, which often left the audience roaring with laughter, but records—with their three-minute maximum length in those days—obviously could not capture this. Records also had the effect of standardizing the blues. Mamie Smith knew this as early as 1921, when she said of her audience: "They have heard my phonograph records, and they want to hear me sing these songs the same

as I do in my own studio in New York." Due to the sensibilities of the age, these records also omitted most of the salty or obscene lyrics found in many blues.

Nonetheless, without records there would not have been the blues craze of the 1920s. All through this period, and especially after World War I, African-Americans were migrating by the thousands out of the poor, rural South to the more urbanized North. Although they were better paid in the North, blacks found working conditions in the factories scarcely better. The blues provided a model of black strength and dignity, and also reminded many of the dislocated workers of their home in the South.

THE DECLINE OF CLASSIC BLUES

The blues queens dominated African-American culture during the 1920s, but their prominence would be short-lived. Two new technologies introduced during the latter part of that decade—radio networks and sound movies—sent the recording industry into a slump. The advent of the Great Depression in October 1929 did even more damage. Total record sales plummeted from 104 million in 1927 to 6 million in 1932, and most of the labels that had recorded the blues women in the 1920s either went bankrupt or were bought out by bigger labels or radio networks. Popular taste in the black community was shifting over to what would soon be called Swing, led by the young, urbane Duke Ellington (see Chapter 8). By the end of the 1930s all the original blues women had either moved over to gospel music, died, or simply faded from view. In their brief heyday, however, as author Daphne Duval Harrison says, their music "introduced a new, different model of black women—more assertive, sexy, sexually aware, independent, realistic, complex, alive."

Signifying

*Bessie Smith
(1894?–1937)*
Photo by Bettmann.
Source: CORBIS.

MUSICIAN BIOGRAPHY 7.2:

BESSIE SMITH *(1894?–1937)*

Bessie Smith was born in Chattanooga, Tennessee, one of seven children of a poor, part-time preacher who died shortly after her birth. Bessie's mother and two of her brothers also died by the time Bessie was eight or nine, and Bessie was left to be raised by her oldest sister. Bessie earned money for the family by singing on the street corners, accompanied by one of her brothers, and by the time she was in her late teens she was performing in a professional minstrel show, working primarily as a dancer. When she got the opportunity to sing, however, she inevitably stopped the show, so great was her natural singing ability. Guitarist Danny Barker said that when she sang in concert, "she could bring about mass hypnotism." For the next decade, Smith traveled the T.O.B.A. circuit, building up an enthusiastic following. In 1923 she made her debut as a recording artist, and her first recording, "Down Hearted Blues," soared to sales of 780,000 in less than six months. By 1924, she was not just another "blues queen"—she was considered the "Empress of the Blues."

Smith's stage show was dramatic: she wore fancy sequined dresses and enormous headpieces made of ostrich plumes, and her gigantic voice filled huge halls without amplification. But her off-stage life was even more dramatic. She loved to drink bootleg liquor, and when she got mad, she would throw punches at men and women alike. Smith was such a larger-than-life personality that stories have circulated about her that may or may not be true. In one of these episodes, she was performing in North Carolina under a big tent when she discovered members of the Ku Klux Klan trying to cut the ropes holding up the tent. When Smith, with her impressive size and costume, marched toward the sheeted men screaming curses like a sailor, she single-handedly scared them off. Despite her troubled life—or because of it—Smith became a model to other women for her strength and bravery, as well as for her ability to sing the blues.

Like the other blues women of her generation, the Depression derailed her career. Unlike many others, however, she pressed on against the odds, changing her repertory to meet the needs of a changing audience. She was on the brink of a career revival when she was killed in a car accident on a lonely highway near Clarksdale, Mississippi.

LISTENING PREPARATION

Bessie Smith, "Poor Man's Blues" (Recorded 1928).

Most of Smith's songs were written by others, but she was a gifted songwriter as well as performer, as this song shows. Although Bessie was not poor herself at the time she wrote these lyrics, she always maintained an acute sensitivity to the plight of the poor, especially the black poor. Some say she really meant this to be a "Black Man's Blues," that the barbs aimed at the rich were really aimed at the wealthy white culture, spoiled and exuberant in the economic boom after World War I. The "battles" she refers to are those of this war, in which African-American men served valiantly and seemed scantily rewarded upon their return home. In a matter of months after this recording, the party of the 1920s came to an abrupt end and there were thousands who would be singing their own "poor man's blues."

Smith is accompanied on this recording by two saxophones, a trombone, and piano. Her voice dominates the music, however. Listen through the crackles of this old recording to the power and expression in her delivery.

Refer to the Appendix at the back of the book for this Listening Activity's complete worksheet. Use the following section to make notes for yourself

LISTENING ACTIVITY 7.2:

Bessie Smith, "Poor Man's Blues" *(CD 1/2)*

1. On your first listening, mark the CD times for the start of each line:

0.00   Introduction

0.12   Mister rich man, rich man, open up your heart and mind,

_____   Mister rich man, rich man, open up your heart and mind,

_____   Give the poor man a chance, help stop these hard, hard times.

_____   While you're living in your mansion, you don't know what hard times mean.

_____   While you're living in your mansion, you don't know what hard times mean.

_____   Poor working man's wife is starving; your wife is living like a queen.

_____   Please listen to my pleadin', 'cause I can't stand these hard times long.

_____   Aw, listen to my pleadin', 'cause I can't stand these hard times long.

_____   They'll make an honest man do things that you know is wrong.

_____   Poor man fought all the battles, he'd fight again today.

_____   Poor man fought all the battles, he'd fight again today.

_____   He would do anything you ask him in the name of the U.S.A.

_____ Now the war is over; poor man must live the same as you.

_____ Now the war is over; poor man must live the same as you.

_____ If it wasn't for the poor man, mister rich man, what would you do?

2. Does Smith sing the same notes in each verse? If not, where does she change the melody?

3. Do you find Smith's voice expressive? Why or why not? Refer to specific lines of text in your answer.

4. Describe the accompaniment, taking special notice of the music during the "breaks." Again, refer to specific lines of text in your answer.

CHICAGO BLUES

By the second decade of the twentieth century, Chicago was the busiest railroad terminal in the world, an important Great Lakes port, and the home to large steel mills and meatpacking factories. Most of the factory jobs were closed to blacks, but this started to change during World War I, due to the increased industrial demand, the loss of manpower due to the military draft, and the sudden cutoff of European immigration. At the same time as Chicago and other northern cities were feeling the pinch of labor shortage, in the rural South a boll weevil infestation and massive flooding wreaked havoc on sharecroppers' crops, leaving families destitute. It was in this context that the Great Northern Drive began, a massive migration of black workers and families out of the countryside and into the cities of the North, which continued for a half century. Although each Northern city saw an increase in its African-American population, Chicago saw the greatest increase, where the number of blacks more than doubled between 1910 and 1920 alone.

The situation in Chicago was far from ideal. African-Americans mostly lived in a small area on the South Side, overcrowded in small ramshackle houses. They were often underpaid compared with their white fellow workers, and many found jobs taken away from them when white servicemen returned from Europe. Despite all this, most black workers considered Chicago a step above sharecropping; here, at least, they were freed from the system of perpetual serfdom.

As the black population moved north, so did musicians. Many played for coins along the Jewish merchant district called Maxwell Street, but more money could be earned in the bars (called _Speakeasies_ until Prohibition was lifted in 1933). Since the bars were larger and noisier in Chicago, most musicians found

Speakeasies

they had to be amplified in order to be heard. The electric guitar—invented in the mid-1930s—became the defining sound of this new breed of blues after World War II, later augmented by amplified blues harp, bass, and drums. Just as with classic blues, records soon spread this new music across the country, led by a small family-run, Chicago-based company called Chess Records. Unlike earlier incarnations of the blues, Chicago-style blues was broadcast over powerful radio stations such as WDIA in Memphis. When white teenagers began to listen secretly to these stations in the early 1950s, the audience for the blues widened even farther and eventually gave birth to rock and roll (see Chapter 9).

Chess Records

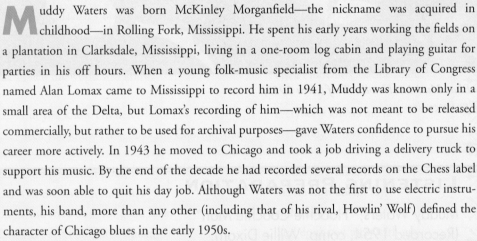

Muddy Waters (1915–1983) Photo by Terry Cryer. Source: CORBIS.

MUSICIAN BIOGRAPHY 7.3:

MUDDY WATERS *(1915—1983)*

Muddy Waters was born McKinley Morganfield—the nickname was acquired in childhood—in Rolling Fork, Mississippi. He spent his early years working the fields on a plantation in Clarksdale, Mississippi, living in a one-room log cabin and playing guitar for parties in his off hours. When a young folk-music specialist from the Library of Congress named Alan Lomax came to Mississippi to record him in 1941, Muddy was known only in a small area of the Delta, but Lomax's recording of him—which was not meant to be released commercially, but rather to be used for archival purposes—gave Waters confidence to pursue his career more actively. In 1943 he moved to Chicago and took a job driving a delivery truck to support his music. By the end of the decade he had recorded several records on the Chess label and was soon able to quit his day job. Although Waters was not the first to use electric instruments, his band, more than any other (including that of his rival, Howlin' Wolf) defined the character of Chicago blues in the early 1950s.

Then rock and roll exploded on the scene. "This hurt the blues pretty bad," he later recalled. Suddenly, audiences no longer liked the slow blues, preferring only the up-tempo numbers. After 1956, Waters never had another hit record. Chicago blues might have completely faded away had not rock musicians ultimately acknowledged the debt their music owed the blues. The members of the Rolling Stones—a band whose very name came from a Muddy Waters song—were among the most prominent rock stars to praise the blues. In the 1960s a full-fledged blues revival ensued, and Waters soon found himself leading his band on international tours and playing for the president of the United States.

Like Robert Johnson and Bessie Smith, Waters had a magnetic effect over his audience. Unlike these predecessors, his personality was more restrained and aristocratic. Although he never learned to read past a rudimentary level, he carried himself with the dignity of a king. He served as a kind of mentor to the next generation of blues performers and ensured the music he helped pioneer would continue on after his death.

CONTEMPORARY BLUES

*B. B. King
(b. 1925)*

*Robert Cray
(b. 1953)*

*Stevie Ray Vaughan
(1956–1990)*

*J*ust as young white listeners were discovering the blues for themselves, young black listeners began to disown it. Soul, led by James Brown, and then funk and rap were all more rhythmically oriented than the blues, and spoke more forthrightly about the nature of the black condition in the United States. To many young blacks of the 1960s, 1970s, and 1980s, the blues seemed to be the melancholy moanings of their grandparents, not the music of the moment. For a while it seemed as though the singing of the blues might have been passed over into the hands of white musicians, such as the talented Stevie Ray Vaughan of Texas.

Black musicians never stopped singing the blues, however, and today the blues seem to be making yet another comeback, this time among a new generation of black musicians. As the blues passes its century-mark, Chicago-style blues has become a tourist attraction in Chicago and other northern cities, led by such outstanding singer-guitarsts as B. B. King and Robert Cray. Meanwhile, young musicians such as Keb' Mo' (Kevin Moore) are reviving a breed of blues enjoyed in the time of his grandfather, including covers of Robert Johnson tunes. Meanwhile, the blues also lives, at least in part, on in the later styles of music that grew out of it: jazz, R&B (rhythm and blues), country, rock, and rap. There is hardly a song in the popular music styles of today which does not have the blues in its ancestry somewhere.

LISTENING PREPARATION

Keb' Mo', "Am I Wrong" (Recorded 1994).

Keb' Mo' (Kevin Moore) is a young, Grammy Award–winning singer, guitarist, and songwriter from California, whose influences seem to range all over the map— from traditional country blues to more electric, band-oriented blues, to gospel. "Am I Wrong," from his self-titled debut album, hews more to the traditional blues sound, with impressive slide guitar work, yet with a contemporary, rhythmic vocal delivery.

Keb' Mo'. Photo by William Allard.
*Source: National Geographic Society. William Allard/NGS
Image Collection.*

Refer to the Appendix at the back of the book for this Listening Activity's complete worksheet. Use the following section to make notes for yourself

LISTENING ACTIVITY 7.4:

Keb' Mo', "Am I Wrong" (CD 1/4)

1. On your first listening, mark the CD times for the start of each line:

0.00	Am I wrong	fallin' in love with you
_____	Tell me, am I wrong	well, fallin' in love with you
_____	While your other man was out there,	cheatin' and lyin', steppin' all over you?

Sweet thing!

_____	Tell me, am I wrong	holdin' onto you so tight?
_____	Tell me, tell me am I wrong	holdin' onto you so tight?
_____	If you other man come between you and me, he'd better be ready, ready for a long, long fight	

_____	Well, I got to be strong	well, I know you're dependin' on me
_____	You know, I got to be strong	I know you're dependin' on me
_____	To give you all my attention, all my time, and all of the love you need	

Oh! Tell me,

_____	Am I wrong	tryin' to hold onto you?
_____	Tell me, am I wrong	tryin' to hold onto you?
_____	Just want to make a home for you baby, and all of your children too	

_____	Tell me, am I wrong	fallin' in love with you
_____	You got to tell me, am I wrong	fallin' in love with you
_____	While your other man was out there, cheatin' and lyin', steppin' all over you?	

_____ While your other man was out there, cheatin' and lyin', steppin' all over you?

2. This song starts with a *pick-up,* a handful of notes before the start of the first measure; the downbeat of measure 1 is on the word "wrong" in the first line. If you listen carefully, you can hear Keb' Mo' making a regular tapping sound, created either by his foot or by his striking the body of the guitar with something metallic, perhaps a ring on his finger. On which beats to these hits occur?

3. Does this song follow the standard 12-bar blues format? Explain.

4. Describe how this song makes you feel.

KEY TERMS

Sharecroppers	Contemporary blues	T.O.B.A
Field holler	Blue notes	Signifying
Call and response	Microtones	Speakeasies
House party	Blues harp	Chess Records
Country blues	Blues form	Stop-time riffs
Classic blues	Vaudeville	
Chicago blues	Vaudeville circuits	

Jazz

CHAPTER
8

Jazz, a musical style known and loved around the world, can be surprisingly difficult to define precisely. Part of the reason for this difficulty is the acquisitive nature of the music, the fact that jazz artists have always borrowed from other styles and even foreign musical cultures. Even at its birth at the turn of the twentieth century, jazz blended elements of the blues, ragtime, the march, and other music stemming from black, white, Creole, and Latino traditions. Later jazz musicians would experiment with aspects of classical music and rock and roll, as well as indigenous music from virtually every continent on Earth. By the middle of the twentieth century jazz was a global phenomenon, with musicians from dozens of countries inflecting jazz with their own musical accents.

Another aspect of jazz that makes analysis difficult is the emphasis on improvisation. In other musical styles, such as rock and classical music, there is a "musical text" that can serve as a focal point—whether it takes the form of a CD, computer file, or musical score. But in jazz, the actual piece of music is secondary to what the musician *does* with the music in performance, spontaneously reinterpreting and even recomposing it on stage. This critical aspect of jazz also makes the style hard to pin down, since a single piece of music can have thousands of incarnations depending on who is performing it. Indeed, a single performer may produce several different versions of the same piece, depending on his or her artistic predilection on any particular night.

These two qualities of jazz—its multicultural character and its emphasis on improvisation—may make the music a "moving target," but they also are key ingredients in making it so wonderful. In fact, one could argue that these two qualities are what make it the quintessential American art form.

This chapter investigates several different stages in the development of jazz: ragtime, Dixieland, swing, bop, the various trends from 1955 to 1975, and the jazz scene today.

RAGTIME

Although jazz was born out of a blending of several different kinds of music, two styles in particular stand out as important precursors: the blues and ragtime. The blues (see Chapter 7), with its twelve-bar structure and emphasis on improvisation in the "breaks" between vocal phrases, provided the model for early vocal jazz and, to some degree, nonvocal jazz. Ragtime was originally an entirely instrumental style, however, and its unprecedented popularity from the 1890s to about the time of World War I paved the way for all African-American music that followed.

Today the name ragtime calls to mind the syncopated piano music of Scott Joplin (see Musician Biography 8.1) and others, but originally it encompassed a variety of instrumental pieces. In fact, in the early days of jazz the terms "ragtime" and "jazz" were used virtually interchangeably. Published "ragtime" pieces were scored for several different groups of instruments, and sometimes even included vocal parts. Ragtime is remembered as piano music, however, mostly because of the tremendous popularity of the living-room piano in middle-class American households at the end of the nineteenth century. Annual production of pianos in America doubled and then tripled over the twenty years starting in 1890, reaching a peak of 350,000 in 1909. The invention of the player piano in 1897—a piano equipped with a machine that would play the piano keys pneumatically by "reading" a roll of paper with holes punched in it, like a giant music box—created an even larger market. The piano was the family home entertainment center at the beginning of the twentieth century.

RAGTIME CHARACTERISTICS

Ragtime pieces (known as *rags*) were based on the most popular music in middle-class America at this time, the *march,* whose most famous exponent was the director of the Marine Band, John Philip Sousa (1854–1932). Like marches, piano rags were generally in duple meter and were built on 16-bar sections of music called *strains,* which were usually repeated immediately. On the largest scale, the format of a typical rag or march might look like Figure 8.1.

Somewhere in the middle of both marches and rags there is a repeated strain called the *trio,* often lighter and sweeter and in a different key. Rags, however, are much more *syncopated* than marches, especially in the right hand (the higher) part of the piano. The ragged rhythms played by the right hand give this style its name. The left hand, meanwhile, is the straight man of this comedy team, usually striking a single low note on each of the two beats of the measure and chords on the off-beats in more or less steady rhythm. This creates an *oom-pah oom-pah* effect similar to the one created by the tuba and banjo in early jazz. As the left hand sets the regular rhythm, the right hand jots to and fro in a delirious display of virtuosity.

The strains of a rag or march are usually sixteen measures long. These 16 measures are typically made up of four *phrases* of four *measures* (or *bars*) each. Think of the structure like a set of Chinese boxes in which smaller boxes nestle inside bigger ones (see Figure 8.2).

The first ragtime piece was published in 1897, but its first bona fide hit came with Scott Joplin's "Maple Leaf Rag" of 1900, which became the first piece of sheet music in American history to sell more than a million copies. The intoxicating rhythms found in this piece were heard in living rooms across the country, played by whites and blacks alike, a state of affairs which left the traditional music establishment worried, according to Ted Gioia in his *History of Jazz.* By the time ragtime faded, a new craze for jazz emerged, which gave the establishment even *more* to worry about.

Rags

March

Strain

Trio

```
AA   BB   CC   DD
          └ trio ┘
```

FIGURE 8.1: *Sample March/Ragtime Format. Each Letter Represents One 16-bar Strain.*

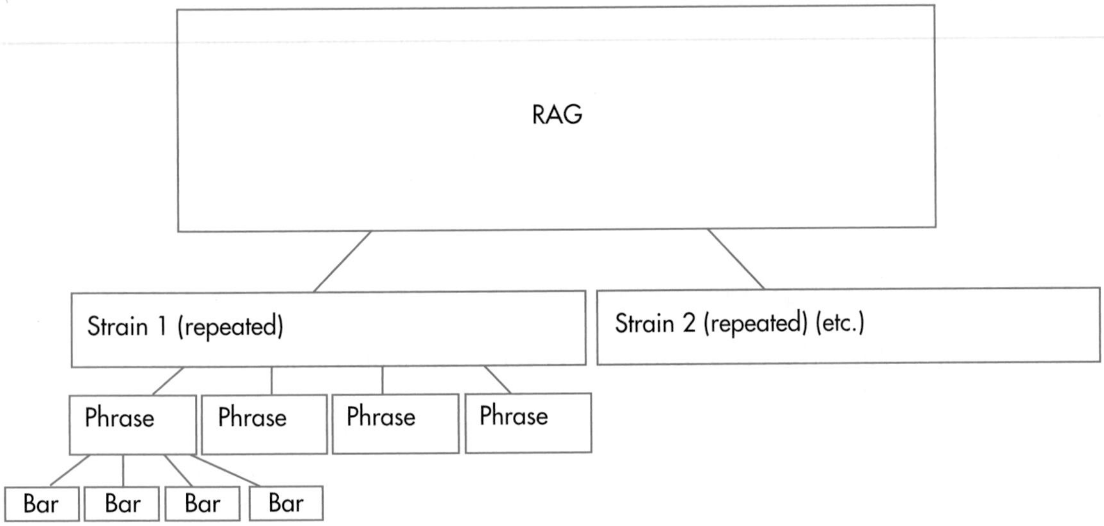

FIGURE 8.2: *The Structure of Strains in Marches or Rags.*

SWING

The jazz discussed so far has all been the work of *combos,* small ensembles with generally one person on each instrument—one trumpet, one saxophone, etc. All through this period, however, there was another kind of jazz played by ensembles of 20 or even 30 musicians, with *sections* of two to five trumpets, saxophones, and trombones each. These ensembles were often called orchestras, but gradually the name *big band* came to designate this kind of group. In the early days the big band work was dominated by such popular bands as the one led by Paul Whiteman, presenting a rather tepid, orchestral version of jazz that bore little resemblance to the original music. With the rise of black bandleaders such as Fletcher Henderson, however, this big band incarnation of jazz gradually captured the attention of serious jazz lovers. By the mid-1930s big band music was sweeping the nation, and for the only time in its history, jazz was the most popular music in the land.

Swing Dancing: More than anything else, what propelled big band music to the top of the pop charts was a shift in dance styles in the United States. Prior to the jazz age, most dancing in white society in the United States was European in origin, dominated by dance steps such as found in the waltz and the fox trot. In the 1910s this began to change, when the Argentine tango got couples to press their bodies together, cheek-to-cheek, in a sensuous march across the dance floor.

In the 1920s and 1930s, dances of African-American origin became the rage across the country, starting with the Charleston. In the 1930s it was the jitterbug (originally known as the Lindy hop), an athletic couples' dance, which can include spins and flips for both partners. More than anything else, the requirements of the dancers shaped the popular music of this time. In the days before amplification larger bands were needed to carry the sound across the dance floor. Also necessary was a particular rhythmic quality called *swing,* in which the beats are subdivided into *long-short* units rather than units of equal length (see Figure 8.8(A) & (B)).

This rhythmic quality eventually came to be used as the name for a whole era of jazz music.

SWING CHARACTERISTICS

The *"swing"* rhythm is just one of several characteristics of this new kind of jazz. Compared to Dixieland, swing has much more polish and élan, a smooth, professional quality, which reflected the more upscale nature of both the musicians and the audience. Other characteristics included:

Rhythm: As in Dixieland, meters are generally quadruple, although occasional triple-meter pieces can be found. Tempos range quite widely, from fast Jitterbug numbers to slow "ballads" for close dancing.

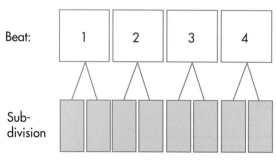

FIGURE 8.8A: *Regular Subdivisions.*

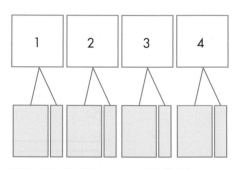

FIGURE 8.8B: *Swing Subdivisions.*

CI-1

Miles Davis playing the trumpet at the Newport Jazz Festival, Newport, Rhode Island. Source: Getty Images, Inc.

CI-2

Jazz singer Diana Krall at the Hollywood Bowl. Photo by Reuters New Media, Inc. Source: CORBIS.

CI-3
James Brown. Source: AP/Wide World Photos.

CI-4
David Bowie. Photo by Neal Preston. Source: CORBIS.

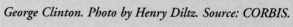

Carmen Miranda. Photo by Hulton-Deutsch Collection. Source:
Getty Images, Inc. © Hulton-Deutsch Collection/CORBIS.

CI-8

A field in the Mississippi Delta Region. Photo by William Allard. Source: National Geographic Society.
William Allard/NGS

Compared to other substyles of jazz and even to later big band jazz, such as the Latin-influenced sound of the 1950s (see Chapter 10), swing is generally less daring rhythmically.

Melody: Since swing was the popular music of the day, melodies tend to be more tuneful here than in any other substyle of jazz. Even in the solos, extremes of range generally are not emphasized. Melodic material tends to be riff-based.

Harmony: Again, the harmony of swing tends to be smooth and predictable, with only an occasional spice of dissonance tossed in. Nevertheless, in the work of Duke Ellington (see Musician Biography 8.3) and others, some harmonic complexity starts to creep in, which presages the techniques of later jazz.

Texture: Here there is a marked change from earlier jazz. In swing, heterophony is almost completely abandoned. The big bands played in a smooth homophonic texture, with a melody line supported by chords. Occasionally there would be one or two countermelodies, creating a texture that approached polyphony, but the freewheeling group improvisation of Dixieland disappears.

Timbre and Instrumentation: A typical big band is divided into sections:

3–5	Trumpets
3–4	Trombones
3–5	Saxophones (with alto, tenor and baritone saxophones)
	Rhythm section (piano, string bass, guitar and drums)

Notice that the clarinet has disappeared from the lineup. The clarinet did appear in the hand of certain bandleaders, however, such as Benny Goodman, Artie Shaw, and Woody Herman. The bass line is now taken by the string bass rather than the tuba, and the banjo is replaced by the guitar, later the electric guitar. Often these sections would be set up in opposition, so that the saxophones might play one phrase in tight harmony, answered by the trumpets as

a group, for example. This kind of organization was called *block voicing*.

Block voicing

In terms of timbre, although polished tone quality was highly valued, many swing players also relished timbral variety and employed a wide variety of mutes, including toilet plungers used in the bell end of brass instruments. Many players would sing or growl through their horns to create a raspy sound.

Form: The overall form continued to follow the scheme outlined in Figure 8.7, with a head followed by solo sections. But there were more differences than similarities. The form of the head now rarely borrowed from the blues or ragtime; more common now was the 32-bar song form, built on four eight-bar phrases in the pattern of AABA. There was also a difference in the way the rest of the music was organized. In swing, the band has more activity during the solos, interjecting riffs or even taking over the music for a time from the soloist. The head, or part of it, may also recur somewhere in the middle. Overall, swing featured more complex arrangements than those found in Dixieland.

32-bar song form

Other Elements: This leads us to what is perhaps the most distinctive feature of swing: the arrangements. In the jazz styles that surround swing chronologically, musicians generally played by ear. The leader of the band decided on a melody, perhaps told the group the order of the solos, and then they just played the music without looking at written notation. With notable exceptions such as the Count Basie band, swing musicians worked from written *charts*. These charts gave all the notes they were to play, except for the solos (although in some bands, even the solos were written out). Thus, in swing music the *arranger* took on a leadership position beyond that of most of the players.

Charts

Arranger

Often the arranger was not even a member of the band, other times he or she was. Occasionally, the leader of the band was also the arranger. The bandleader/arranger who explored the artistic potential of the swing arrangement more than any other was Duke Ellington.

Duke Ellington and his band at the Oriental Theatre, Chicago, Illinois.
Source: Getty Images, Inc.

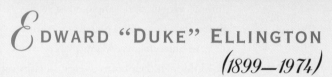
MUSICIAN BIOGRAPHY 8.3:

EDWARD "DUKE" ELLINGTON
(1899–1974)

Duke Ellington was the son of a butler for a wealthy Washington, D.C. doctor. He began piano lessons at age seven, taught himself harmony at seventeen, and soon after worked both as a performer and manager. In the early 1920s he moved with his band to New York City and eventually found a steady gig performing at the Kentucky Club. As band members left, Ellington replaced them with superior musicians, and by the mid-1920s he was making recordings for several different labels. In 1927, the Ellington band moved up to the Cotton Club, perhaps the premiere nightclub in Harlem. In the 1930s Ellington scored several popular hits with his band, among them "Mood Indigo," "Don't Get Around Much Anymore," and "It Don't Mean A Thing (If It Ain't Got That Swing)," and a phenomenally successful tour of Europe in 1933 demonstrated that the band's popularity was international.

Despite his popular success, Ellington always had aspirations for his music beyond the charts. Even when he was just getting started in the 1920s he wrote extended compositions for his band such as the *Black and Tan Fantasy,* which presented a level of complexity in arrangement beyond any other in jazz at that time. Most of these extended compositions were examples of program music, that is, it was meant to tell a story as the music unfolds. A famous example is his *Black, Brown, and Beige,* a three-movement, 45-minute work from 1943. Ellington also worked with associate arrangers, such as the brilliant Billy Strayhorn (1915– 1967).

Ellington struggled during the decline of big bands in the late 1940s and early 1950s, but his career got a second wind as the composer approached his sixtieth birthday. Ellington took his band on numerous overseas tours, composed music for films, and wrote a popular autobiography. Among his many honors and awards were honorary doctorates from Howard and Yale universities, membership in the American Institute of Arts and Letters, election as the first jazz musician member to the Royal Music Academy in Stockholm, and recipient of the Presidential Medal of Freedom. After Ellington's death in 1974 his son Mercer took over leadership of the band, and today it continues under the leadership of his grandson, Paul Mercer Ellington.

LISTENING PREPARATION

Duke Ellington, "It Don't Mean A Thing (If It Ain't Got That Swing)" (1932).

Although not one of Ellington's celebrated extended compositions, this number remains one of his most memorable tunes, and it gave the era its name. Featuring vocalist Ivie Anderson in her first recording with the band, the song shows Ellington's skill as both a songwriter and arranger.

One of the trademarks of the Ellington sound was the unusual timbres his players created; notice how muted trumpeter Cootie Williams seems to talk through his horn when he solos through the first verse. The background brass players, too, toy with their timbre through different placements of their mutes. Ellington was intrigued by tone color, and often used exotic instruments or musical elements in his compositions.

There are also elements of "It Don't Mean A Thing" that are typical of the swing sound as a whole. You can hear sections of the band working as one unit at times (block voicing). At the beginning of the song you can hear the string bass, played by Wellman Braud, playing a *walking" bass line,* going up and down the scale in a steady, on-the-beat fashion, which was also increasingly popular in the swing era. And governing it all, of course, is that compelling swing rhythm, giving the song a buoyant, danceable quality.

Refer to the Appendix at the back of the book for this Listening Activity's complete worksheet. Use the following section to make notes for yourself

"Walking" bass

LISTENING ACTIVITY 8.4:

Duke Ellington and his Orchestra, "It Don't Mean A Thing (If It Ain't Got That Swing)" (CD 1/7)

1. This song is in a quick tempo, quadruple meter, with the walking bass hitting two notes per measure. The intro lasts until the muted trumpet comes in. How many measures long is the intro? _____

2. Besides the bass, what else do you hear happening in the intro?

3. Here is an example of Ellington toying with form: instead of presenting the vocals right after the intro, he lets the trumpet outline the tune, *then* he lets Anderson present the head (a 32-bar song, in an AABA format). Listen through to the head. What lyrics does she sing in the "B" section?

4. What is the band doing while she sings?

5. After the head, Ellington strays again from the standard setup, giving the alto saxophone (Johnny Hodges) a solo over a new twelve-bar pattern that repeats. How would you characterize the saxophone solo over these 24 bars?

6. Now, at about 1:50 on the CD timer, Ellington returns to the 32-bar format of the head, continuing the saxophone solo. What happens in the "B" section of this pass through the pattern?

7. The final run through the 32-bar pattern starts with the whole band. At what point in the AABA pattern do you hear Ivie Anderson singing some scat? _____

8. How does Ellington end the song?

9. Make a diagram of the whole song, inserting details to make a good roadmap to this song.

MODERN JAZZ

Jazz musicians must have been pleased with the popularity of their music during the swing era. The music's widespread appeal provided at least one kind of validation of their work, and the increased employment opportunities must have been welcome. Nevertheless, many musicians felt restless in the age of the big band. The early days of jazz had been performer-oriented, with plenty of soloing opportunities for anyone who wanted them. The arrangements of the big band placed the musicians under tighter musical control, with far fewer opportunities for improvisation. Many players were relegated to permanent background roles. And the popularity of the music had its downside, too, with bands having to play the same songs the same way night after night.

Many of these musicians found their greatest pleasure in the informal jam sessions held after the concerts were over. Usually these would involve only a few players, a return to the informal combos of jazz's earliest days. This was an opportunity for musicians to play for other musicians, to leave the charts behind and just play from the soul. Sometimes these jam sessions would take the form of *cutting contests,* where musicians would trade solos in a kind of contest of virtuosity. These cutting contests, too, were a holdover from the early days of jazz.

These jam sessions eventually took over as the mainstream of jazz. As swing fever subsided in the early and mid-1940s, more and more nightclubs began hiring the less expensive combos for their musical entertainment. Many listeners abandoned jazz at this point, following a new passion for vocal-based pop music and eventually, in some cases, rock and roll. In the place of these listeners arose a new kind of jazz lover—one less interested in dancing and more focused on the virtuosity of the solos. These fans were fewer in number but far more dedicated. Although jazz would go through several transformations in the postwar years, all would be a part of this new musician-oriented final phase of jazz history. Now, jazz had become art music.

BOP

The atmosphere of the cutting contest played an important role in the formation of the first modern jazz style, *bebop* (later shortened to *bop*). The originators of bop, such as trumpeter Dizzy Gillespie and alto saxophonist Charlie Parker (see Musician Biography 8.4), were big band side musicians who blew their competitors off the stage in the after-hours jam sessions. Because of the hothouse atmosphere of those jam sessions, bop developed into a virtuosic, complex breed

of jazz that intentionally left some listeners baffled—and most musicians intrigued.

DIFFERENCES FROM SWING

Some of the differences between bop and swing have already been touched upon: bop was music for combos, not big bands, and it emphasized improvisation over arrangements. Other characteristics of bop include:

Rhythm: Perhaps the defining feature of bop compared to the other styles of modern jazz is the speed of the tempos. Although bop musicians in nightclubs would play a variety of pieces, including slow ballads, the most characteristic numbers flew by at a breathtaking speed, sometimes over 300 beats per minute. Most musicians had trouble just keeping up, let alone improvising at that tempo.

Cutting contests

Melody: Bop melodies tend to be angular and disjunct, a deliberate break from the smooth tunefulness of swing melodies.

Harmony: Complexity in harmony is another hallmark of bop. The bop musicians rewrote standard tunes to add unusual and *extended chords,* those with four, five, or even six notes instead of just three. Because of the fast tempos, the harmony often changes quickly as well, adding another layer to the complexity.

Extended chords

Timbre and Instrumentation: Bop combos ranged in size—Dizzy Gillespie even experimented with a bop big band—but a typical ensemble might consist of four or five musicians: perhaps a saxophone, trumpet, string bass, piano, and drum set. The guitar, when used, moved from an accompanying role to a more melodic one. A distinctive element of bop drumming is the use of the suspended cymbal for timekeeping, rather than the snare drum.

Form: This is perhaps the only element in which bop is *less* complex than swing. Bop most often follows the traditional jazz format shown in Figure 8.7, with a direct presentation of the head (often played in unison by the melody instruments) followed by solos. In bop, solos are often played over two, perhaps even three or four passes through the head

Bop

pattern, rather than one, giving the players more space to work out their improvisations.

Other Elements: Even though bop is complex and extraordinarily difficult to play, there is also an element of humor in the music—or perhaps wittiness is a better word. Bop musicians were fond of quoting other music in the middle of their improvisations, sometimes from a wildly different kind of music from the jazz at hand, anything from pop hits to operatic arias. Part of the fun for listeners of bop was the challenge of catching these sly quotes in the midst of a blistering solo. This, incidentally, is also an element of the enjoyment of rap—identifying the sampled musical "quotes" and seeing how the original music is transformed in its new context.

Charlie Parker, New York City (1949). Source: Getty Images, Inc.

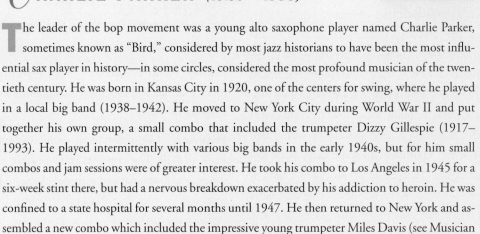

MUSICIAN BIOGRAPHY 8.4:

CHARLIE PARKER *(1920—1955)*

The leader of the bop movement was a young alto saxophone player named Charlie Parker, sometimes known as "Bird," considered by most jazz historians to have been the most influential sax player in history—in some circles, considered the most profound musician of the twentieth century. He was born in Kansas City in 1920, one of the centers for swing, where he played in a local big band (1938–1942). He moved to New York City during World War II and put together his own group, a small combo that included the trumpeter Dizzy Gillespie (1917–1993). He played intermittently with various big bands in the early 1940s, but for him small combos and jam sessions were of greater interest. He took his combo to Los Angeles in 1945 for a six-week stint there, but had a nervous breakdown exacerbated by his addiction to heroin. He was confined to a state hospital for several months until 1947. He then returned to New York and assembled a new combo which included the impressive young trumpeter Miles Davis (see Musician Biography 8.5), but his struggle with drugs and alcohol continued. When he died from a bleeding ulcer at the age of 34, a doctor tending him thought he was between 50 and 60 years old.

In this abbreviated career Parker transformed jazz. His style of playing was vastly different from the warm, mellifluous quality of the swing saxophonists; Parker's solos were crisp, acerbic, and stunningly quick, with swift jabs and dodges. His solos were also abstract. Instead of being tied to the three or four pitches in any given chord, Parker experimented with notes more distantly related, or not related at all. He once said an improviser should feel free to use any note with any chord, as long as he or she places it in a *context* that makes sense. In lesser hands, this would have created nonsense, but Parker's solos find their energy in their proximity to chaos. His solos were also aided by his rich melodic gift. Like Mozart (see Musician Biography 12.5), melodies seem to spill out of Parker's horn almost by accident. Fifty years after his recordings were released, young jazz saxophonists still carefully copy his recordings as a kind of apprenticeship to the language of modern jazz.

LISTENING PREPARATION

Charlie Parker Quintet, "Mohawk" (Recorded 1950).

This piece, written by Parker, is not as fast as many bop numbers, but does provide a good example of many bop elements, as well as an all-star roster (Dizzy Gillespie on muted trumpet, Thelonious Monk on piano, Curley Russell on bass, and Buddy Rich on drums). The melody of the head is not especially tuneful, yet it is appealing. But the real action, as is typical of bop, is in the solos.

Refer to the Appendix at the back of the book for this Listening Activity's complete worksheet. Use the following section to make notes for yourself

LISTENING ACTIVITY 8.5:

Charlie Parker Quintet, "Mohawk" (CD 1/8)

1. What instrument dominates the intro? _____

2. The melody of the head is played in (circle one) *unison* or *harmony?*

3. Which instruments are playing the melody of the head?

4. Comment on the **melody** of the head. Consider the melody's *tunefulness* and *contour*. Do you like it? Why or why not?

5. Parker takes the first solo. Comment on the nature of his solo.

6. Gillespie takes the next solo. Describe his solo, comparing it to Charlie Parker's.

7. The next solo is divided between the pianist and the bass player. Describe Thelonious Monk's piano solo.

8. The final solo is by Russell on the bass. What other instrument(s) do you hear during the bass solo?

9. How is the piece ended?

10. Make a diagram of the entire piece, as you have done before, indicating which instrument takes the solos.

COOL JAZZ

By the late 1940s bop had come to dominate the jazz scene, and its success drew a counterreaction. The swing establishment, naturally, denounced the music, calling it fakery or "just noise." But the transformation of jazz was inevitable, and one by one, the great swing bands of the 1930s and early 1940s folded. Some listeners never took to bop, however, and instead became collectors of early jazz records. This prompted an early jazz revival, providing a second wind to the careers of several Dixieland musicians who had been forgotten during the swing era.

Another reaction to bop was a new style that eventually came to be called *cool jazz*. Led by Charlie Parker's former sideman Miles Davis, among others, cool jazz featured much more sedate tempos than were found in bop, and a more contemplative, relaxed ambiance. The solos were less explosive, and there was a gentle rhythm propelled by the soft swishing of brushes on the snare drum. The relative calm of cool jazz should not suggest a retreat from the intellectual rigor of bop, however. Cool jazz musicians were even more experimental than their bop predecessors in their own way, exploring unusual meters (such as five or eleven beats per measure), new timbres (such as the French horn and the vibraphone), advanced harmony, and a more compositional approach to form.

MUSICIAN BIOGRAPHY 8.5:

*M*ILES DAVIS *(1926—1991)*

No other musician in the history of jazz can be credited with launching so many new trends in jazz or so many unknown sidemen into great careers. Davis was also influential as a soloist, showing that the trumpet had potential beyond the typical fireworks bravado of earlier trumpeters. Davis liked to perform with a mute, and experimented with compressing the trumpet's valves only halfway, to provide an eerie, cracked tone that seemed to express the anguish of his soul.

Davis grew up in St. Louis, the son of a well-off dental surgeon. He was accepted at New York's Juilliard, one of the most prestigious schools of music in the country, but once he arrived in New York he was quickly seduced by the nightclub scene and soon dropped out. Before long, Charlie Parker took the teenager under his wing and eventually hired him as the replacement to Dizzy Gillespie. Davis left because of Bird's increasingly erratic behavior and drug addiction. Soon, Davis would be plagued by his own punishing addiction to heroin.

In 1949 he started his first group, a nonet (nine musicians), which recorded only one album, *Birth of the Cool,* heralding the new style. The album was derided by most jazz fans and the group soon broke up, sending Davis into one of several spells of depression which hounded him throughout his life. Today, the album is considered a classic. By the time cool jazz was becoming the dominant form of jazz in the early 1950s, Davis was experimenting with something new, *modal jazz,* using a collection of pitches neither major nor minor. In the late 1950s he put together what was probably his greatest combo, including Bill Evans on piano, alto saxophonist "Cannonball" Adderley, tenor saxophonist John Coltrane—all of whom went on to successful solo careers—along with bassist Paul Chambers and drummer Jimmy Cobb. In the mid 1960s the Davis band included another set of rising stars, among them pianist Herbie Hancock and tenor saxophonist Wayne Shorter. At the end of the decade Davis revolutionized jazz yet again with the addition of electrified instruments, launching the fusion between jazz and rock. Throughout a career which stretched from the 1940s to the 1990s Davis continually rethought his approach to jazz, almost never returning to an earlier style of playing.

Modal jazz

LISTENING PREPARATION

Miles Davis, "Flamenco Sketches" from *Kind of Blue* (Recorded 1959).

Like the other numbers on his seminal album *Kind of Blue,* Miles Davis gave his musicians just the barest bones of raw material to work with in "Flamenco Sketches." All the pieces on the album were sketched out by Davis just before the recording session, where the musicians met and recorded the music almost without rehearsal and alternate "takes." The result is an album that captures the spontaneity of excellent musicians at the moment of discovery.

"Flamenco Sketches" has no head, no melody to work with, nor even a pattern of harmony. The band was given five scales—some of them major, some modal—over which the soloist would improvise new melodies. When to move from one scale to the next would be up to the soloist at that time (the accompanying instrumentalists had to listen carefully to know when to change chords). After a vamping introduction by the piano, bass, and drums (with brushes on the snare), the order of solos is trumpet (Davis), tenor sax (Coltrane), alto sax (Adderley), piano (Evans), then trumpet again. With such an open structure and slow tempo, the soloists were free to explore a wide range of emotion and melodic expression.

Refer to the Appendix at the back of the book for this Listening Activity's complete worksheet. Use the following section to make notes for yourself

LISTENING ACTIVITY 8.6:

Miles Davis, "Flamenco Sketches"

1. On your first listening, record the CD timer information for the start of each solo:

   Muted Trumpet: _____
   Tenor Saxophone: _____
   Alto Saxophone: _____
   Piano: _____
   Muted Trumpet: _____

2. Each of these players does a different thing with this raw material. How is each solo different in melodic contour, mood, and other musical characteristics?

   First Trumpet Solo:

   Tenor Sax Solo:

   Alto Sax Solo:

Piano Solo:

Second Trumpet Solo:

3. Which is your favorite solo? Why?

THE FRAGMENTATION OF MODERN JAZZ

*T*he modal-inflected jazz of Miles Davis was just one of several trends in modern jazz. At about the same time as Davis's *Kind of Blue,* alto saxophonist Ornette Coleman (b. 1930) was experimenting with *free jazz,* an avant-garde style in which musicians improvise with no reference to any underlying structure, often over the top of one another. In the 1950s and 1960s *Latin jazz* was also popular, fueled by a *bossa nova* craze (see Chapter 10) led by Antonio Carlos Jobim (1927–1994). In the late 1960s Davis pioneered jazz/rock *fusion,* the most popular kind of jazz since swing, exemplified in the 1970s by bands led by keyboardists Herbie Hancock (b. 1940), Chick Corea (b. 1941), guitarist John McLaughlin (b. 1942), and the group Weather Report. In the 1980s fusion subdivided into what may loosely be called New Age music and Light Jazz, both of which are still popular. Jazz purists, meanwhile, objected to what they perceived as watered-down jazz and launched a wholesale revival of the combo jazz of the 1950s, led by a new generation of virtuoso players such as trumpeter Wynton Marsalis and his older brother, soprano saxophonist Branford.

JAZZ TODAY

*D*espite the various forms of popularized jazz from the fusion era to today, jazz has never regained the central position in popular taste it enjoyed in the swing era. And yet there has never been a time when more *kinds* of jazz have been enjoyed by more people around the world than today. The combo jazz aesthetic founded in the 1940s and 1950s is alive and well along side fusion players who have built on their work from the 1970s and 1980s. Ragtime sheet music still sells briskly, and Dixieland clubs and ensembles have an international presence. The big band jazz ensemble has become almost as ubiquitous in high schools and colleges across the country as the traditional marching band, and a vibrant swing revival in the late 1990s found young people once again learning swing dance steps.

A sign of jazz's continuing popularity can be seen in the success of Ken Burns' ten-part PBS documentary on Jazz, watched by millions in 2001.

Free jazz

Latin jazz

Fusion

New Age
Light jazz

LISTENING PREPARATION

Cole/Mills, "Straighten Up and Fly Right," arr. Diana Krall (Released 1993).

Diana Krall, a young Canadian singer-pianist, is one of the rising stars of the jazz world. Winner of a Grammy in 1997, she has a distinctive, expressive voice and a brilliant piano style.

In this recording—a tune originally recorded by Nat King Cole—Krall accompanies herself on piano, along with stand-up bass and drums. Listen to the way she delivers the song, elastically stretching and accelerating the beat, bending the pitch, all to the effect of adding impact to the song.

Refer to the Appendix at the back of the book for this Listening Activity's complete worksheet. Use the following section to make notes for yourself

LISTENING ACTIVITY 8.7:

Diana Krall, "Straighten Up and Fly Right" (CD 1/9)

1. Describe how the song begins, up to the entry of the vocals.

2. At what point in the lyrics does the rest of the band come in?

3. What are the meter and tempo of this song?

4. Where does Krall show signs of flexibility in her vocal delivery? Cite examples from the text.

5. This song is in the 32-bar song format, with a vocal introduction. Assuming the text cited in Question 2 above represents the start of the first "A" section (of AABA), write down the lyrics to the "B" section below:

6. Discuss Krall's improvised solo in the middle of the song.

7. What happens after the solo?

8. How does the song end?

9. Describe the work of the bass and drums in this song.

10. What is the overall mood of this song? How is this achieved?

KEY TERMS

Rags	Combo	Bop
March	Sections	Extended chords
Strains	Big bands	Cool jazz
Trio	Swing	Modal jazz
Syncopation	Swing rhythm	Free jazz
Cakewalk rhythm	Block voicing	Latin jazz
Glissando	32-bar song form	Fusion
Flat four meter	Charts	New Age
Head	Arranger	Light jazz
Trading fours	"Walking" bass	
Scat singing	Cutting contests	

CHAPTER
9

Rock

Rock is a popular music style that can be hard to pin down. Not only are there dozens of substyles, such as heavy metal, folk rock, and others, but the definitions of these substyles often seem arbitrary. Many times the names for substyles are determined by music retailers, who seem to decide on a whim which bin to put a new CD into. This decision is bound to be different from store to store, even in the days of huge retail record chains. One store's "Alternative" CD might be another's "Grunge." Or a CD bin's title might be changed from "Grunge" to something else simply because the term "Grunge" has become passé—and thus less marketable. This chapter will make use of the most common terms in circulation.

The commercial nature of rock presents other challenges to the intelligent listener as well. There is a peculiar bias in our culture to be suspicious of that which is popular. The more popular something is, the more its artistic quality is called into question. This bias pervades all musical styles, especially a mass culture art form such as rock. Perhaps you have encountered listeners who like a rock group, then quickly abandon this preference once the group achieves widespread popularity. With rock, the groups you prefer say something about who you are as a person, and for many listeners, the statement they want to make through their listening preferences is that they are outside the mainstream, iconoclastic rogues out on the frontiers of musical taste.

If this describes your typical listening habits, for the purposes of this book, you will be asked to put aside this mode of operation. Only a naïve listener would suggest that if a song is popular, it must be of high quality. But it is just as intellectually lax to argue that if a song is popular, it must *lack* quality. This book will not tell you what to like and what to dislike, but it will demand that you judge the music on the basis of the music itself.

Of course, rock cannot be assessed by the music alone. Rock has also been a visual art form, starting with Dick Clark's *American Bandstand* television program of the 1950s, through the beginning of MTV in the 1980s and on to the internet visuals of the 1990s. Rock music, like all others, also exists in a broader cultural context. In this chapter these other matters will be addressed as they arise.

THE DEVELOPMENT OF ROCK

The musical style known as rock began in the mid-1950s as a blend of three distinct popular music styles: rhythm and blues (R&B), country, and gospel. The particular mix of these three styles was different from artist to artist and even song to song, but in general, rhythm and blues made up the most important element of this new hybrid style, followed in influence by country and gospel. Like other popular styles, rock's acquisitive nature continued long after its founding, on to the present day, always absorbing elements of external musical styles to refresh and invigorate the music. Indeed, the three "parent" styles (blues, country, and gospel) have continued to be reinserted into the rock style from time to time in rock's history.

NONMUSICAL FACTORS

Rock music could only have appeared at a particular moment in United States history—after World War II—when several nonmusical factors coalesced:

Post-War Economic Boom: The years after World War II were heady times for Americans. Since the crash of the stock market in 1929, the U.S. economy had been mired in the Great Depression. By 1933, stock prices had fallen 80 percent, and thousands of banks had failed in the United States alone. Unemployment had reached 25 percent, and more than 200,000 people had become homeless. Although the

Roosevelt administration provided some relief, the Great Depression only really lifted with World War II, when the country devoted massive resources and energy to war production. When the Allies emerged victorious from the war, only the United States did not have to rebuild bombed cities, and thus the economic boom continued with barely a glitch into the 1950s. After years of privation during the Depression and World War II, Americans were ready to have fun, and they spent their new money on cars, televisions, and records.

The "Invention" of the Teenager: The development of rock was closely associated with the teenagers of the 1950s. The concept of the teen years as a special time of life, however, only really emerged at this time. During the Great Depression, most teens had to work to help support their families, but with the economic boom after the war, teens now had allowances from their parents. As teens spent this money, corporations soon realized that this was a unique market, with tastes distinct from those of their parents. Teens have always been fond of shocking their parents; indeed, the parents of these teenagers may have shocked their own parents during the jitterbug craze of the 1930s, when they were teens. But in the 1950s, teens had more leisure time and money to devote to their own passions.

Bland Suburbs: Home ownership rose dramatically after World War II, with many people choosing to live in the newly developed suburbs rather than cities. This exodus was fueled by cheap gas prices and a new government devotion to building interstate highways. These suburbs were quiet, safe, and rather bland. Teens growing up in this antiseptic environment began to seek means of excitement, a need rock and roll would soon fill.

The Civil Rights Movement: The United States at midcentury was a largely segregated nation. Blacks and whites lived in separate areas and worked in separate jobs, with a large proportion of the wealth and power in the hands of the whites. Slowly, however, African-Americans asserted their rights to be equal participants in the American dream. In 1947, Jackie

Teenage girls playing their 78 rpm records.
Source: Getty Images, Inc.

Robinson broke the color barrier of Major League Baseball, joining the Brooklyn Dodgers. In 1950, Gwendolyn Brooks became the first African-American to be awarded a Pulitzer Prize for poetry. In 1954, the Supreme Court struck down the notion that schools could be "separate, but equal," starting a period of desegregation. In 1955, Rosa Parks refused to give up her seat on a bus to a white man in Montgomery, Alabama, launching a black boycott of the city's bus system. The boycott was led by Dr. Martin Luther King, Jr. These changes were slow in coming, and often painful, but were significant not only for the moral health of the nation but also for the blending of musical cultures that eventually resulted in rock.

Advent of Television: Television had been invented in 1928, but became important as a consumer product only after World War II in the late 1940s and early 1950s. Prior to this time, radio had dominated home entertainment, led by big national networks such as NBC, CBS, ABC, and the Mutual Broadcasting System. All but Mutual dived into television in the late

1940s, and as TV grew in popularity, advertisers abandoned radio for the new medium. Before long, the great radio networks were being dismantled. This may seem like a sad state of affairs for radio—it certainly seemed that way at the time—but radio emerged from the ashes of the network system as a new niche medium. In the old network system, stations mostly put on live shows, featuring symphonic music and thrilling radio dramas; in the new age of radio, with less funding, stations presented phonograph records, with just one radio personality in the studio: the so-called disk jockey. No longer bound to the network system, radio stations sought to define themselves individually—and to everybody's surprise, some of the most popular stations (with both black and white audiences) were those that broadcast black music. Radio gave many white teenagers of the 1950s their first taste of black music, providing the spark that ignited rock and roll.

Battle of the Record Speeds: In the late 1940s the two biggest record companies, Columbia (affiliated with the CBS radio-TV network) and RCA-Victor (affiliated with NBC) launched two new record formats, both of which were meant to replace the old, fragile 78 RPM records then in circulation. The CBS model, spinning at 33⅓ RPM, was two inches larger in diameter than the 78 record (12 inches vs. 10), but could hold up to 25 minutes of music on each side (and was thus called a *long-playing record,* or *LP*). The RCA model, which operated at 45 RPM, held the same amount of music on each side as a 78— about three minutes—but was much smaller and cheaper. In the end, both formats were adopted, the LP for the "adult" market, dominated by classical music, and the 45 for the popular market. The 45 record, called a *single,* became the medium of choice for the early years of rock.

Other New Technology: Rock and roll would not have been possible without the development of several other new pieces of equipment. Two of these, the solid-body electric guitar and the multitrack tape recorder, were pioneered by a jazz guitarist and engineering hobbyist named Les Paul (b. 1916). Paul created the prototype solid-body electric guitar in the late 1930s, and in the 1950s the Gibson guitar company began to mass produce these bearing Paul's name. Les Paul also made the first successful recordings using a technique called *overdubbing,* where the same musician can lay down tracks separately on top of one another—becoming, in effect, a one-person band. Paul developed an eight-track recorder that was marketed by Ampex in 1957, but the true potential of the multitrack recorder would only be realized by rock artists of the 1960s like the Beach Boys and the Beatles. In 1951, the Fender company produced the first electric bass, and several instrument makers would soon develop electric pianos. With the amplification of all the instruments (except the drum set, which hardly needed amplification at this time), a band of three or four musicians could suddenly make music of enormous volume, an important ingredient of the rock style. Equally important, these newly amplified instruments also had different timbres from their acoustic forerunners, timbres which would help define the rock sound.

Overdubbing

THE BIRTH OF ROCK AND ROLL

The birth of rock and roll was a slow process, moving in fits and starts. The essential ingredients were in place by about 1950: not only the nonmusical factors mentioned above, but also many of the musical qualities soon to be considered part of the rock and roll sound. One of the important musical precursors was the development of an electrified Chicago blues style (see Chapter 7), led by Muddy Waters, Howlin' Wolf, and others. These blues bands contained similar instrumentation (but not identical) to future rock bands (electric guitars, acoustic basses, drum sets, and harmonicas). Another important precursor was something called *jump music,* a danceable musical style similar to swing jazz but with a smaller ensemble and faster tempos. Louis Jordan (1908–1975) and Louis Prima (1911–1978) were popular jump band leaders in the late 1940s and early 1950s.

LP

Single

Jump music

Les Paul (b. 1916)

Bill Haley and his Comets at a rehearsal. Photo by Bettmann.
Source: CORBIS.

AM radio stations with strong signals in Memphis and elsewhere started playing these blues and jump records (then collectively known as rhythm and blues, or R&B for short), and white teenagers in the early 1950s tuned in secretly, not wanting their parents to know what they were listening to. A white Cleveland disc jockey named Alan Freed (1922– 1965) started a famous radio show in 1951 called *Moon Dog's Rock and Roll Party,* playing only the latest R&B records. This may have been where the name *rock and roll* was coined. Freed certainly thought so: a few years later, he copyrighted it. He also organized R&B concerts and tirelessly promoted the music. In 1960, Freed made history again with the *payola* scandal, when he was found guilty of accepting bribes to promote certain records on his shows.

By the early 1950s it was clear that R&B was increasingly popular with white teenagers. A savvy young recording engineer in Memphis, Sam Philips (b. 1923), saw that the market would be even bigger if it weren't for racism. He later recalled that "distributors, jukebox operators, and retailers knew that white teenagers were picking up on the *feel* of black music. These people liked the plays and the sales they were getting, but they were concerned: 'We're afraid our children might fall in love with black people.'" Philips opened his own recording studio in 1950,

and launched his own little record label, Sun Records, two years later. At first he recorded only black artists, including an important R&B single by Ike Turner and the Kings of Rhythm called "Rocket 88" in 1951, considered by many to be the first rock and roll record. The band had accidentally dropped their guitar amplifier off the top of a car, but Philips liked the fuzzy sound made by the broken speaker cone and insisted they use the broken amplifier—a precursor to distortion.

Philips enjoyed some success with these R&B records, but he knew that, as he put it, "If I could find a white man who had the Negro sound and Negro feel, I could make a billion dollars." An early attempt along these lines on another label was made by a Texas swing band called the Comets, led by Bill Haley (1925–1981), covering "Rocket 88" and another popular R&B song originally recorded by Joe Turner (no relation to Ike), "Shake, Rattle and Roll." Many radio stations refused to play records by black artists, but happily broadcast these cover versions. But Bill Haley and the Comets' biggest hit, "(We're Gonna) Rock Around the Clock" (1955), was not a cover, and some consider it the first rock and roll song by a white band. Still, Philips only found what he was looking for when a young truck driver named Elvis Presley walked through the doors of Sun Records in 1953.

Elvis Presley.
Source: AP/Wide
World Photos.

*E*LVIS PRESLEY *(1935—1977)*

Elvis was born in Tupelo, Mississippi, the son of a farmhand and a sewing machine operator. The family was poor and moved from town to town in search of better wages, eventually ending up in Memphis, Tennessee. The Presleys were religious, attending revivalist camp meetings, where the young Elvis learned an ecstatic breed of gospel music that influenced his later music. "I also dug the real low-down Mississippi [blues] singers, although they would scold me at home for listening to them," he later recalled.

Legend has it that Sam Philips recognized Elvis' genius when the teenager walked through the doors of the Memphis Recording Service to make a record for his mother in 1953, but in truth, Philips wasn't even there. The Sun Studios office manager, Marion Keisker, recorded Elvis that day, and kept pressing Philips to use Elvis in a commercial recording. Eight months later, Philips called Elvis in to make a country record. These initial sessions were failures until Philips suggested Elvis try some blues. Elvis' first record, "That's All Right, Mama," a cover version of a blues song by Big Boy Crudup, was first played on Memphis radio station WHBQ in the summer of 1954, and the station was immediately flooded with calls and telegrams asking for more information about the singer.

Elvis and his band made more records and took to the road. Elvis was so nervous on stage his legs shook—a gesture his female fans took to be sexual, adding to the excitement of his performance. Elvis became a phenomenon, and by 1956 he was on national television with a coveted spot on the popular *Ed Sullivan Show.* He was televised only from the waist up so his gyrating hips would not scandalize the television audience. By this time, Philips had sold Elvis's recording contract to RCA Victor for $40,000 and Elvis's management to a somewhat shady character named Colonel Tom Parker.

Elvis had a string of number-one and top-ten hits in the late 1950s that has never been surpassed, but his career became sidelined when he was drafted into the army in 1958. While serving in Germany for two years, he met 14-year-old Priscilla Beaulieu, whom he married in 1967. When he came back to civilian life in 1960, the music scene had shifted, and his kind of music was no longer in style. Nonetheless, his continuing popularity allowed him to pursue a secondary career as a movie star, and he eventually made 32 films within the span of about a decade.

In 1968 he launched a come back with a national television special, presenting new songs. He used this as a springboard to the final phase of his career as a Las Vegas nightclub singer. From 1969 until his death he was the most popular entertainer in Las Vegas. But the strains of his stardom were already taking their toll. Protected by a group of friends known as the "Memphis Mafia," secluded in his strange mansion called Graceland, Elvis's life became more and more bizarre. He began to take drugs to control his weight, and then drugs to help him fall asleep and drugs to wake up. This all contributed to his death at age 42.

The fascination with Elvis seemed to grow after his death. Supermarket tabloids reported Elvis sightings. Elvis impersonators recreated the performance style of the "King of Rock and Roll." For those who know Elvis only from films, his Las Vegas days, or tabloid reports, he has become something of a joke, a caricature of a lounge singer with sequined suits. But those who saw Elvis perform live tell a different story: the story of a singer with enormous charisma, even in his final days. And his critical role in the creation of rock and roll is without question.

THE 1950S

*A*fter Elvis appeared on the scene, dozens of performers tried to match his success. Sam Philips used the money he earned from selling Elvis's contract to launch the careers of Carl Perkins (b. 1932), Johnny Cash (b. 1932), Jerry Lee Lewis (b. 1935), and Roy Orbison (1936–1988), among others—for the most part, country singers who experimented with R&B elements. There were also experiments in the other direction, music by black musicians who dabbled in country music such as Chuck Berry (see Musician Biography 9.2). Other black artists, such as Little Richard (Penniman, b. 1935) and Ray Charles (b. 1930) infused popular music with the emphatic vocal acrobatics of gospel music and a pumping piano style, which added to the excitement of early rock and roll. Another gospel-influenced breed of early rock and roll was *doo-wop*, featuring four or five singers—usually all of the same race and gender—singing in tight harmony, often with nonsense lyrics backing up the melody line.

This early rock and roll seems pretty tame by later standards, but at the time the music shocked the adult world. It was louder and faster than any of the previous styles from which it was born, and it contrasted sharply with the sedate pop fare with sentimental lyrics then enjoyed by most grownups. Some of the

Little Richard (b. 1935)

Backbeat rhythm

Doo-wop

lyrics of rock and roll made veiled references to sex, and the emotional, energetic stage acts of the performers seemed to defy the stiff decorum of the late 1950s. This was music meant for uninhibited dancing, and teens loved it.

In general, the characteristics of early rock and roll are as follows:

Rhythm: The most striking aspect of rock and roll rhythm was the tempo: *fast.* Rock and roll songs often clocked in at 120 BPM or faster, and the tempos only increased in the excitement of the concert setting. The meter was universally quadruple, with a particular quality borrowed from R&B called *backbeat emphasis.* The "backbeats" of a four-beat measure are beats two and four, beats which get extra emphasis in rock music, sometimes even more than the downbeat. Rock and roll drummers typically strike the kick drum on beat *one,* then the louder snare drum on beats *two* and *four* (Figure 9.1).

Melody: The melodies of early rock and roll were very simple and tuneful, which helped propel the

| One | Two | three | Four | One | Two | three | Four |

FIGURE 9.1: *Backbeat Emphasis in Rock and Roll.*

MUSICIAN BIOGRAPHY 9.2:

CHUCK BERRY *(b. 1926)*

Chuck Berry, born and raised in St. Louis, Missouri, learned to play the guitar as a teen and became a professional musician in his early twenties. In the mid-1950s he sought out legendary blues performer Muddy Waters (see Musician Biography 7.3) for career advice. Waters directed him to the Chicago-based Chess Records, where Berry made his first recordings. Waters may have regretted this advice, because Berry's first release, "Maybelline" (1955) became an instant hit. Soon, Berry's records were selling more than all the other Chess artists *combined*.

Chuck Berry deserves at least as much credit as Elvis Presley and Little Richard as a founder of rock and roll. Berry was a masterful blender of styles, placing the single-string country guitar solo style over a boogie-woogie rhythm and a blues chord structure. Berry was a talented songwriter—which Elvis was not—and his hit tunes from 1956 through 1958 have become rock and roll classics, including "Roll Over Beethoven," "School Day," "Rock & Roll Music," and "Sweet Little Sixteen." Even today, novice rock guitarists cut their teeth on Berry's opening solo to "Johnny B. Goode."

After the 1950s, Berry's career became increasingly troubled. After serving a three-year jail term in the early 1960s he made a brief come back, then faded back into obscurity while he fought with his new record company, Mercury. He had only one more top-ten single in the early 1970s, then retired to run a restaurant and other businesses. Berry published an autobiography in 1987 and has made only rare appearances since then as a performer.

Berry's legacy as a rock and roll icon is undeniable, however. He pioneered not only the sound of early rock and roll, but much of the tough, aggressive attitude. His one- and two-string guitar solos set a precedent for future guitarists, and helped make the electric guitar the dominant instrument in rock. His energetic stage antics, including the famous "duck walk," served as an important model for future rock acts.

songs to popularity. The songs were made up of repeating, generally short phrases sung in a narrow range. Even the most unmusical fan could sing along to the music—and often did.

Harmony: The harmony was also simple in the early days of rock and roll, usually just three or four chords, often in the blues pattern (see Chapter 7).

Texture: The texture of early rock and roll was almost exclusively homophonic.

Timbre and Instrumentation: The main instruments of the early rock and roll band included the hollow-body electric guitar, the stand-up acoustic bass, and a simple three- or four-piece drum set (kick drum, snare drum, hi-hat, and crash cymbals). Acoustic or electric pianos were also common, and some bands even featured a *horn section* (made up of trumpets and saxophones, usually). Harmonized singing was popular in this time, growing out of the doo-wop tradition.

"Cover" songs

Form: Early rock and roll was closely related to the blues in structure—often in a repeating form of twelve bars (see Chapter 7). In the blues, there had been space at the end of each four-bar phrase for a guitar "response" to the vocal line, but in early rock and roll, the singing tends to run all the way through the four bars. Solos are taken separately, over the whole twelve-bar structure, in between verses of music. Slowly during the late 1950s, the verse-chorus structure of rock music started to develop, becoming solidified in the 1960s.

Lyrics: Much of the early rock and roll music consisted of *covers* of R&B songs, as mentioned above. Many times, these covers would include new lyrics, or simplified versions of the original lyrics.

LISTENING PREPARATION

Chuck Berry, "Johnny B. Goode" (1958).

"Johnny B. Goode" is one of a certain class of rock and roll songs that simply talk about rock and roll, in this case about the rise of "simple country boy" to fame and fortune through his uncanny ability to play the guitar. The song was recorded in the Chess studios with members of the studio band on acoustic bass, piano, and a small drum set—and, of course, Chuck Berry's famous guitar and voice.

Refer to the Appendix at the back of the book for this Listening Activity's complete worksheet. Use the following section to make notes for yourself

LISTENING ACTIVITY 9.1:

Chuck Berry, "Johnny B. Goode" (CD 1/10)

"Johnny B. Goode" is an interesting song, historically, because it demonstrates—in one song—how rock and roll was evolving from a traditional blues structure to the verse-chorus structure of later rock. The entire song is blues-based, but the first lines of the verses do not repeat, and every other pass through the blues structure is a twelve-bar blues "chorus," featuring the words "Go! Go, Johnny, go!" followed by guitar licks.

The song opens with one of the most famous guitar licks in the history of rock and roll, a three-note *pick-up* followed by a series of rapid syncopated notes, played on two strings at once:

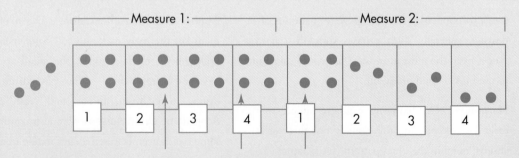

(The circles represent notes; the rectangles represent the four beats in each of the first two measures, with the number of each beat indicated by the numbers in boxes below; and the arrow shows the placement of the *accent,* providing syncopation. This whole diagram represents less than four seconds of music).

1. At the start of the third measure, the kick drum comes in to orient the listener to the downbeat of the third measure, followed by two more measures of guitar solo before the rest of the band kicks in. Counting these four measures of solo guitar and the guitar plus the band, how many measures of introduction are there total, before Chuck Berry begins to sing? _____

2. The first verse is twelve measures long. Write out the words to this verse below, up to just before the start of the chorus (the chorus begins with the words "Go! Go, Johnny, go!")

3. What differences do you notice between the verse and the chorus?

4. After this verse, the chorus, a second verse and chorus, we hear a guitar solo. How many measures long is it (that is, how long between the second chorus and the third verse)? _____

5. Finish the diagram of the song started below. Include the beginning line of each verse and chorus, and boxes representing the length of the section.

Opening solo	
Verse 1	"Deep down in Louisiana. . ."
Chorus	"Go! Go, Johnny, go!"
Verse 2	"He used to carry his guitar. . ."

6. Does this song possess *backbeat rhythm?*   Y   N

On the whole, lyrics were an element of relatively little importance in early rock and roll. Indeed, many times listeners simply ignored the lyrics and applied their own meaning to the songs, often in collusion with the artist. When Little Richard sang, "Womp-bomp-a-loo-bomp, a-lomp-bomp-bomp!" in the 1955 song "Tutti Frutti," everyone seemed to understand that something very naughty was implied.

ROCK AND ROLL'S FIRST "DEATH"

One of the unusual features of the history of rock and roll is the ongoing speculation about its demise. Every few years, music critics announce that rock has lost all its power and "honesty" and is now no longer in existence. The first of these crises occurred just a few years after the style was born.

It was rock and roll's popularity that triggered this first crisis. When the music first appeared, the major record companies thought it was a passing fad. But the enormous amount of money being made by small independent labels soon became impossible to ignore, and the major record companies developed a quick interest in rock and roll. Some of the major labels bought recording contracts from the small labels, as RCA Victor did with Elvis; in other cases, the major record companies swallowed the little companies whole, eventually leading to today's situation where big media conglomerates house dozens of specialty labels. The result was a new consolidation of power: in 1957, 60 percent of the top ten records were produced by independent labels, but by June of 1960, just 30 percent were independent. In still other cases, the big record companies groomed their own teen idols, such as Pat Boone, Ricky Nelson, and Frankie Avalon—handsome, wholesome white boys who could cover R&B numbers and bleach away any offensive material. These recordings lost some of rock and roll's original rawness and became more polished, but teens seemed to love them just as much.

Meanwhile, the founders of rock and roll were sidelined. Elvis was drafted in 1958, and in the same year, Jerry Lee Lewis's meteoric career suddenly crashed to earth when a newspaper leaked a story that he had married his 13-year-old cousin before his divorce from his first wife was final. Two very promising rising rock and roll stars, Ritchie Valens and Buddy Holly, were killed in a plane crash in 1959; Valens had the potential to build a bridge to the Latino market, and Holly was creating a unique rock and roll sound, the first significant artist to use a solid-body electric guitar. Also in 1959, Chuck Berry was arrested for allegedly transporting a minor across state lines "for immoral purposes." About this time Little Richard experienced one of his periodic conversions to fundamentalist Christianity and dropped out of the rock and roll scene altogether. The payola scandal of 1960, mentioned above, ruined the careers of many of the early proponents of R&B and rock and roll.

These events at the end of the 1950s were very important in the development of rock, for several reasons. Although the pop-rock of the era has left little memorable music, the attention to craftsmanship and more polished recordings would leave a lasting impact on future rock. The dominance of "bubblegum" music also forced the lovers of more raw, authentic music to look to other musical styles, styles that would eventually be folded back into rock and roll and reenergize the music. And the sidelining of the major stars of the 1950s left open the door of opportunity for the major new stars of the 1960s.

THE 1960S

Brill Building

At the beginning of the 1960s, rock music showed few signs of the powerhouse style it would become by the end of the decade. Teen idols dominated the pop charts, singing songs written by others. Many of the great songwriters of this time worked in the famous Brill Building in New York City, writing carefully written pop songs designed to be hits. These songwriters often worked in teams, such as Jerry Leiber and Mike Stoller, Burt Bacharach and Hal David, and Gerry Goffin and Carole King—teams that produced an astonishing number of hits in the early 1960s.

Some of these songwriters became frustrated with the way their songs ended up on record. Once the songs left their hands, record producers had complete control over the final product. Thus an important development began: some songwriters began to take a more active role in record production. Perhaps these songwriters knew that the record was more important in rock music than it had been in any previous style. More than the singer, more than even the songwriter, it was the record producer who was the "author" of rock music.

Perhaps the most influential record producer of this time was Phil Spector (b. 1940). Seeking to maximize the power and effectiveness of the little monophonic 45-RPM single, Spector produced songs with full, lush orchestral backing. His goal, he said, was to create a "wall of sound" for the listener. Although his records usually lack the fire of regular rock and roll, his experiments with timbre pointed the way to the rich productions of the acid rock and progressive rock eras.

MOTOWN AND SOUL

Another songwriter-turned-producer was Berry Gordy, Jr. (b. 1929). Although he had enjoyed some success as a songwriter, Gordy quickly understood that in order for black artists to succeed they needed their own record label. With money from his family and from his earnings as a songwriter and producer, Gordy launched two record labels starting in 1959, Tamla and Motown (named for his city, Detroit, the "motor town" of automobile manufacturing). Gordy had an uncanny eye for up and coming talent, and quickly signed several great artists to his labels—Smokey Robinson and the Miracles, Diana Ross and the Supremes, Mary Wells, and Marvin Gaye. Gordy maintained tight control over his operation, even to the point of hiring a lady from a finishing school to teach the singers how to carry themselves so they looked aristocratic. His singers wore ball gowns and tuxedos, and performed with synchronized movements onstage, a subtle symbol of black discipline and classiness. Motown had its own house band and house songwriting team (Holland-Dozier-Holland), producing hit after hit in the Phil Spector wall-of-sound mode.

Phil Spector (b. 1940)

The Supremes. Photo by Bettmann. Source: CORBIS.

Other record companies soon followed the Motown model. Atlantic Records, run by the white entrepreneur Jerry Wexler, emerged as a new major record label largely through its black artists such as Ruth Brown and Arethra Franklin. Atlantic, like Sun, found many of its artists in Memphis, as well as in a small community called Mussel Shoals, Alabama. Atlantic Records did as much as Motown to popularize the black popular music of this time—known as *soul music*—although the Atlantic sound was leaner than Motown's, with more emphasis on electric guitar and organ.

The "godfather of soul" was James Brown (b. 1933), a singer-songwriter with an enormously compelling stage presence and a gift for rhythmic energy. His singing style is famous for its leaps, screams, and grunts, which he copied from gospel performances. Called by some "the hardest-working man in show business," he put together his own band in the early 1960s and instilled an almost military discipline in them, fining them when they made mistakes and demanding perfection. The result was the tightest ensemble of the mid-1960s, a band which paved the

Berry Gordy, Jr. (b. 1929)

Motown Records

James Brown (b. 1933)

way for *funk,* an exciting, rhythmically rich style of the 1970s, and the *rap* grooves of the 1980s and 1990s.

SURF MUSIC

Surf music

While this was going on, musicians on the west coast of the United States were launching yet another distinct substyle of rock and roll. Guitarist Duane Eddy (b. 1938) was a pioneer of *surf music,* playing near the bridge of his guitar to give it a brittle, sharp quality; he also used a tremolo bar, which bent the pitch—a wavering sound that reminded listeners of ocean water. Several surf groups emerged in the early 1960s, singing carefree songs that celebrated the beach lifestyle.

The Beach Boys

The most successful of these was the Beach Boys. The band consisted of the three Wilson brothers, Carl (guitar), Dennis (drums), and Brian (the brains behind the outfit, who played bass), plus a cousin and a neighbor. The group combined the surf music elements listed above with the tight vocal harmony of 1950s doo-wop, the lush recording studio techniques of Phil Spector, and the guitar work of Chuck Berry, to create a new, vibrant sound. Brian Wilson suffered from that plague of most geniuses, or near geniuses—depression. By 1966, he had a nervous breakdown that forced him to stop touring with the band, but this enabled him to focus on his songwriting and producing. His masterpiece album, *Pet Sounds* (1966), along with the single "Good Vibrations" (1966, not on that album), mark the high tide of his accomplishments with the band and served as inspirations for the Beatles and others.

THE FOLK REVIVAL

The folk revival

Yet another important musical movement of this time was the revival of folk music. Folk music has a long tradition around the world, songs sung by traveling minstrels and everyday people who learn the tunes from one another. In

the 1950s, spurred on by the release of recordings by the Smithsonian Institution, collected by the ethnomusicologist Alan Lomax and others out in the fields and farms of America, folk music found a new popularity. In coffee shops in Greenwich Village in New York City and on college campuses across the country, young people took up the acoustic guitar and sang folk songs together. Perhaps there was something about the *authenticity* of the music that appealed to these students, the fact that it existed outside the commercial culture of the 1950s. Just as was the case with rock and roll, however, commercial interests soon became involved with folk music, and "professional" folk groups such as Peter, Paul, and Mary and the Kingston Trio soon topped the charts.

The darling of the folk music scene in the early 1960s was a talented young songwriter named Bob Dylan, who seemed to represent folk music's best hope for the future—and then derailed the movement by turning toward rock.

R&B AND ROCK AND ROLL OVERSEAS

While Americans drifted away from the raw energy of early rock and roll in the early 1960s, listeners overseas were just discovering it. In the port cities of England, such as Liverpool, sailors brought back R&B and rock and roll records from visits to the United States, and a new passion for the music spread over the country. Soon, teens all over England and Europe were forming blues bands in imitation of Muddy Waters, Howlin' Wolf, and Chuck Berry, copying lead guitar lines lick for lick. It would be these foreign bands, ironically, that reawakened America's interest in blues-based rock and reignited the passion in popular music.

The first of the British bands to make an international mark on rock music was the Beatles, probably the most influential band in the history of rock music.

Bob Dylan during a recording sessions (circa 1965). Source: Getty Images, Inc.

MUSICIAN BIOGRAPHY 9.3:

BOB DYLAN *(b. 1941)*

Robert Zimmerman, a student at the University of Minnesota, was one of those college students from the late 1950s who was swept away by the folk music revival. His passion ran deeper than most, however; at the end of his freshman year he changed his last name to Dylan (after the poet Dylan Thomas), grabbed his guitar and harmonica and hitchhiked across the country in order to meet his hero, the ailing Depression-era folk singer Woody Guthrie. Soon after arriving in New York he started performing in the famous coffee houses of Greenwich Village, and by 1961 he had a debut album out on Columbia Records, *Bob Dylan.* By 1963 he was a leading light of the folk scene. His songs had even taken on a political cast, with "Blowin' In the Wind" sung by Peter, Paul, and Mary at the famous civil rights March on Washington that year, and "The Times, They Are A'Changin'" becoming a kind of anthem of the era.

Dylan's voice is raspy and unsteady, his guitar-playing unremarkable; his gift is in his songwriting. Dylan's lyrics, influenced by the Beat movement of the 1950s, have a poetic quality to them, at once intensely personal and universal; his melodies are both tuneful and interesting. Like all important folk artists, Dylan's songs have been covered by many artists, but no one delivers his songs quite like Dylan himself.

The first of many changes of direction in Dylan's career came in 1965, when he performed for the first time with an electric guitar and rock band backup at the Newport Folk Festival. The traditionalist folkie crowd booed the performance, but it was too late: Dylan had cemented something already in the air, the merging of folk and rock music. Folk-rock would combine the thoughtfulness and political stance of Dylan's lyrics—along with some of the musical elements of folk music—with the energy of rock music to become an important strand in subsequent rock history.

A serious motorcycle accident forced Dylan off the scene in 1966, and when he returned in the late 1960s, he changed directions again, this time incorporating country music into rock (and again, helping launch an important substyle of rock). In the late 1970s Dylan, who was born Jewish, converted to Christianity, and his songs from this time, such as "Gotta Serve Somebody," reflect this development. He later returned to Judaism—as well as folk music—and wrote songs of a more personal nature in the 1980s and 1990s.

Bob Dylan continues to write songs and perform, touring recently with members of the Grateful Dead on one occasion and with Paul Simon on another. In 1997, and every year since then, he has been nominated for the Nobel Prize in Literature.

MUSICIAN BIOGRAPHY 9.4:

*T*HE BEATLES

In 1957, two Liverpool teenagers, John Lennon (1940–1980) and Paul McCartney (b. 1942), put together a *skiffle* band called the Quarry Men. Skiffle was a popular kind of English folk music in the 1950s, featuring acoustic guitars, banjos, and a variety of other instruments. When the R&B craze hit Liverpool, the band changed its name to the Silver Beatles, after Buddy Holly's band the Crickets, and changed its musical directions too. By 1960, the group was playing a continuing gig at a bar in Hamburg, Germany, specializing in Chuck Berry covers. When a British record-store owner named Brian Epstein heard the Beatles playing as a backup band on a recording, he recognized their talent and offered to be their manager. Epstein made the Beatles toss out their leather jackets for suits and clean up their stage act. At this time the fourth member of the group, drummer Ringo Starr (b. 1940), joined Lennon and McCartney and lead guitarist George Harrison (1943–2001). By 1962, after months of diligent work, Epstein had scored them a record contract at Capitol-EMI.

In those days, due to licensing restrictions, most of the recordings released by a band had to be original songs. As fate would have it, Lennon and McCartney happened to be two of the greatest songwriters of the century, naturally gifted, and they fused together the American musical theater tradition of sophisticated harmony and coy lyrics with the energy of rock and roll. At Capitol Records, they were assigned to the novelty record producer George Martin, the final ingredient to this potent mixture of musical talent.

From this point, their ascension was rapid. Their first record was released in September 1962; by November, the group was featured on British television. Their second record reached number 1 the following February, when they launched their first national tour. By the end of 1963, the Beatles had a string of hits and were soon flying overseas for a tour of the United States. The popularity of the group was astonishing, especially to the Beatles themselves. If you listen to concert recordings of the Beatles from this time, all you can hear is the screaming of the ecstatic fans. On a tour in 1965, the Beatles sold out a concert at New York's Shea Stadium, the first "arena" rock show.

By 1965, the Beatles were showing signs of restlessness. Their popularity continued unabated, making them quite wealthy, and allowing them to make zany movies such as *A Hard Day's Night* and *Help!* The example of Bob Dylan, however, demonstrated that rock music could be more than "silly love songs," to borrow a phrase from Paul McCartney. The Beatles began to push the envelope in the studio, experimenting with classical instruments (which George Martin scored for them, since none of the Beatles could read music) and, in the case of George Harrison, the sitar, an Indian instrument. Lyrics became more thoughtful, and the songs more carefully crafted. The Beatles began to seek spiritual growth, through the guidance of an Indian yogi, through experimentation with mind-altering drugs, and through expanding the artistic possibilities of their music.

In 1966, they made a decision which angered many of their fans: they stopped touring. No longer would they replicate their songs in concert, and the Beatles were ready to move beyond the teen-idol stage. Their next project, *Sgt. Pepper's Lonely Hearts Club Band* (1967), was a landmark album, telling a loose story with songs that blended together in a rich tapestry of timbre. This was one of the first *concept albums,* meant to be listened to as a whole, rather than as a collection of singles.

By this time, the Beatles were starting to disintegrate as a band. Brian Epstein died in 1967, an important force of cohesion for the group. Lennon, who had recently married the artist Yoko Ono, was becoming interested in political causes. Still, the four men were reluctant to call it quits, because they knew there was a special kind of alchemy to the group. In the late 1960s they returned to their roots, recording again as a band, even doing some R&B numbers, but the tension between them was too much and they broke up in 1970.

All four launched solo careers, and Lennon and McCartney especially found success as solo artists, but artistically they had all been stronger as members of a band. Fans dreamed of a reunion, but this hope was shattered when Lennon was murdered by a deranged fan in 1980. The remaining Beatles finally reunited—briefly—in the mid-1990s for a television special and a new recorded collection of their outtakes called *Anthology.* George Harrison died of cancer in 2001.

THE BRITISH INVASION

*I*t is not surprising that other British bands tried to follow the Beatles. What *is* surprising is how successful this wave of British bands was—and how good they were. The next in line was the Rolling Stones, a grittier, more blues-based band out of London, a band that miraculously still tours around the world, four decades after its founding. By the mid-1960s, dozens of British bands were either touring the United States or hoping to, among them the Animals, the Yardbirds, Cream, the Kinks, and the Who. In the late 1960s and early 1970s, a second wave of British bands swept across the Atlantic, including Led Zeppelin, Pink Floyd, Genesis, and Yes. Bands and singers have continued to make this trans-Atlantic trek throughout rock history, from David Bowie and the Police in the 1970s and 1980s to Oasis, Seal, and the Spice Girls in the 1990s.

The first wave of the British Invasion focused on blues-oriented rock. When the Rolling Stones toured the United States, they made a point of performing with the original blues performers who had been their inspiration. Blues finally got some of the attention it deserved in its home country, and a blues revival emerged across the United States. Later British bands, however, expanded on the experimental work of the Beatles' *Sgt. Pepper's,* launching what has been called *progressive rock* (discussed below). Throughout rock history, Great Britain and the United States have had a symbiotic relationship, influencing each other across the Atlantic and spurring the music on to greater artistic heights.

ACID ROCK

*T*he 1960s were a time of great social unrest in the United States and around the world. Although the U.S. economy

*The British
Invasion*

Acid rock

was strong, poverty and crime were on the rise in America's blighted inner cities, problems which were increasingly blamed on government policies that seem to favor whites over blacks. America's involvement in the Vietnam War had been generally supported when it began in the late 1950s, but was sharply criticized by the mid-1960s. Many young men burned their draft cards, refusing to serve in a war that seemed to serve no immediate national purpose. Young people began to look upon the U.S. government and other figures of authority with suspicion. They began to defy authority in a variety of ways—growing their hair long, abandoning traditional career paths leading to a corporate job, taking illegal drugs, having premarital sex, and living together before marriage.

The epicenter of this cultural earthquake was in San Francisco. Young people from across the country gravitated toward this California city, always known for its open-mindedness. By 1967, thousands of *hippies* had moved to the city. They centered around the Haight-Ashbury district, and lived in a continuous party. The soundtrack to this new kind of life was a new breed of rock called *psychedelic rock* or *acid rock,* named after the nickname for the drug LSD.

Bands such as the Grateful Dead and Jefferson Air-plane developed this music, meant to enhance the experience of the hallucinating audience, it featured long, improvisational songs that gradually morphed into other songs. Acid rock seemed to exemplify the principles of the movement: it was loud; it was free of traditional rules; and parents hated it. Although some of this music was undisciplined and self-indulgent, it was also powerful and *important* as no rock music had been before.

ROCK'S SECOND "DEATH"

*J*ust as it was at the end of the 1950s, several events coalesced around 1970 to call an end to rock's second era. There were several deaths of important stars, including Jimi Hendrix (d. 1970), Janis Joplin (d. 1970), Mama Cass Elliot of the Mamas and the Papas (d. 1974), and Jim Morrison of the Doors (d. 1971), although now the cause of death was more likely drug abuse than plane crashes. Just as significant was the break-up of the Beatles, the band that had led the way in rock for most of the decade. Rock suddenly lacked leadership and, some thought, direction.

Grateful Dead and Bruce Hornsby. Photo by Matthew Mendelsohn.
Source: CORBIS.

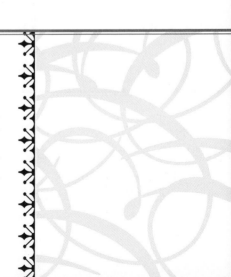

Jimi Hendrix (August 1970). Source: Getty Images, Inc.

MUSICIAN BIOGRAPHY 9.5:

JIMI HENDRIX *(1942—1970)*

James Marshall Hendrix was born in Seattle, Washington. He acquired his first guitar at age 16, which he played left-handed. After a brief stint in the army, he became a session musician, working with R&B stars such as the Isley Brothers and Jackie Wilson in the early 1960s. While performing with a band in New York City in 1966, Hendrix was discovered by Chas Chandler, formerly of the British Invasion band the Animals. Chandler became Hendrix's manager, brought him to England and suggested he spell his first name "Jimi." Chandler helped him form a trio, with a bassist and a drummer, called the Jimi Hendrix Experience, and within a year the group had achieved international stardom.

Hendrix's legacy is his transformation of the electric guitar. Experimenting with guitar *effects* such as reverb and distortion, he greatly expanded the range of timbres that could be created on the instrument. Jimi could play with blazing speed, but even more impressive was the lyrical, emotional quality of his solos. As a songwriter, he produced a wide range of works, from songs of heart-thumping excitement to delicate atmospheric pieces. His exciting performances at the Monterey Pop Festival (1967), where he set his guitar on fire, and the Woodstock Festival (1969), where he gave a riveting, ironic performance of the U.S. national anthem, made rock history. No rock guitarist that followed was untouched by his influence.

The Experience trio released three albums in a year and a half, then disbanded. Hendrix formed a new trio, Band of Gypsies, in 1969, and was preparing to record a double album when he died from complications from a drug overdose at the age of 27.

Effects

LISTENING PREPARATION

Jimi Hendrix Experience, "Purple Haze" (1967).

One of Hendrix's landmark songs, "Purple Haze" describes a mystical underwater adventure dream, or so Hendrix reported. The opening cut on his debut album *Are You Experienced,* "Purple Haze" announced a new range of intensity and color for rock music. From the opening dissonant, distorted octave leaps on the guitar through the final fade out, this song burns with unrelenting energy and excitement.

Refer to the Appendix at the back of the book for this Listening Activity's complete worksheet. Use the following section to make notes for yourself

LISTENING ACTIVITY 9.2:

Jimi Hendrix Experience, "Purple Haze"

"Purple Haze" is in quadruple meter, with Jimi outlining the tempo at the opening with his guitar. As you listen to the opening, say "one, two, three, four" along with each note to establish the tempo.

1. Hendrix's introduction is in three parts. Fill in the remainder of the chart below, describing each of the three parts of the introduction and determining their length in bars:

PART	LENGTH	DESCRIPTION
First	two bars	Dissonant, distorted guitar notes, leaping up and down an octave.
Second		
Third		

2. Instead of a chorus, at the end of each of the three verses, Hendrix halts the music to emphasize the final line of that verse. Describe what the electric bass and guitar play after this "stop time" segment.

3. After the second verse, we hear a guitar solo, with indistinct spoken voices in the background. Why do you think the band chose to do this?

4. Describe how the song ends, from the last line of the third verse through the fade out.

Woodstock Festival (1969)

Simultaneous with these losses, rock also lost steam as the hippie movement dissipated. The *Woodstock Festival* of 1969 had been a high water mark for the counterculture, when approximately 400,000 young people had gathered on a farm in upstate New York for several days of free food, free love, free drugs, and free music. Alas, the days of free concerts were numbered. When the Rolling Stones gave one at the Altamont Speedway in California later that year, a concert-goer was stabbed to death by a member of the Hell's Angels, a motorcycle gang the band had hired for "security."

Photo by R. P. Angier.
Source: Stock Boston.

The hippie movement began to lose its cohesion. The assassination of Dr. Martin Luther King, Jr., left many African-Americans devastated and less optimistic about racial harmony. Other segments of the counterculture soon split off to pursue separate agendas—the legalization of abortion, equal pay for women, environmentalism, gay rights, and so on. As the hippies grew older, their idealism seemed to be substituted with pragmatism. By 1980, most hippies had shorn their hair and joined the establishment they had once sought to overthrow.

Rock music, likewise, seemed to splinter in the 1970s into several different camps—and become more a part of the establishment.

THE 1970S

Popular music was scattering in several different directions during the 1970s. Some bands were taking rock into a more distorted direction, leading toward hard rock and heavy metal, while others, such as the Carpenters, were softening it. There was a return to dance music, in the form of disco, then a rejection of it. This was the era of the rock arena concert, with big-name bands selling out stadiums around the world. This increased commercialization angered some people and helped give rise to punk rock, an antiart movement still reverberating more than twenty years later. Other bands went the opposite direction, trying to infuse rock with more intellectual and artistic qualities. Some artists dabbled in different trends at different times or even on a single album.

SINGER-SONGWRITERS AND COUNTRY ROCK

One of the important trends of the early 1970s was the emergence of the *singer-songwriter*. Before the 1960s, popular-music songwriters had mostly stayed in the background, writing songs for professional entertainers to sing. With the arrival of Dylan and the Beatles on the rock scene, however, a new interest developed in hearing the songwriter present his or her songs with his or her own voice. By the end of the 1960s, an important dividing line developed between pop music and rock: pop singers sang songs written by others, while rock bands generally created their own.

Singer-songwriter

Dylan, the Beatles, and other excellent songwriters also brought renewed attention to the craft of songwriting, and the singer-songwriter trend was an outgrowth of this. These songwriters were generally young acoustic-guitar players who focused their attention almost exclusively on their songs, rather than on their singing style, their appearance, or flashy stage shows. The focus of their work was writing songs that transcended the rather plain quality of their voices—and in this they succeeded, writing some of the most beautiful, enduring songs of the entire rock era. One of these artists, Carole King (b. 1942), had been a Brill Building songwriter before beginning her solo career. Others, such as James Taylor (b. 1948), Carly Simon (b. 1945), and Joni Mitchell (b. 1943), emerged out of the coffee house scene in the late 1960s. Another important 1970s singer-songwriter, Paul Simon (b. 1941, no relation to Carly), had made his name in folk rock with the duo Simon and Garfunkel in the mid-1960s.

Southern rock

Singer-songwriters most often work in the rock-band format, fronting with an acoustic guitar, or, occasionally, as is the case with Billy Joel (b. 1949) and Elton John (b. 1947), a piano. Many, however, experimented with unusual instrumentation, such as world instruments. Whatever instruments they choose, the intention is to highlight the emotional expressiveness of their songs.

Hard rock

The heyday of the singer-songwriter lasted only through the 1970s, when other trends in rock took center stage, but new singer-songwriters continued to captivate audiences in the 1980s and 1990s, artists such as Suzanne Vega (b. 1959), Tracy Chapman (b. 1964), Sarah McLachlan (b. 1968), and Alanis Morrisette (b. 1974).

Country rock

Country Rock: We have seen how country music played a decisive role in the birth of rock; in the late 1960s and early 1970s, a new infusion of country elements again colored rock mainstream. Bob Dylan was a pioneer of this style with his 1968 album *John Wesley Harding,* but other groups, such as the folk-rock bands the Byrds and Buffalo Springfield, were also moving in that direction. The instrumentation of country rock was similar to a rock band's, but often included the sliding sound of the pedal steel guitar. Country rock also sometimes featured two lead guitarists (taking up the country-music tradition of dueling solos) or both an acoustic and an electric guitar.

Probably the most successful country-rock bands were Creedence Clearwater Revival and the Eagles, both of which found great chart success in the early 1970s. While country rock faded from the scene in the late 1970s, another blending of country and rock caught fire in the 1980s and 1990s, this one a blending in the reverse direction: rockified country music. Led by Garth Brooks (b. 1962), Reba McEntire (b. 1955), and others, this new breed of country music has found wide mainstream appeal.

Southern Rock: Another blending of country music and rock in the 1970s produced an entirely different substyle, now known as southern rock. Unlike country rock, which often had a soft, acoustic quality, southern rock had a harder edge, with blistering, distorted electric guitars. The lyrics often presented an outlaw image, but also with a deep affection for the South, as is found in Lynyrd Skynyrd's 1974 song "Sweet Home Alabama." Perhaps the best of the southern rock bands was the Allman Brothers Band, led by Duane Allman, then by his brother Gregg after Duane died in a motorcycle accident in 1971.

HARD ROCK AND HEAVY METAL

The substyle of rock called *hard rock* emerged out of the second wave of the British Invasion groups in the late 1960s and early 1970s. These bands, such as the Who, Led Zeppelin, and the various bands of guitarist Eric Clapton (b. 1945), originally played a blues-based rock, or, in the case of the Who, a precursor to progressive rock (as exemplified by their experimental rock opera *Tommy* in 1969). As these bands became more popular and played in larger arenas, their sound became louder, faster, more distorted, and more exciting, with crowd-pleasing displays of virtuosity on the electric guitar. Hard rock bands prided themselves on the intensity of their live shows. As these bands lost steam in the late 1970s and early 1980s, new bands such as AC/DC and Van Halen—with even more virtuosic guitarists—took up the mantle and rocked the stadiums into the 1980s.

At the same time, a parallel development produced a branch of hard rock called *heavy metal*. Again, this started with British bands in the late 1960s, including such bands as Judas Priest and Black Sabbath (with its colorful lead singer, Ozzy Osbourne, b. 1948). Heavy metal rock later spread to the United States.

Heavy metal features some of the most complex music in rock, with virtuosic playing from all the instruments and songs which seem bent on disorienting the listener, changing tempos and meters throughout. Heavy metal is among the most riff-oriented of all rock substyles. The most infamous aspect of heavy metal, however, is its association with evil. This association grows out of similar associations connected with the blues (see Sidenote, Chapter 7), but was more intentionally cultivated by some heavy metal artists through their aggressive, screaming vocals, disturbing lyrics, somber dress, and off-stage behavior. Some heavy metal bands, such as Metallica, have little interest in this connection, but it seems to be a common one nonetheless. This artistic fascination with the "dark side" has occurred throughout human history (see Chapter 13), and is also expressed in the *horror* movie genre.

GLAM ROCK AND PROGRESSIVE ROCK

Two more trends that emerged from the second wave of British Invasion groups were glam rock and progressive rock. *Glam rock* represented an exploration of rock's visual side, with artists wearing ever-more elaborate and bizarre costumes in performance. Sometimes this was display just for the sake of display, as seen in Elton John's sequined suits and gigantic eyeglasses. In other cases, the costume was meant to be a part of a kind of concert narrative, as when David Bowie (b. 1947) took on the role of Ziggy Stardust, with make-up and spiky, colored hair, the interplanetary bandleader of

the Spiders from Mars. In some cases, as with the bands Queen and the Village People, glam rock intersected with homosexual culture, although many straight record buyers remained unaware of this context.

Progressive rock bands took their cue from the Beatles' *Sgt. Pepper's Lonely Hearts Club Band,* intent on stretching the expressive and narrative boundaries of rock. In some cases, glam rock and progressive rock overlapped: Bowie's 1972 glam-rock release *The Rise and Fall of Ziggy Stardust and the Spiders from Mars* was a concept album, while the lead singer of the progressive rock band Genesis, Peter Gabriel (b. 1950), was fond of dressing up in outlandish costumes in concert. For the most part, however, progressive rock bands were interested more in the sonic qualities of their art rather than in the visual qualities. Some progressive rock groups, such as the band of Emerson, Lake, and Palmer, and the band Yes, had dreams of blending rock with classical music, just as musicians had hoped of blending jazz with classical music 40 years earlier. The best progressive rock, exemplified by Pink Floyd's chilling epic, the double-album *The Wall* (1979), managed to find new expressive power within a rock framework.

Although there continue to be bands recording in the progressive rock style, with some producing excellent concept albums, the peak of this style had passed by 1980.

FUNK AND DISCO

The innovator of *funk* was the soul artist James Brown, whom we have already encountered. Starting in the mid-1960s, Brown started making more complicated, "upside-down" arrangements; that is, what were once melody instruments (trumpets, saxophones, and electric guitars) would play rhythmic figures, and what were once rhythmic instruments (bass and drums) would take on an almost melodic role. Chord changes are minimal, and the singing becomes chantlike, related to African-American work songs. The rhythmic element of funk is emphasized, not only because it made the music

Heavy metal
Progressive rock

Funk

Glam rock

exciting and danceable, but also because it served as a gesture of African-American pride, since rhythm is the element of greatest interest in African-based music.

In the early 1970s, funk bands became increasingly popular, especially among African-American audiences, featuring large bands with full horn sections such as Kool and the Gang and the group Earth, Wind, and Fire. The most memorable of funk performers was George Clinton, leader of the bands Parliament and Funkadelic, who performed with outrageous costumes and spaceship sets.

Over the course of the 1970s, funk and similar music became increasingly popular in nightclubs. Nightclub DJs, sitting in glass booths with two turntables, developed a specialized skill called *spinning,* the art of blending together two or more records into a continuous dance mix. Before long, musicians were creating music specifically for this emergent dance culture, called *disco.* Because of its function, disco records tended to have similar tempos, less emphasis on the *backbeats,* and extended nonvocal sections called *breaks* where one record might be blended with another. Spurred on by the popularity of the 1977 movie *Saturday Night Fever,* disco music and dancing swept the United States and beyond in the late 1970s, with particular dance steps

Spinning

Disco

Breaks

and a polyester-look clothing style. Pop artists such as Donna Summer (b. 1948), the Bee Gees, ABBA, and Chic dominated the charts, and rock artists from the Rolling Stones to Kiss were soon recording their own disco songs to crack into this chart success.

By the end of the decade, a serious disco backlash swept the United States and elsewhere. In July 1979, a "Disco Sucks" rally was held at Chicago's Comiskey Park—where admission to a White Sox baseball game was 98 cents plus a disco record, which was to be destroyed. The rally proved so popular that the game was sold out and tens of thousands of fans were turned away at the door. The main reason for this backlash was simple oversaturation: disco dominated radio programming and media attention, and the very qualities that made the music successful for dancing made it repetitive for listening. But the backlash also had something to do with the fact that this was an African-American style—and one that had a not-so-hidden connection to gay culture in America.

Although disco seemed to be dead by the start of the 1980s, dance music certainly didn't die. The musical descendents of disco live on into the twenty-first century, now known by different names (most recently, *house, drum, and bass,* and *jungle*) but serving the same function.

The Sex Pistols on stage at the 100 Club, Oxford Street, London.
Source: Getty Images, Inc.

ROCK'S THIRD "DEATH" AND THE ADVENT OF PUNK ROCK

By the mid-1970s, many critics were suspecting rock was dead (for the third time). Popular music was now big business, controlled by a handful of global record companies. Pop albums were produced on multitrack machines, leaving many with the feeling that rock's original rawness had been sacrificed for commercial appeal. New bands had trouble breaking in, and the older bands seemed to have lost their edge. Many thought that disco had conquered popular music.

In England, this situation was compounded by the most severe recession since the Great Depression. These two factors—the complacency of the pop music scene and hard times—gave rise to *punk rock,* which would launch the third wave of British Invasion groups. The origins of punk date back to the 1960s with New York bands such as the Velvet Underground and to the 1970s with groups like the Ramones, Television, Patti Smith, the Talking Heads, and Blondie. London store-owner Malcolm McLaren heard some of this music while visiting the United States and thought it especially fitting for the mood of the times at home. Returning to England, he put together the first British punk band, the Sex Pistols, in 1975. Punk was a kind of antiart: very loud, distorted, noisy, with few chords and no discernable melody. The point was to shock, with lead singer Johnny Lydon screaming profanities and the rest of the band flailing away on their instruments almost at random.

There was plenty of precedent for antiart movements; McLaren was well aware of an early twentieth-century visual antiart style called *dada.* And in the late 1970s, the time was ripe for punk, and the noise of the Sex Pistols' first single—a bitter rant called "God Save the Queen," released during Elizabeth II's silver jubilee year—soared to number 11 on the British popular music charts. Soon, dozens of British punk bands appeared, including the Clash and Souixie and the Banshees, all playing a brazen, fast-tempo, distorted, angry breed of rock.

The Sex Pistols themselves were a short-lived phenomenon, ending in 1978 with the death of bass player Sid Vicious from a heroin overdose. But the band opened the door to a new, invigorated breed of rock. Punk is the direct ancestor of the grunge movement of the early 1990s, and some of the punk aesthetic—such as body-piercing—is still with us at the turn of the new century.

Punk rock

THE 1980S

Rock in the 1980s was renewed by several technological advances. The first of these was cable television. Cable had been around for years before this time, but it was in the late 1970s that it began to extend its reach beyond those far-flung communities that couldn't get antenna reception. As this happened, new cable stations arose that no longer simply replicated traditional broadcast television. One of these was MTV, which in 1981 began to broadcast rock videos around the clock, opening the door to a whole new group of artists and making rock a far more visual art form.

Compact discs were the second technological advance of the 1980s to affect rock music. At first, some listeners rejected CD's, complaining that the new digital format sounded cold and brittle, and bemoaning the loss of artwork space on the record album covers and sleeves that the 12-inch LP format had afforded. Most listeners, however, quickly perceived advantages to the CD: the sound was clearer; the dynamic range was wider; in a space about one-third the size, it could hold about 50 percent more music; and with no parts wearing out the CD in the player's mechanism, the disc was far more reliable and long-lasting. Many listeners were already switching from

Compact discs

MTV

MIDI

LP's to tape cassettes, and CD's surpassed both older formats in sales by 1991. The music industry got a temporary boost as listeners bought their favorite LP's on the new CD format. Recording companies also profited from the higher prices they changed for the new CD's. The advent of CD's also changed the nature of rock music, making it better suited to digitization and no longer bound by the length of the LP record side.

A third technological advance in the 1980s, although hidden from consumers, also had a deep impact on rock music: with the increased computerization of retail check-out, the services that charted the popularity of records by their sales became far more accurate. Prior to this time, some of the music industry statistics had been compiled by phoning record store owners and asking what records were popular that week; now, the information was relayed with computerized precision. Suddenly, it became clear that certain kinds of music—rap and country, for example—were far more popular than had ever been known. Rock was still the dominant music style, but its position would no longer be as secure as it had been in the 1970s.

Michael Jackson (b. 1958)

NEW WAVE

New Wave

The first new rock style of the 1980's was originally called *new wave*. This term encompassed groups covering a wide range of styles, from serious punk bands to image-oriented groups seeking exposure on MTV (derisively called "haircut bands"). Many of the new wave bands, such as the Police and Duran Duran, came to North America in the fourth wave of the British Invasion, but there were also many bands developing in certain regions of the United States, such as Athens, Georgia (the B52's and R.E.M., among others).

It is difficult to assess such a wide range of music encompassed by the new wave umbrella, but one common feature of these bands was an interest in synthesizers. Rock bands had been using synthesizers since the 1960s, but advances in technology in the

1980s made them far more flexible and affordable. One of these advances came in 1983, when synthesizer makers agreed on a standard format, called *MIDI* (for Musical Instrument Digital Interface), to allow digital synthesizers to communicate with each other (and, ultimately, with computers). For a time in the early 1980s synthesizers seemed poised to supercede electric guitars as the dominant instruments in rock. Synthesizers were used differently by different bands; some, such as Kraftwerk and the Eurythmics, seemed to relish the mechanistic quality of "synths" and used them to create a "futuristic" sound; others used them as a substitute for acoustic instruments such as orchestral strings.

A large proportion of new wave was dance music. Although the sound of the music was quite different from disco, much of the function was the same—recorded music to be played in nightclubs. This function was made clear in the accompanying music videos of the time, which now, more than ever before, rewarded those artists who could dance as well as sing.

One of the first important video artists was Michael Jackson (b. 1958), formerly of the Motown group the Jackson Five. He was the first black artist to receive significant exposure on MTV, with the videos made for his blockbuster 1982 album *Thriller*. Michael Jackson has had a difficult career, partly due to his eccentricities, partly due to the rabid tabloid culture of our time. These problems have tended to obscure his actual work as an artist—work which has been enormously creative, both musically and visually. One of Michael's sisters, Janet (b. 1966), has had success rivaling her brother's.

The dominant figure of 1980s dance music, both on the charts and on MTV, however, was Madonna.

THE SEARCH FOR AUTHENTICITY

An ongoing theme in this brief history of rock has been the search for authenticity, an issue rock musicians and listeners have

MUSICIAN BIOGRAPHY 9.6:

Madonna *(b. 1958)*

Madonna Louise Veronica Ciccone was one of eight children born to working-class parents in Bay City, Michigan. She had early dreams of becoming a ballerina and moved to New York City in 1977, where she worked in various stage shows as a dancer. By 1980 she was recording dance music demos, eventually landing a record contract in 1982. After a few minor releases, Madonna became a star in 1984 when her single "Borderline" reached the Top 40. This was the first of an amazing run of seventeen consecutive Top-40 singles, lasting over several albums and the rest of the decade. In 1984 she also starred in her first commercial movie, *Desperately Seeking Susan.*

Before long, young girls across the globe (known derisively as "Madonna Wannabes") were imitating Madonna's clothing style, with undergarments provocatively exposed. Madonna proved to be a moving target, however, changing her image radically with every new music video. Although she made little effort to be a spokesperson for any cause, Madonna became a role model of sorts: she was undeniably sexy, and yet in no way weak (as other media images of sexy women have been). No woman in popular music before her (and perhaps no man) had taken such firm control of her career.

It was a career that did have some set-backs: some of her movies flopped, and her impressive string of hits stalled temporarily in the early 1990s. About that time, she released a pornographic book called *Sex,* which received scathing reviews. She also has had her share of personal troubles, including a rocky marriage to actor Sean Penn, which ended in divorce in 1989. But Madonna's talent for endless reinvention has served her well. She won a Golden Globe award for her title role in the film adaptation of the musical *Evita,* released in 1996, and continues to find chart success. Her daughter, Lourdes, was born in late 1996, and her son Rocco in 2000.

wrestled with from the start. Bands rise to stardom, then suffer a backlash because of their very popularity (often being accused of "selling out"), then perhaps launch a comeback by "returning to their roots," whatever those might be. Singers or bands are sometimes heralded as saviors of rock, capable of returning the music to its supposedly honest earlier state. In the mid-1980s, Bruce Springsteen (b. 1949) was such a savior, with his popular album *Born in the U.S.A.* (1984), a mainstream rock album that spoke powerfully to the concerns of working-class Americans.

World Beat: Other rock bands that have played what has been called *world beat* have sought renewal in the music of other peoples. The Jamaican rock styles *reggae* and *ska* had found popularity in the

LISTENING PREPARATION

Madonna, "Material Girl" (Written by Peter Brown and Robert Rans; produced by Nile Rodgers, 1984).

The release of "Material Girl" in the heart of the Reagan Era was one of several signs of the tremendous change in American society from just 15 years earlier. Liberal idealism was out; greed was in. In this playful song, Madonna not only captured the new mood of the decade but also demonstrated a subtle form of feminine strength. As shown in the video, it is the female protagonist who is in control, tossing aside those tuxedoed suitors who cannot meet her cynical financial requirements.

"Material Girl" is a highly synthesized dance song. The producer, Nile Rodgers, perhaps took a little too much liberty with the vocal effects processor. The effects work well for parts of the song, such as when Madonna chirps into the microphone and the digital delay chirps back at her, but tend to cloud her voice during most of the song. Nevertheless, these effects added to the bright, bouncy character of the song and helped make it a hit.

LISTENING ACTIVITY 9.3:

Madonna, "Material Girl"

"Material Girl" consists of at least twelve distinct musical layers. Some of these layers are more prominent than others; some are heard throughout the song, while others appear only occasionally—but all are important in the structure of the song. In order to truly understand how popular music is constructed, we must learn to sort out all the layers. This sorting process is made more difficult because most of these layers are created by synthesizers. When talking about the layers in a classical or jazz piece, we can label them by instrument, but this isn't possible when most of the layers are made by the same instrument (even though the synthesizer is functioning in a similar way to an ensemble, creating a variety of timbres). Here is how I describe these twelve layers:

1. Drums.
2. Synthesized bass.
3. Background syncopated synthesizer comping (a "pointed" sound).
4. Warbly synthesized organ sound.
5. Distorted electric guitar riff: a high ascending leap, then falling.
6. Synthesized Bells ("ding ding").
7. Madonna's voice.
8. Men's voices accompanying her (or singing "Li-ving in a material world" on a single pitch).
9. Women's voices echoing her (actually Madonna herself, overdubbed).
10. Soft synthesized organ "groan," low in pitch.
11. Warbly electric guitar, playing a counterpoint to Madonna's melody.
12. Occasional, jagged synthesized chords in the background.

Using this list and the formal outline you completed in Listening Activity 6.1, write a short paper (1 to 2 pages) describing the musical events of the song. Include reference to both form and texture.

United States in the late 1970s and early 1980s and soon found their way into the musical vocabulary of bands such as the Police. Former Genesis lead singer Peter Gabriel began to incorporate complex west African rhythms into his solo albums of the early 1980s to great effect, and this, too, spread to other bands. The most famous of these efforts was made by Paul Simon, whose excellent 1986 album *Graceland* featured extensive work by South African musicians (and caused a controversy, since South Africa at that time was supposed to be boycotted due to its apartheid policies). Rock was now a global phenomenon, and bands from around the world could participate in the music and bring in elements of their own culture. Ireland's U2 was one of the most popular bands of the late 1980s, and we can expect this trend to increase as the world's interconnectivity grows in the twenty-first century.

RAP

Another kind of American popular music stimulated by world beat was *rap,* which developed from a similar art form from Jamaica called *toasting.* American rap emerged from the hip-hop culture of South Bronx, one of the most troubled neighborhoods in the nation in the 1970s. Jamaican immigrant Kool Herc began to put on street parties as he had done back home, spinning records and chanting his inventive rhymes over the top. A new dancing style emerged from these parties, called *break dancing,* combining stiff, robotic movements with fluid ones, and including acrobatic, upside-down spins. In 1979, the first rap hit, "Rapper's Delight" was scored by the Sugar Hill Gang, and by the mid-1980s, rap groups like Run-D.M.C. and Public Enemy were nationwide stars.

Rapping has deep sources in African-American culture. *Signifying,* playfully insulting another person in a creative way, was an important source for rap (as it was for the blues; see Chapter 7). The best MC's (*masters of ceremony*) are the ones who can improvise the best rhymes on the spot. The DJ, who spins records (like a DJ in a disco), creates a multilayered

Queen Latifah (1990). Photo by Neal Preston.
Source: CORBIS.

Rap

rhythmic backdrop for the MC, touching on the same rhythmic complexity found in African drumming. Later on, the addition of *drum machines* and *samplers*—which digitally record a snippet of sound that can be used as a kind of riff—gave rap musicians more tools to work with. Samplers also stirred up copyright issues, and courts are still trying to sort out what constitutes "fair use" in sampled material. Rap also stirred up controversy when some of the songs seemed to celebrate violence.

Twenty years later, rap is still going strong—and has expanded its reach. Rap at first seemed a male-dominated scene, but women such as Queen Latifah (b. 1970) and the group Salt 'n' Pepa quickly found strong voices and legions of fans. White groups started rapping in the 1980s, and rock and rap have blended in many bands. Just as in the early days of rock, rap has proved to be more substantial and long-lasting than critics thought, becoming one of the most popular and important styles of the 1990s.

Hip-hop culture
Drum Machines
Digital Samplers

MC
DJ

MUSICIAN BIOGRAPHY 9.7:

*K*URT COBAIN *(1967—1994)*

Kurt Cobain was raised in Aberdeen, Washington, a depressed logging town outside Seattle. He was the son of an auto mechanic and cocktail waitress. After his parents' divorce, when he was 7, Cobain was shuttled between relatives and even lived under a bridge for a time, homeless. When he was 11, he heard a recording of the Sex Pistols, igniting a life-long love of punk rock. Originally a drummer, Cobain formed a garage band in the mid-1980s with his friend, bassist Krist Novoselic, also from Aberdeen. By 1987, Cobain had switched to guitar and drummer Chad Channing had joined the band, which had been christened Nirvana. (Drummer Dave Grohl replaced Channing in 1990.) The band's first album, *Bleach* (1989), was recorded for $600 and released on the local Seattle label Sub Pop. For their next album, *Nevermind* (1991), the band moved up to Geffen Records. This album was a surprise success, selling more than 10 million copies and making the band members instant millionaires—but also unraveling Cobain's life.

Nirvana's success stems from the band's unique blend of qualities. Some songs are sweet, but most are desperate, frenzied screams—and often the band combined these extremes into the same song. Nirvana is driven by the angry distortion of punk rock, yet often incorporates catchy riffs and tuneful, memorable melodies. Cobain once said that lyrics were the least important element of his art, just random cut-ups thrown together. If this is true (and it seems to be in many of his songs), he managed to occasionally combine words with resonance and power. And so Nirvana's music is one of opposite poles, somehow held together—popular and yet anti-popular; cynical yet sentimental; meaningless yet meaningful; fierce yet vulnerable.

Sudden success is hard for anybody, but especially for those, like Cobain, who already battle depression. Cobain observed that many of Nirvana's new fans were just the kind of people he hated—the kind who used to beat him up in high school for being different. Many of these fans seemed to love the music without really understanding it, thinking, for example, that the song "Polly" was prorape, when it was actually the opposite. Cobain began to suffer a variety of physical ailments, including ulcers, perhaps connected to his depression, and soon turned to heroin to relieve the pain. In February, 1992, he married his pregnant girlfriend, the singer Courtney Love, another heroin addict, and his band continued to tour and record, releasing the successful follow-up album *In Utero* in 1993 and making a stunning appearance on the MTV *Unplugged* show later that year. But Cobain's life was in a downward spiral. While the band was on a European tour the following winter, Cobain attempted suicide through an overdose of prescription pills. After he was released from the hospital, he went home to Seattle and killed himself with a shotgun. He was 27.

THE 1990S

At the time of this writing, the decade of the 1990s is still a bit too close to warrant adequate historical perspective. At the start of the decade, the Soviet Union collapsed, ending the Cold War and accelerating the drive toward global capitalism. The 1990s will also be remembered for the rise of the internet, which was virtually unknown at the start of the decade and virtually universal by the end. The full ramifications of the internet are probably unknown, although already it has transformed the way the world communicates, works, and recreates. The ramifications of the internet for music are also unknown. It could be that the new music formats found on the World Wide Web, such as MP3, will soon supercede CD's and transform the music business yet again. Or it could be that CD's still have some life to them yet, and that their replacement will be some technology as yet unconceived.

LISTENING PREPARATION

Nirvana, "Smells Like Teen Spirit" from *Nevermind* (Lyrics by Cobain, 1991).

As Cobain himself conceded, the lyrics to the megahit "Smells Like Teen Spirit" are hard to decipher. But the underlying anger is not. The song oscillates between bone-crushing distortion and eerie quiet sections, a kind of false serenity that makes the distorted parts all the more effective. As in many of Nirvana's other songs, "Teen Spirit" also features unusual harmony, chords outside the scale of the song that add to the song's disorienting effect. Cobain's voice sounds broken and plaintive at first, then full of venom. The band is "tight"—meaning completely together in rhythm—which adds even more to the excitement of the song. The result is music both harrowing and powerful.

Refer to the Appendix at the back of the book for this Listening Activity's complete worksheet. Use the following section to make notes for yourself

LISTENING ACTIVITY 9.4:

Nirvana, "Smells Like Teen Spirit"

In the space below, make your own diagram for this song that illustrates the song's organization. You may use lyrics, if you know them, or boxes, or both; make the diagram as clear as possible.

As for rock, it is also difficult to know what will be remembered and which trends will be considered most significant in retrospect. Many of the trends of the 1980s continued and expanded—rap, alternative rock, dance music, heavy metal, world beat, and "mainstream" rock. It was also a great time for women in rock, exemplified by the continuing Lilith Fair tours organized by singer Sarah McLachlan. The one trend we can say for certain that will be remembered, however, is the so-called *grunge* movement of the early 1990s, centered in Seattle and led by a young power trio called Nirvana.

Grunge

Checkpoint

Rock music was born in the 1950s as a combination of R&B, country, and gospel music, and out of a potent mixture of social and historical factors. The title of "King of Rock and Roll" has been given to Elvis Presley, but it could as easily have been given to Chuck Berry or Little Richard, both of whom contributed to the early style. After about 1960, rock split into several directions: a watered-down version of rock and roll featuring "teen idols," the polished Motown soul, surf music, and folk music. The arrival of the Beatles in 1963 reenergized rock and opened the floodgates to dozens of "British Invasion" bands that followed. Rock became more powerful, more meaningful, and closely associated with the hippie counterculture of the time.

In the early 1970s, rock again split into several different directions: singer-songwriter rock, country rock, southern rock, hard rock and heavy metal, glam rock and progressive rock, funk and disco, and punk rock. In the 1980s, fueled by the advent of MTV and the CD, rock entered one of its most lucrative phases, dominated at first by dance music, but soon featuring a wide variety of substyles, including rap and world beat. Most of these substyles persist into the 1990s, with the strengthening of alternative rock, influenced by the early 1990s grunge movement out of Seattle.

KEY TERMS

LP	Acid rock	MTV
Single	Effects	Compact discs
Overdubbing	Woodstock Festival	New wave
Jump music	Singer-Songwriters	MIDI
Payola	Country rock	World Beat
Sun Records	Southern rock	Reggae and Ska
Doo-wop	Hard rock	Rap
Backbeat rhythm	Heavy metal	Hip-hop culture
"Cover" songs	Glam rock	MC
Brill Building	Progressive rock	DJ
Motown Records	Funk	Drum Machine
Surf music	Spinning	Digital Sampler
The Beach Boys	Disco	Grunge
The Folk Revival	Breaks	
The British Invasion	Punk rock	

Latino Music

The term *Latino* refers to people living in the United States of Latin American descent. Latinos represent one of the most important ingredients in the ethnic makeup of this nation, soon, in the twenty-first century, to become its largest minority group. But the term *Latino* itself also encompasses enormous diversity, from recent immigrants from the "cone" of South America to fifth-generation Mexican Americans living on ancestral land in California. Along with diversity of origins comes diversity of music, making generalization all but impossible. Two relatively common features of Latino music—although by no means universal—are sophisticated rhythmic elements and a close association between the music and dancing.

This chapter is an introduction to Latino music as it is practiced in the United States, including a brief historical sketch of the various Latin dance crazes to sweep the country during the twentieth century, and a closer examination of two distinct kinds of Latino music, *tejano* and *mariachi*.

HISTORICAL BACKGROUND

*P*robably the best way to describe Latino culture is through the concept of *blending*. The most fundamental aspect of Latino culture throughout the hemisphere is the blending of the nationalities that created it. Mexicans and Mexican-Americans speak proudly of their *mestizo* heritage, the intermarriage of Spanish *conquistadores* and their descendents and the American Indians native to the land. In much of the Caribbean and Brazil, the eastern edge of Latin America where the slave trade was most active, there is a mixture of three races, European, Native American, and African. It is this history of blended cultures that makes Latino music so vibrant and so readily adaptable to other kinds of music.

Mestizo

Hunter-gatherer people have lived in the Western Hemisphere for more than 20,000 years. By the time of the Spanish invasion of the early sixteenth century, however, powerful Native American empires were forming, most notably the Aztecs of what is now central Mexico, and the Incas, whose empire included parts of modern-day Ecuador, Peru, Bolivia, and Chile. Both of these were highly sophisticated cultures, with artistic, architectural, and engineering skills rivaling those of any nation on Earth. Both, however, were easily conquered by the Spanish in the 1520s and 1530s, who brought with them deadly weaponry and germs for which the native population of the Americas had no immunity. Germs, in fact, were what made the difference. According to historian Jared Diamond in his book *Guns, Germs and Steel*, just before Hernán Cortés made his final assault on the Aztecs in 1520, smallpox swept through the native empire and killed half the population, including the emperor. Francisco Pizarro had the same smallpox advantage when he began his conquest of the Incas in 1531. In the two centuries after Columbus' voyage of 1492, the native population of the New World plummeted 95 percent, most of the decline attributable to the spread of Old World diseases.

For the next 300 years, these lands were colonies of European nations, primarily Spain and Portugal (which controlled Brazil). Spanish America was divided into four regions, one of which, the viceroyalty of New Spain, included what is now Mexico and the U.S. Southwest. Much of the latter was left to the remaining Native American population until the founding of the California missions in the late eighteenth century by Catholic missionaries. The Mexican presence in the north increased more rapidly after the New Spain colony achieved independence from Spain in 1821. But in 1848, Mexico lost possession of this entire northern region to the United States as a result of the Mexican-American War. The Mexicans living in this area were offered U.S. citizenship, and to this day the Southwest has maintained the largest Latino population of any region in the United States. The relationship between Mexican-Americans and the conquering Anglo-Americans, however, has often been troubled, especially along the U.S.–Mexico border.

Mexican-Americans constitute the largest segment of the Latino population in the United States, but they are by no means the only members of this community. Another important Latino people are those of Puerto Rican origin. After the Spanish-American War of 1898, Puerto Rico became a territory of the United States. This meant that Puerto Ricans were U.S. citizens and could move freely to and from the mainland. Most Puerto Ricans who have moved to the contiguous United States have chosen to live in New York City, where they contribute significantly to the culture. A third significant segment of the Latino community are Cuban Americans, who have settled in great numbers in the Miami area, especially after the Communist revolution in Cuba led by Fidel Castro in 1959. Immigrants from other Latin American nations, from the Caribbean to the tip of South America, are also increasing in numbers and political strength in the United States.

LATINO MUSIC IN THE UNITED STATES

*I*n addition to their importance in the ethnic make-up of the United States, Latinos have contributed significantly to the character of the nation's popular music. Music is a vital part of the Latino community, and different kinds of Latin music have periodically entranced the broader U.S. public, usually in combination with a popular new dance step. The music writer John Storm Roberts in his book *Latin Jazz* reports that the first "Latin craze" came as early as 1884, when New Orleans hosted the international World's Industrial and Cotton Centennial Exhibition. The Mexican government sent the Eighth Regiment of the Mexican Cavalry, a highly polished band of between 60 and 80 members, to the exhibition. The band proved to be extremely popular in New Orleans and prompted several music publishers to quickly print copies of its most beloved tunes. Even more widespread was the *tango* craze, which hit the nation in 1913 and continued in popularity—among whites, blacks, and Latinos—for more than two decades. The tango, of Argentine origin, involves a couple gliding across a room, closely embraced, moving with long, dramatic steps in accompaniment to a moderate quadruple meter. A new dance-music craze arrived in 1930:

the *rumba,* another sensual couples' dance, this one with origins in Cuban music. Rumba dancers hold each other somewhat apart and move in a "box" step (somewhat similar to the outline of the waltz; see Chapter 15), all the while moving their hips provocatively from side to side.

The rumba is one of several kinds of Latin dances that make use of the *habanera rhythm,* a term derived from Havana, the capital of Cuba. The habanera rhythm is a one-measure repeating pattern in quadruple meter with syncopation in the middle, so that the 8 eighth notes of the measure are organized into a pattern of $3 + 3 + 2$. You can understand the rhythm best if you practice clapping it. Using the following diagram, try alternating between "straight" eighth notes (the second line of the diagram) and the habanera rhythm (the third line), clapping louder on the numbers in bold as shown in Figure 10.1.

This simple rhythm, subtle yet elegant, is the foundation of much of the Latino dance music that has been popular in the United States over the years.

The rumba remained popular throughout the 1930s, both in its more exciting "uptown" version and the more commercial "downtown" form, led by such bandleaders as Xavier Cugat (1900–1990), who

Rumba

Habanera rhythm

Tango

Xavier Cugat (1900–1990)

1. Four beats in quadruple meter:	**1**		**2**		**3**		**4**	
2. Subdivision of the four beats:	1	2	3	4	5	6	7	8
3. Habanera syncopation:	**1**	2	3	**4**	5	6	**7**	8

FIGURE 10.1: *Habanera Rhythm.*

Mambo

Conga

conducted the house band at New York's Waldorf Astoria Hotel. Cugat was one of the pioneers of the next dance craze as well, the *conga,* which calls for dancers to march around a room in a serpentine line, kicking out on the heavily emphasized fourth beat of the quadruple meter.

Conga drums

Bongos

Claves
Timbales

Güiro
Cubop
Maracas

The *conga dance* is not to be confused with the *conga drum,* one of the most important Cuban instruments to arrive with the rumba craze. Other important Cuban instruments include the *bongos,* smaller drums held between the knees and typically played with the fingers and the hands; the *claves,* two wooden sticks hit together; the *timbales,* metal drums attached to a stand and played with drumsticks; the *güiro,* a notched gourd which is scraped by a piece of wood; and the *maracas,* pairs of gourds with pebbles or seeds inside that rattle when shaken.

*Carmen Miranda
(1909–1955)*

Samba

Bossa nova

*Tom Jobim
(1927–1994)*
*João Gilberto
(b. 1931)*

In addition to his music-making, Xavier Cugat was also featured in several Hollywood films of this era. Another Latin musician/movie star was the Brazilian singer Carmen Miranda (1909–1955), who helped launch the next Latin music phase, the *samba,* around 1940. Like the previous Latin trends, the samba is in a moderate quadruple meter, but features much more complex rhythm. Miranda, referred to at the time as the "Brazilian Bombshell," with her trademark flashing eyes and fruit-salad headdress, was enormously popular on both stage and screen in the 1940s. She suffered, however, from Hollywood's perennial temptation to stereotype Latino and Latina characters, and never succeeded in breaking out of her two-dimensional screen persona.

Perhaps the most exciting time in the history of Latin music in the United States was the late 1940s and the 1950s, the time of the *mambo* craze. This was a return to Cuban-influenced music, but with more emphasis on the traditional Cuban percussion instruments and a new incorporation of the big brass sound from swing bands. Indeed, some jazz scholars believe that mambo—led by the three great New York band leaders, Machito, Tito Rodriguez, and Tito Puente (see Musician Biography 10.1)—revitalized big band music in the late 1940s and forestalled its demise. At this time there was also a great deal of crossover in the other direction, with jazz incorporating the rhythm and even some of the instruments of Latin (especially Cuban) music. Trumpeter Dizzy Gillespie (1917–1993; see Chapter 8) was the leader of this so-called *Cubop* movement, along with bandleader Stan Kenton (1911–1979). Latin music continues to influence jazz to this day.

LATER LATIN MUSIC TRENDS

While the mambo and its related dances, such as the Cha Cha Chá, were brass- and percussion-dominated, the next important Latin trend, *bossa nova,* was more subdued. Developed in Brazil by the song composer Antonio Carlos (Tom) Jobim (1927–1994), the guitarist-singer João Gilberto (b. 1931), and others in the late 1950s as a combination of Samba and jazz, bossa nova held an immediate appeal to U.S. jazz musicians and audiences alike. By 1962, when Gilberto and Jobim released their hit song "The Girl from Ipanema," bossa nova was the most popular kind of

MUSICIAN BIOGRAPHY 10.1:

*T*ITO PUENTE *(1923—2000)*

*T*ito Puente, *El Rey del Timbal* (the Timbales King), was born the eldest son of Puerto Rican immigrants (a factory foreman and his wife) in Harlem Hospital in New York in 1923. By the time he was seven, his family's neighbors were complaining so much about his constant banging on pots and pans that his mother scrounged up money for 25-cent piano lessons to try to channel his musical energy. By the age of ten, however, Puente had switched to drums, which would be his primary instrument throughout his six-decade career.

At the age of 18, Puente landed a position as percussionist in the leading Caribbean-music band in New York, Machito's Afro-Cuban All-Stars. After a three-year stint in the Navy during World War II and a couple of years of formal study in music composition and arranging at the Juilliard School, Puente formed his own band in 1947, the Picadilly Boys, named after *picadillo,* a spicy Cuban dish. In Puente's band, he moved his primary percussion instruments, the *timbales,* to the front of the band so that his musicians could follow his direction. This move also heightened the popularity of the band, highlighting his astounding skill on the instrument, which he played in a whirlwind of frenetic energy. He also played the vibraphone, which he introduced to mambo music.

The Picadilly Boys and the other leading mambo bands alternated nights at New York's Palladium, a large dance hall then known as the House of Mambo. In the mid-1960s Puente moved to Hollywood, where he continued his career long after the initial Mambo craze had dissipated. In the 1970s the rock guitarist Carlos Santana had a hit with Puente's song *"Oye Como Va,"* and Puente is credited with paving the way for the success of many subsequent Latin musicians. During his long career Puente released over 100 albums, earned five Grammy Awards, appeared in several Hollywood films and won many honors and honorary degrees.

music in the United States. Compared with other Latin music, bossa nova featured a more subtle sound, with more complex harmony and intriguing melodies. Singers such as Gilberto sang in hushed tones, almost at a whisper, while gentle tropical rhythms were suggested by the acoustic guitar and percussion instruments. Bossa nova faded from the U.S. pop charts by the mid-1960s, but its imprint on jazz still remains.

Many of the subsequent Latin trends in U.S. pop music involved even more integration of various styles than before. The term *salsa* (meaning "spice") was coined in the early 1970s to refer to the hot Cuban-jazz-rock hybrid then popular in New York, a style of music that also incorporated Puerto Rican and other Latin music. Salsa remains broadly popular in the United States and around the world, as does a similar kind of dance music originating from

Salsa

Merengue

the Dominican Republic, the *merengue*. Meanwhile, some of the most famous Latin musicians of the time, such as Linda Ronstadt (b. 1946) and Carlos Santana (b. 1947), found most of their success in non-Latin music. Latin musical elements were also becoming increasingly mainstream. By the 1980s and 1990s, star performers such as Gloria Estefan (b. 1957), the Miami Sound Machine, and Ricky Martin (b. 1971) were producing Latin-inflected pop music that soared to the top of the charts, while several non-Latino musicians were recording pop songs with a prominent Latin element, sometimes

even singing in Spanish. Other kinds of crossover, such as Spanish rap, are also becoming increasingly popular.

But this "new" integration was not really new. Latin music has not only been a sequence of dance crazes, but has been intertwined with popular music in the United States for more than a century. The habanera rhythm, for example, was common in ragtime (see Chapter 8), as well as in early rock and roll. Without the Latin element, the entire history of American popular music would have been very different—and far less interesting.

LISTENING PREPARATION

Tito Puente, "Mambo Gozón" (Recorded 1957).

Son
Danzón

The mambo is descended from traditional Cuban dances called the *son* and the *danzón*, giving more emphasis to brass and percussion than the earlier styles. The *"Mambo Gozón"* (The Happy Mambo) appears on one of the best selling of Puente's more than 100 albums, *Dance Mania Volume 1* (RCA, 1958). It features his orchestra in full flight, his blazing trumpets, and his tight percussion section. The music invites dancing with its driving rhythm and exciting buildup of texture.

The words in mambo tunes do not carry as much weight as they do in other kinds of Latino music; they are used to carry the voices, which are here for their musical rather than lyrical potential. The back-up singers simply repeat the first line of the text, while the lead singer (Santitos Colón) sings a countermelody (these words are in italics below):

A gozár este rico mambo	Enjoy this tasty mambo
A gozár	Enjoy
Pero baila mi mambo	*Dance my mambo*
Que bueno baila tu mamá	*Your mama is a good dancer*
Te invito a bailar	*I invite you to dance*

Montuno

At the beginning of the "Mambo Gozón," the entire orchestra plays rhythmically in synch (although not in *unison,* because some players are playing different notes). The ensemble hammers out the opening rhythm to alert the dancers that the mambo is about to begin, that it's time to get into position to dance. Then, the piano presents the *montuno,* a repeating segment used as a foundation for the buildup that follows. The saxophones soon take up the montuno, then the trumpets present an exciting countermelody, building up the intensity until the band comes to a screeching halt to make way for the vocalists. This kind of strategy—the incremental increase of instruments and volume, followed by a halt, only to resume the build up again—is the main ingredient in the success of this song.

LISTENING ACTIVITY 10.1:

Tito Puente & His Orchestra, "Mambo Gozón" (CD 1/11)

1. There are four main instrumental groups playing in the *"Mambo Gozón"*: percussion, saxophones, brass (specifically, trumpets), and the piano, in addition to the vocals. After the introductory flourish, we hear the piano montuno. After the montuno is played once, we hear the saxophones and percussion join in. How many times do the saxophones play their pattern before the trumpets come in? _____

2. At what CD time do the trumpets enter, after the repeating saxophone pattern? _____

3. At what CD time do the voices first enter? _____

4. What group or groups of instruments accompanies the voices?

5. At the end of this first vocal section, we hear an exclamatory statement by most of the band. At what CD time does this occur? _____

6. Now we start another buildup. What group of instruments plays a repeating pattern, used as the basis for this buildup? _____

7. Describe what happens in the trumpet part from about 0:53 through 1:16 on the CD timer:

8. What happens next?

9. There are two brief percussion solos in this piece. When do they occur? _____ and _____

10. Describe what happens after the second percussion solo.

MEXICAN-AMERICAN MUSIC

While none of the Latin music crazes outlined above were Mexican or Mexican-American in origin, Mexican-Americans have nonetheless played a critical role in the musical and cultural life of Latinos in the United States. Not only are Mexican-Americans the largest group in the U.S. Latino population, they have also made significant contributions to Latino arts and literature. Since Cesar Chavez's (1927–1993) successful organization of Mexican-American migrant farm workers in the 1960s and 1970s, Mexican-Americans have also held increasing political power. In 1993, President Bill Clinton appointed two Mexican-Americans, Henry Cisneros and Federico Peña, to his cabinet, and Mexican Americans are finding increasing representation in city councils, state legislatures, and the U.S. Congress.

This increasing presence in the broader U.S. society has not been won easily, however. For much of the time since the Mexican-American War, Mexican Americans have been second-class citizens, working the farmlands of the Southwest and other regions for substandard wages. One of the most important ways Mexican Americans have held onto their cultural identity has been through music.

MUSICA TEJANA

The site of the most intense cultural interaction, both positive and negative, has generally been along the border between the United States and Mexico. The longest stretch of this border is in the state of Texas, and the *tejanos*—Texans of Mexican heritage—have produced some of the most vital and influential music of all Hispanic America.

Manuel Peña in his book *Musica Tejana* says there are two main tejano ensembles, the *conjunto* and the *orquesta.* The central instrument of the conjunto is the accordion, originally accompanied by the guitar and either the double bass or the *bajo sexto,* a six-string acoustic bass guitar. More recent conjuntos have added rock instrumentation—electric guitar, electric bass, and drum set, as well as saxophones and other instruments, but still the focus remains the accordion. Conjuntos were originally dance bands, and played a wide range of ethnic music, including the waltz, the polka, the schottische and mazurka, as well as a lively regional Mexican dance called the *huapango,* notable for the loud stomping of the dancers' feet.

Another important kind of tejano ensemble is the orquesta, a larger ensemble with a broader range of instrumentation than found in the conjunto. Nineteenth-century orquestas were modeled on European string-based orchestras or concert bands, but by the 1930s, the orquesta resembled swing bands, with trumpets, trombones, and saxophones. By the 1960s and 1970s, the orquesta adopted rock instruments, just as the conjunto had done. Unlike the conjunto, however, the orquesta has always been an ensemble designed to cross musical boundaries—to play both Mexican and American music, both *ranchero* (country) and *jaitón* (sophisticated) kinds of Mexican music. Manuel Peña argues that this "bimusical" aspect of the orquesta mirrored the bilingual and bicultural identity of the middle-class tejanos who listened to this music.

Just as important as the instrumental music played by conjuntos and orquestas is the vocal music of the Mexican culture. The *corrido,* which dates from the seventeenth century, is a kind of ballad, a song of numerous verses but usually no choruses or bridges, telling an epic tale. In Mexico's colonial times, traveling corrido singers provided remote villages with news of the outside world through these narrative songs, usually based around true events. After the Mexican-American War, some corridos told of heroic Mexican-Americans outsmarting the *gringo* powerholders. The *canción,* on the other hand, is usually a more romantic song. A particularly popular

Bajo sexto

Huapango

Ranchero and Jaitón

Corrido

Tejanos

Conjunto
Orquesta
Canción

MUSICIAN BIOGRAPHY 10.2:

Selena (1971–1995)

Selena Quintanilla Perez, the "Queen of Tejano," was born in Freeport, Texas, in 1971, the youngest child of a restaurant owner and his wife. Selena demonstrated unique gifts as a singer at a very early age and was performing in public by the age of eight. Her father, who had been a tejano musician in the 1960s, gave her performing opportunities at his restaurant, and later abandoned his business to become her full-time manager. Selena's success was very much a family project; her sister and brother were the drummer and guitarist-songwriter, respectively, in her band, Selena y Los Dinos.

Throughout the 1980s the band's success grew. After signing to a regional independent record company in 1985, the band scored a hit in the tejano market with its single "Dame un beso," and two years later Selena won the Tejano Music Awards title of Female Entertainer of the Year, an honor she would repeat several times in her short career. In 1989, the band signed with one of the major labels, Capitol/EMI, and the group's first album, *Selena y Los Dinos,* made waves throughout Spanish-speaking North America. By 1993, she was performing before crowds of 60,000 at the Houston Astrodome. In 1994, her *Selena Live* album won a Grammy as the Best Mexican-American Album.

By the early 1990s Selena was a role model in the tejano community. Unlike some pop stars, she was a singer of real talent, with an expressive and flexible voice. While she clearly pursued fame eagerly and maintained a sexy image onstage, off stage she remained modest and kind, a "girl of the people." She eloped with her bass player Christopher Perez in 1992, and was on the brink of crossover success with her first English-language album when she was shot to death at age 23 by the president of her fan club. Selena is credited with paving the way for the next wave of popular tejano crossover groups such as La Mafia and Limite.

kind of canción is the *canción-ranchera,* an old-fashioned song associated with rural life. In addition to these traditional Mexican songs, tejano singers include in their repertory songs in English (or in both Spanish and English) that resemble the U.S. country-western musical style.

In the 1980s and 1990s tejano music began to find a wider audience. Singers such as Emilio Navaina (b. 1962) and Selena (see Musician Biography 10.2) began to find success in the broader Mexican-American, U.S., and even South American market. As they did so, the younger tejano stars began to internationalize their music, singing more songs in English and from other Latin-American regions. Selena in particular received acclaim for her *cumbias,* a kind of dance music originating in Colombia that has become popular throughout the Spanish-speaking world. Some observers have worried about the loss of traditional tejano music in this internationalization process.

Cumbia

Chicano movement

LISTENING PREPARATION

Little Joe y la Familia, *"Margarita"* (Written by R. Melon and R. Sanchez).

Little Joe, born Jose Maria DeLeon Hernandez in 1940, is one of the pioneers of tejano music. His band, originally called Little Joe and the Latinaires, was formed with family and friends in the mid-1950s in rural Texas. In the late 1960s and early 1970s, with the rise of the *Chicano movement* emphasizing pride in the Mexican-American heritage, Joe changed the name of his band to Little Joe y La Familia and gradually reached larger and larger audiences. Little Joe and his band have released over 50 records and won two Grammys.

Listen to the bicultural quality of *"Margarita"*—how it blends elements of country music and traditional tejano accordion-based sounds, and Spanish and English lyrics:

SPANISH	ENGLISH
Está es para todas las Gringitas bonitas.	*This goes out to all the pretty Gringitas.*
Margarita, Margarita	*Margarita, Margarita*
No te subas tan arriva	*Don't climb up too high*
Qué las hojas en el arbol	*That the leaves of the tree*
no duran toda la vida.	*Do not last forever.*
	From the distance I can see you
	As you step there by the window
	I can see your pretty blue eyes
	Shining like "cielito lindo."
Hay que lástima, qué lástima me da	*It's a pity to see Margarita cry.*
De ver a Margarita que llorando está.	
Hay. . . pícale Gringo.	*. . . hurry Gringo.*
Hay. . . echale Gringo.	*. . . way to go Gringo.*
	Gonna get you a pretty red dress
	and a pair of cowboy boots
	We'll drive to San Benito
	and we'll dance the "Taquechito"
Desde aquí te estoy mirando	*From a far I have been watching you*
Cara a cara, frente a frente	*Face to face in front of you*
Pero no eres pa' decirme	*But you do not ask me*
chiquitito vente, vente.	*Chiquitito come to me.*
	It breaks my heart to see
	Pretty Margarita crying over me.
	It breaks my heart to see
	My pretty Gringita crying over me.

Refer to the Appendix at the back of the book for this Listening Activity's complete worksheet. Use the following section to make notes for yourself

LISTENING ACTIVITY 10.2:

Little Joe & La Familia, "Margarita" (CD 1/12)

1. What is the meter of this song? _____

2. Is the tempo closest to (circle one): 50 BPM 100 BPM or 150 BPM?

3. What family of instruments dominates at the beginning of the song? _____

4. Name an aspect of this song that connects it with Anglo-country music.

5. At what CD time do you hear the tejano accordion come in? _____

6. What is the general mood of this song? _____

7. How is this achieved?

MARIACHI

The *mariachi* band is one of the most recognizable symbols of Mexican culture. The term *mariachi* refers to the band itself, covering a wide variety of ensembles from the *típico* or traditional to the contemporary, from the local restaurant band to popular groups releasing commercial CD's.

The origins of the mariachi are somewhat foggy. Probably originating in what is now the western Mexican state of Jalisco, the ensemble is likely a descendent of the theater orchestras popular there during the Spanish colonial times. Mariachi music remained a regional musical style until the Mexican Revolution of 1910–1917. After the revolution, there was massive immigration from the countryside to

Mexico City (which would eventually become the world's most populous metropolitan center), and the country folk brought regional styles with them to the capital, and from there into national circulation. The new leadership of Mexico became particularly enamored with the mariachi, and hired bands for political rallies and other events. The music of the mariachi, led by the famous band Mariachi Vargas de Tecalitlán in the 1930s, now became closely identified with the Mexican people.

Mariachi bands can vary greatly in size. The largest ensembles consist of up to eight violins, two trumpets, a guitar, plus some traditional Mexican instruments: the *vihuela,* a small, high-pitched, round-backed guitar, and the *guitarrón,* a large, deep guitar,

Mariachi

Vihuela
Guitarrón

San Antonio, Texas: Mariachi Band. Photo by Joe Sohm.
Source: The Image Works.

Traje de Charro

Serenata

which provides the bass for the ensemble. Also appearing on occasion is the Mexican folk harp. Smaller ensembles may include just three or four instruments, most typically the vihuela, guitarrón, violin, and trumpet. Most of the musicians can sing as well as play their instrument. Mariachi musicians usually wear a traditional outfit called the traje de charro, black waist-length jackets and pants that flare out at the ends; both jackets and pants are decorated with embroidery or silver buttons in a variety of shapes.

Mariachis play at restaurants and bars, but are also hired for special occasions. In earlier times in Mexican society, when the sexes were kept apart, a young man might hire a mariachi band to perform a *serenata* beneath the window of his beloved. Mariachis are hired to play at all kinds of events: weddings, birthday parties, the *quince años* celebration (a kind of coming-out party for girls turning fifteen), patriotic holidays, even funerals. Since the mid-1960s, *mariachis* have sometimes been featured at church in special *mariachi* masses.

The music played by mariachis varies as much as the setting—and often, with the setting. Most mariachis are used to taking requests from the audience,

and must maintain a large repertoire ranging from older rancheros to the latest cumbia or pop tune on the Latin charts. Sometimes the band is meant to be listened to; in other settings, the audience or members of the band might dance. The songs are typically sung high in the voice range, in tight parallel harmony, with vocal sections trading off with instrumental flourishes.

Women have had a steadily increasing role in the mariachi world. Since the 1940s, when the Mariachi Las Coronelas was formed in Mexico, there have been several all-female mariachi bands. Today it is not uncommon to find mariachi bands made up entirely from a single family, including the mothers and daughters.

Checkpoint

Music has been an important part of the cultural life of Latinos since before the arrival of the conquistadores in the sixteenth century. From time to time, Latin music crazes have swept through the broader U.S. society—the tango in the 1910s and 1920s; the rumba and conga in the 1930s; the samba in the 1940s; the mambo in the late 1940s and 1950s; the bossa nova in the 1960s; salsa and reggae in the 1970s; and the international Latin popular music sound in the 1980s and 1990s.

In tejano music there are two main kinds of ensembles, the conjunto and the orquesta. Vocal music, which can appear with conjunto, orquesta, or other kind of backing, is also very important. Corridos, or narrative ballads, tell epic stories through music, while cancións are the traditional love songs of the Mexican people. Stars such as Selena have given music from southern Texas international attention. The traditional mariachi band, however, remains among the most familiar symbols of Mexican culture.

KEY TERMS

Mestizo
Tango
Rumba
Habanera rhythm
Conga
Conga drums
Bongos
Claves
Timbales
Güiro
Maracas
Samba

Mambo
Cubop
Son
Danzón
Montuno
Bossa nova
Salsa
Merengue
Tejanos
Conjunto
Orquesta
Bajo sexto

Huapango
Ranchero and Jaitón
Corrido
Canción
Cumbia
Chicano movement
Mariachi
Vihuela
Guitarrón
Traje de Charro
Serenata

CHAPTER 11

Intermezzo:
Introduction to Art Music

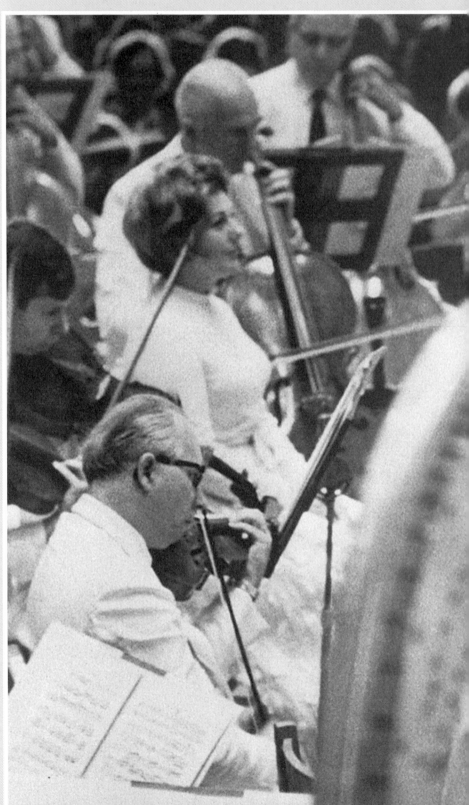

An *Intermezzo* is a short opera heard during the intermission of a longer opera, a diversion from the main event but very popular in its own right. In fact, for a while during the eighteenth century the Intermezzo was more popular than the original opera. The term was also used in the nineteenth century for a short piano piece. Like its operatic counterpart, this chapter serves as a break in the middle of the *Styles* part of this text, between the popular and classical styles. It will prepare you for the last four chapters of this book, all of which focus primarily on classical music.

Art Music versus Classical Music: Before we begin, we need to clarify some terminology. The term *classical music* is generally used today to refer to all kinds of serious music that developed out of a European tradition. As we shall see, this includes several different styles that are distinct from one another in both character and chronology. One of the style periods is known as the Classical Period, referring only to the music created in the late eighteenth and early nineteenth centuries. To avoid confusion, musicologists sometimes use the term *art music* to encompass all serious music drawn from the European tradition, reserving the term *classical* for the music of this single style period.

For the purposes of this book, the term *classical music* will be used in the way most people use it, as a global term for a collection of styles.

Intermezzo

Art music

Classical music

LISTENING TO CLASSICAL MUSIC

Listening to classical music presents different challenges from other kinds of music. The first challenge is simply the length of the music. Classical pieces are often quite long, sometimes stretching out over hours. The pace of the music can also be slow, with a long preparation before the first *theme,* or melody, begins. Our impatience with this music says something about the sound-bite culture of modern life, where information is processed by the nanosecond and we are accustomed to quick and direct results. Much of our entertainment is geared toward abbreviated attention spans. In order to enjoy classical music, we must retrain ourselves to extend our entertainment envelope, to be patient for the music to unfold. This is probably the most important step to enjoying classical music.

Another challenge in listening to classical music is its instrumental nature. Although there is a great tradition of classical vocal music, classical music is often purely instrumental. Most popular music today is voice-oriented, and listening to just instruments can take some getting used to.

Classical vocal music can present even more of a challenge than classical instrumental music, however. Most of the lyrics are in another language—typically Italian, French, or German—and so unless the listener is bilingual a translation is critical. The character of classical vocal music also surprises newcomers. Classical vocal music developed before the days of amplification, so singers were trained to project their voices across large distances. Amplification enabled singers from the jazz era onward to be heard at a whisper. Classical voices therefore often sound big and loud, with a fair amount of *vibrato,* when a pitch seems to waver up and down quickly.

Classical music also possesses a certain musical density that can surprise those who have not listened to it attentively before. Musical ideas are stacked up, turned around, extended, shrunk, and mutated into something different. The music can have prickly passages that make you wince or want to hit the CD "skip" button. Like a great novelist wringing the most out of his or her characters, classical composers often seem bent on extracting every possible idea out of a simple musical theme.

Theme

Vibrato

WHY BOTHER?

If classical music presents so many challenges—and if there are so many other fine styles of music that are more easily accessible—why should we bother with it? Part of the answer to this question is circular: we listen to classical music simply because it's "classical," just as we enjoy the classics of literature, film, and other arts. Artists such as Shakespeare, Rembrandt, and Hitchcock created works that engage the minds and souls of generation after generation, and the same is true of Mozart, Beethoven, and the other classical composers. To explore these works is to tap into a rich vein of cultural treasures. To put it another way, we listen to classical music in part just to see what the buzz is about.

If you were to ask a classical-music lover why he or she listens to the music, they would probably explain that the music rewards repeated listenings. Some of the most popular music has a very short "shelf life." A tune might zoom to the top of the charts one week, then crash the next. Indeed, from a purely marketing standpoint, a record company does not care how many times you listen to a CD, but rather how many new CD's you buy. Obviously this does not mean all popular music is worthless; the point is that overall, popular music is not intended to last. Most classical music, on the other hand, can be listened to hundreds of times because of its richness and complexity. Some music scholars spend years studying just one piece of music, always discovering nuances and beauty they had never found before.

For some kinds of classical music, the enjoyment comes more from the music's complexity than its beauty. Certain composers—usually clustered together in certain times and places in music history, such as late fourteenth-century southern France and early twentieth-century Vienna—delighted in composing in an intellectual manner, which has challenged listeners and other composers to decode the music. So with this kind of music, in addition to its aesthetic qualities, there is a puzzle to work out, so the brain and the heart are both attended to.

WAYS TO NAVIGATE THE CLASSICAL MUSIC TERRAIN

The first thing to realize about classical music is that it isn't just one style of music, but rather several styles that cover a millennium. We will talk more about these different styles in a moment. Since there are many varieties of classical music, it is important to learn the context of the music—details about the composer's life, the times, the audience of the day, and so forth. In the chapters that follow we will discuss different strategies for different kinds of classical music.

The most important thing, however, is simply to stay tuned in. We have a habit in our society of using music as wallpaper; the purpose of this book is to shake that habit off. Any time you find your mind wandering, stop the CD. Come back to it when you are ready. Keep careful notes as you listen. The Listening Activities found in these chapters will help, but they are not the only way to listen to the music. There are probably as many different listening styles as there are music lovers. As with any other kind of music, the more you listen, the more you will trust your own instincts.

SOME CLASSICAL TERMS

CLASSICAL TEMPO MARKINGS

Classical musicians refer to tempo using the Italian names listed below. Why Italian? The reason has to do with music history:

the first people to develop music printing were Italians, and they established much of the standard terminology for music using their own language. Note that these terms sometimes have a broader connotation than just tempo: they can also indicate the *way* in which a piece of music is to be played. Tempo markings usually appear at the very beginning of a piece of music. This is a list of the most common *classical tempo markings,* with the approximate range of beats per minute:

Prestissimo	As Fast as Possible	200 BPM +
Presto	Extremely fast	about 168–200 BPM
Vivace	Lively, with great speed	150 BPM +
Allegro	Fast	about 120–160 BPM
Moderato	Moderate tempo	about 108–120 BPM
Andante	Slower, but still moderate; walking tempo	about 76–108 BPM
Adagio	Slow	about 66–76 BPM
Larghetto	Very slow	about 60–66 BPM
Largo	Extremely slow	about 40–60 BPM

You might also encounter supplementary Italian tempo terms, such as *piu,* meaning "more;" so that *piu presto* means "more quickly." In addition, in classical music, tempo markings are often accompanied by terms of expression such as *maestoso,* "majestically;"

cantabile, "in a singing manner;" and *appassionato,* "with great passion." Usually the tempo term comes first, then the term of expression: *adagio maestoso* (slowly and majestically). There are also Italian terms for those times when music changes in tempo. Here is a list of *classical tempo changes:*

Accelerando	Getting faster
Ritardando	Getting slower
Rallentando	Getting slower
Ritenuto	Suddenly slower

In the early nineteenth century the German inventor Johann Maelzel (1772–1838) developed and patented a machine he called a *metronome,* the clicking of which provided for the first time an accurate measure of tempo. Starting with his friend, the composer Ludwig van Beethoven (see Musician Biography 13.1), some composers began to supplement or replace these Italian terms with specific *metronome markings,* a number or range of numbers in beats per minute. In classical music today, composers are free to use whatever tempo markings they like—the traditional Italian terms, metronome markings, even tempo designations in their own language.

Cantabile

Appassionato

Classical tempo markings

Classical tempo changes

Metronome

Metronome markings

Piu

Piu presto

Maestoso

STYLE PERIODS

The styles we have studied so far—the blues, jazz, rock, and Latino music—have overlapped each other to varying degrees. When we talk of classical music, however, we think of styles *succeeding* on another, the romantic style following the classical style, and the twentieth-century style following the romantic, and so forth. This is actually something of a historical fiction; in art music, styles overlapped as much as in popular music. At the same time the composer J. S. Bach was composing in a late baroque style, for example, his own sons were composing in the new classical style. Nevertheless, for the sake of clarity we will adhere to

the tradition of specific cutoff dates for the years of the style periods:

Medieval:	A.D. 600 to 1450
Renaissance:	1450 to 1600
Baroque:	1600 to 1750
Classical:	1750 to 1815
Romantic:	1815 to 1900
Twentieth Century:	1900 to 2000

In this book we will study late baroque music through the classical music of the twentieth century; this is the classical music most likely to be found on

Early music

concert programs. This means we will miss some great music from the early baroque, Renaissance, and medieval periods, known collectively as *early music.*

Once you become acquainted with the classical styles in this book, I urge you to explore the wealth of great music written before 1700.

GENRES

Chamber Genres
Genre

W hen discussing classical music, we need to introduce a new musical term, *genre,* referring to a kind of piece. All styles of music make some distinction between different kinds of pieces, but often this distinction is rather fuzzy. Usually, different genres are primarily a function of tempo (for example, slow ballads versus fast numbers). In classical music, however, the distinction is based primarily on instrumentation—different kinds of pieces for different groups of instruments. Sometimes, however, you will find two different genres for the same group of instruments; the difference here is probably a matter of the piece's form. Genres are more important in classical music than in most other styles.

There are three broad groups of genres in classical music: instrumental, vocal, and music drama. Within instrumental genres, there are two subgroups, pieces for large ensembles (*orchestral* genres) and pieces for

Orchestral Genres

small ensembles or soloists (*chamber* genres). The word "chamber" refers to any room where music might be heard, rather than a concert hall. As for the individual genres in these two subgroups, as mentioned above, the differences mostly have to do with instrumentation, although some have to do with the form and/or the number of *movements,* or sections of the piece (see below).

The following are lists of the most common genres in classical music:

ORCHESTRAL GENRES

Symphony: A piece for full orchestra in several movements (typically four).

Concerto: A piece for full orchestra plus one or more soloists, usually in three movements.

The Syracuse Symphony performs at Emerson Park on July 3rd before the fireworks on Owasco Lake (1977). Photo by Lisa Krantz.
Source: The Image Works.

Overture: A piece for full orchestra in one movement. Some overtures were originally written for plays or musical theater productions, and some were written just for orchestral concerts. The latter are referred to as *concert overtures.*

Suite: In the baroque period, this referred to a collection of dance pieces of varying tempos and meters. Today, a suite refers to music for the concert hall that was originally written for another setting. For example, a composer might take the music he or she wrote for a movie, extract some choice selections, then rearrange them to make an appropriate piece for an orchestral concert. Suites can also be drawn from ballets, operas, even television shows.

Tone Poem: A piece for full orchestra in one movement that tells a story, also known as a *symphonic poem.*

CHAMBER MUSIC GENRES

*C*hamber music refers to pieces for relatively small ensembles—typically nine musicians or fewer, who usually play without a conductor. In chamber music, each instrument plays a separate part, while in orchestral music, some of the parts have several instruments playing the same notes. There are some standard terms used for chamber ensembles, which should be familiar to you: a *duet* is a piece for two musicians, a *trio* for three, a *quartet* for four, a *quintet* for five, and so forth. These can be for any combination of instruments. There are also certain common chamber music ensembles with set instruments, and therefore set genres. The genres for these common ensembles are listed here.

Duet
Trio
Quartet
Quintet

Sonata: A multimovement work for piano solo or a solo instrument plus piano accompaniment.

String Quartet: A work for four string instruments: two violins, one viola, and one cello.

Woodwind Quintet: A work for five wind instruments, one of which is actually a brass instrument: flute, oboe, clarinet, French horn, and bassoon.

A string quartet playing in the Schloss Hellbrunn Gardens, Salzburg, Austria.
Source: The Image Works.

Brass Quintet: A work for five brass instruments: two trumpets, French horn, trombone, and tuba.

VOCAL GENRES

Madrigal

Art song

Like instrumental classical music, vocal music can be broadly grouped into chamber music and music for large choral ensembles. As with instrumental music, chamber music for voice is designed for one musician on a part, while larger choral music involves several singers on each part. An example of chamber music for voice is the *madrigal,* popular during the Renaissance, written for three to five singers. Another kind of vocal chamber music is the *art song,* written for solo voice with piano accompaniment.

This brings up another important point about vocal music: the nature of the accompaniment. Some vocal music is sung with the support of an entire orchestra; some is accompanied by just a piano; and some is sung without accompaniment at all—

A cappella

referred to as *a cappella* singing (meaning "in the style of the church," a term originating in a time when church music was almost always sung without accompaniment).

Sacred
Secular

A final distinction regarding vocal music concerns the nature of the text, whether it's *sacred* (with religious words) or *secular* (featuring nonreligious words). The two chamber genres listed above, the madrigal and the art song, are both secular genres. Most of the common genres of large choral works are sacred.

Mass: Music used in the Eucharist service of the Roman Catholic Church, with specific words used each time.
Requiem: A mass to honor the dead.
Motet: A religious choral piece, usually *a cappella,* using varying texts.
Anthem: Like a motet, but for English-speaking countries. Originally anthems were written

for the Church of England. Note that this is different from a *national anthem,* a secular piece associated with political functions and nation-states.
Hymn: A simple sacred piece sung by the entire congregation in Protestant church services, in German-speaking countries, known as a *chorale.*
Cantata: A sacred choral piece in several movements featuring one or more soloist, a chorus, and a small orchestra. Cantatas are usually built on a particular hymn.
Oratorio: Like a cantata, only longer, with larger performing forces, and usually relating a story (although it is not *staged,* as are music drama works).

Photo by Steve Liss.
Source: TimePix.

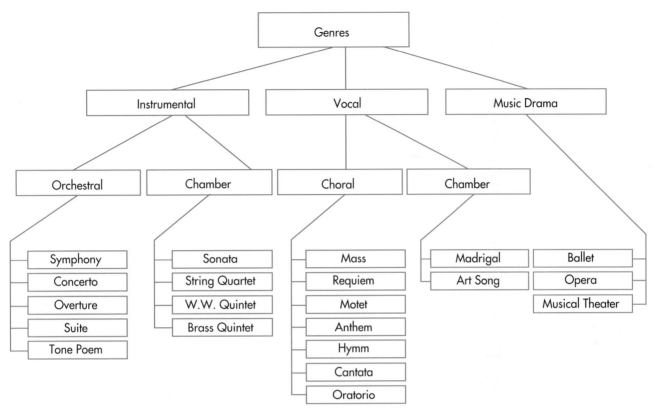

FIGURE 11.1: *Organization of Classical Genres.*

MUSIC DRAMA GENRES

Music and drama have a long association, dating back perhaps to the beginnings of both art forms. The connection is a natural one, since these are the two main art forms that unfold over time (as opposed to painting and sculpture, for example, which usually deal with static physical materials). Music drama genres are distinguished by the means in which the drama is presented:

Ballet: A music drama genre featuring orchestral music, in which the drama is presented through dancing.

Opera: A music drama genre in which the drama is presented primarily through singing and acting.

Musical Theater: A music drama genre in which the drama is presented through singing, acting, and spoken dialogue. Musical theater (*musicals,* for short) is usually considered a popular, rather than a classical genre.

A diagram of the classical music genres discussed in this chapter might look like Figure 11.1.

MOVEMENTS

In instrumental classical music, as well as some vocal classical music, a single piece almost always has several distinct sections called *movements.* Movements are distinguished by tempo, with successive movements usually alternating between slow and fast tempos. In fact, when we

Movements

refer to the movement of a classical piece, we often use the tempo marking as a substitute for its name. The first movement of Beethoven's Fifth Symphony, for example, may be referred to as the *allegro con brio* movement (fast, with energy).

Different genres have different numbers of movements. A symphony usually has four (fast, slow, moderate, fast), while a concerto typically has three (fast, slow, fast). Sometimes in concert or on CD (especially compilation CD's) you might hear just one movement of a piece, but performers usually like to present all the movements so that we hear the music the way the composer intended it to be heard.

TITLES

Narrative titles

Generic titles

Catalog number

Opus numbers

The last matter for us to consider in preparing to study classical music is the way pieces are named. In classical music there are two main kinds of titles of pieces: *narrative* and *generic*. Narrative titles are used for musical works that are connected to a story, such as Richard Strauss's tone poem *Death and Transfiguration,* where the title prepares the listener for the story told by the music. A generic title is one which tells the listener about the genre of the piece (note that the words *generic* and *genre* are cognates). An example of a generic title would be the word "symphony"— we know from the title that this will be a work for orchestra without soloist, probably in four movement.

A problem with generic titles comes when a composer writes more than one piece in the same genre. To help distinguish between different pieces of the same genre, we usually add several other bits of information:

A. The number of that kind of piece that the composer has written, usually in order of composition (Symphony *No. 5*);
B. The musical key (Symphony No. 5 *in C Minor*);
C. The *opus number*. Opus means "work," abbreviated "Op." This is the number assigned by composers to their pieces as their work gets published, so the first work of any kind is Op. 1, then Op. 2, and so forth. The opus number thus helps listeners understand whether the work was written early in a

composer's career or later. Many composers have between 100 and 200 opus numbers, but some have more than a thousand (Symphony No. 5 in C Minor, *Op. 67*);
D. The composition number included within the opus number. In the Baroque and Classical periods, publishers sometimes bundled together works in groups of six or twelve. So, if you talk about Handel's Op. 3 Concertos, you have to indicate which concerto you are referring to in the set of six (Handel, Concerto Grosso in G Major, Op. 3 *No. 3*).
E. Some composers never managed to publish much in their lifetimes. In these cases, we use the number from the catalog of their complete works instead of an opus number. When Mozart's Symphony No. 40 appears on a program, for example, usually the *catalog number* from the catalog assembled by Ludwig Köchel is appended to the title. For pieces by Mozart, look for the "K" number (for Köchel); for Schubert, look for the "D" number (for Otto Erich Deutsch). (For example, Mozart, Symphony No. 40 in G Minor, *K. 550.*)
F. The movement number (usually given in Roman numerals) and the tempo marking of that movement (Mozart, Symphony No. 40 in G Minor, K. 550, I, *Molto Allegro*). If all the movements are being performed in a concert, the movements are usually listed beneath the main title, one on each line.

Symphony No. 5 in C Minor, Op.67   Ludwig van Beethoven

> *Allegro con brio*
> *Andante con moto*
> *Allegro*
> *Allegro*

FIGURE 11.2: *Sample Program Entry on a Classical Program.*

Here is an example of a generic title as it might appear in a concert program (Figure 11.2).

From this entry, we know what kind of piece we will hear, who the composer is, approximately where in his output this piece falls (his fifth symphony, and not an early work—and if we know that he completed 135 opuses during his career, we know that this work was composed approximately in midlife); we also know that the piece has four movements, and we even know how fast each movement will go.

FINAL WORD

Some of you have heard classical music before and are well prepared for what follows; for others, although you may have heard classical music in shopping centers and TV commercials, this is relatively new music. Some of you will take to it immediately and never look back; other will find it hard to like. Give the music time, be patient with yourself, and any music can make sense to you.

KEY TERMS

Intermezzo	Appassionato	Quintet
Art music	Classical tempo changes	Madrigal
Classical music	Metronome	Art Song
Theme	Metronome markings	A cappella
Vibrato	Early music	Sacred
Classical tempo markings	Genre	Secular
Piu	Orchestral genres	Movements
Piu presto	Chamber genres	Narrative titles
Maestoso	Duet	Generic titles
Cantabile	Trio	Opus numbers
	Quartet	Catalog number

CHAPTER

12

Eighteenth-Century Music

This chapter discusses the art music of two style periods, the late baroque and the classical. The baroque period began around the year 1600, but it is the music written after about 1700 that is more commonly heard in concerts today, written by composers such as Vivaldi, Handel, and J. S. Bach—and so it is with this late baroque music that our classical music discussion begins. About midway through the eighteenth century a new musical style emerged, the classical style, centered in Vienna, Austria, and brought to perfection by composers such as Haydn and Mozart. Around the turn of the nineteenth century, a brash young composer in Vienna, Ludwig van Beethoven, transformed the classical style of Haydn and Mozart into a new music now called romantic, discussed in Chapter 13.

THE BAROQUE ERA

Before 1700, only about 10 percent of Europe's population lived in cities. Most people lived in the countryside and grew food to feed their immediate family. Extra food might be sold at a nearby town, but for the most part everything a family needed was grown or made at home. Some people were craftsmen instead of farmers, creating goods for use in exchange for food, and a few people worked as merchants, earning profit by buying and selling goods in the small towns, but agriculture dominated the economy.

This situation gradually began to change in the eighteenth century. A new kind of merchant emerged who became more involved in the manufacturing of goods, supplying the raw materials to craftsmen and buying the end products. Over the course of the eighteenth century these merchants, called *entrepreneurs,* moved most of the production out of people's houses and into centralized locations called *factories,* where the entrepreneurs could exert more control over the workers and improve their productivity. And gradually, much of the work done by hand was replaced by mechanized processes that were faster and more consistent. This was the *Industrial Revolution,* one of the greatest upheavals in human history. By 1850 much of Western Europe's peasant population had left their family farms and moved to the growing urban centers to work twelve-hour days often in unsanitary and dangerous conditions. During this time, too, the merchant class had grown in power and wealth and were challenging the power of the nobility, the landowning aristocrats who inherited their land and their titles (such as *duke* or *count*) and who had held power in Europe for centuries. The end of the eighteenth century and the beginning of the nineteenth century would be marked by bloody revolutions that would eventually lead to the end of the power of the European aristocracy in the early twentieth century.

During the baroque period (1600–1750), however, these revolutions were a long way off, and the increasing wealth of European nations seemed to be consolidating the power of the rulers, not eroding it. Absolute monarchs such as France's Louis XIV (r. 1643–1715) held complete control over their countries and lived lives of opulent wealth and privilege. Almost all the art music of the baroque period was written either for these rulers or for the church (Protestant or Roman Catholic) and reflects their refined, grandiose tastes.

THE BAROQUE AESTHETIC

Refinement and grandiosity—these two terms seem to characterize the baroque style in all the arts. Architects created sumptuous palaces for the kings and aristocrats of the day, with ornate columns and huge spaces, sometimes emphasized by interior paintings that added visual embellishment and expanded the sense of space. Outside the palaces were large formal gardens, where the order of the buildings was continued in

Industrial Revolution

carefully planted and trimmed flowers and bushes. Although baroque painting styles varied a great deal from country to country, all across Europe artists created works of large size, with sharp contrasts of light and color to heighten the dramatic subject matter. In the 1720s a late baroque painting style called *rococo* became popular, emphasizing pastel colors and frilly decoration.

The music of the baroque was also grandiose, elegant, and carefully constructed. The music's grandiosity comes from two different aspects of size: the number of musicians performing and the length of the works, both of which generally increased over the course of the baroque period. Elegance was highly valued: singers and instrumentalists were expected to execute elaborate *ornaments* to any melody, little decorations not actually written down, but always added by musicians who were considered tasteful. The craftsmanship of the music was also important. Baroque composers believed there was a precise and proper way to write music, with definite rules for the way one note, rhythm, or harmony followed another. This sense of craftsmanship appears in many of the characteristics of the baroque style.

Ornaments

Basso continuo

Recitative

Rhythm: Baroque music featured two extremes of rhythmic regularity. On one hand, there was a vocal style of music called *recitative* (from the word "recite") which was meant to emulate the varied rhythm found in human speech. In recitative—used mostly in opera—it is virtually impossible to determine the meter or even the tempo, because both elements fluctuate according to how a person might speak the words. Other kinds of music in the baroque period, however, were known for their rhythmic regularity. Baroque instrumental music, especially, features steady, unyielding tempos and meters throughout an entire movement. For this reason some people refer to baroque music as having *motor rhythm,* as if a machine were governing the pace of the music.

Melody: Baroque melodies tend to be built on long, sometimes rather complex phrases. Often, the melodies are built out of a single motive, used as the building block for all the melodies of the music. As mentioned above, baroque melodies were often considered incomplete unless a musician added ornaments not written into the original scores.

Harmony: It was in the baroque period that the modern sense of harmony emerged with a clear division between major and minor. Baroque composers thought carefully about the succession of chords, often structuring their pieces around a series of modulations.

Texture: Baroque music featured a balance between homophonic and polyphonic textures, although polyphony became increasingly dominant toward the end of the era. J. S. Bach, especially, excelled at writing elaborate, intellectual polyphonic compositions, which represent a level of musical craftsmanship that has never been matched since.

Timbre and Instrumentation: The ensemble we now call an orchestra was invented during the baroque era, combining violins, violas, cellos, double basses, flutes, oboes, bassoons, and sometimes brass and timpani. The most important element of baroque instrumentation was something called the *basso continuo*. In baroque musical scores, the bass line featured chord symbols, and the players of both the bass instrument (such as the double bass or cello) and the keyboard instrument (usually a harpsichord, although sometimes an organ) read this line, the keyboardist improvising chords based on the symbols in the written music. In this regard, baroque keyboard players were similar to jazz keyboard players, who also improvise chords based on symbols, rather than written notes (although the symbols for jazz are different than those used in the baroque period).

The combination of the bass and keyboard instrument was called the basso continuo, since they both read the same bass part, and because their music was virtually continuous throughout the piece. In fact, if you train your ears to recognize the sound of the harpsichord, you will have found a simple way to identify baroque music, since the instrument was used almost all the time during this period, but fell out of fashion in the classical era.

Form: The baroque attention to detail and craftsmanship shows up in the structure of the pieces. Although the structure of any given piece may be complex, there was usually an attention to both balance and detail that make the music satisfying to listen to and to study.

Genre: Probably the most popular kind of music in the baroque was *opera,* performed with elaborate sets and beautiful costumes in the ornate, full-sized theaters in the regal palaces. During the religious season of Lent, when opulent opera performances were considered inappropriate, *oratorios* were substituted, similar in music but without scenery, costumes, sets, or acting, and featuring a plot drawn from the Bible. In Italy and in northern Germany, another multisection vocal genre, the *cantata,* was also popular. In Germany, this was heard in conjunction with weekly Lutheran church services. The vast improvements in the design of keyboard instruments prompted composers to create new works such as the *prelude* and *fugue* for themselves to perform on the harpsichord and the organ. Another popular instrumental genre of the baroque was the *trio sonata,* written for two violins plus basso continuo (bass or cello plus harpsichord). Therefore, this is one type of trio that actually includes four instruments; it was considered a trio because two instruments read the third line of music together, and are thought of as one part.

THE CONCERTO

When it came to orchestral music the *concerto* and *concerto grosso* dominated the baroque repertoire. The concerto grosso is similar to the concerto—with its three-movement structure and contrast between soloist and the large group—but with the difference that it usually features two or more soloists rather than just one. The contrast between soloist or solo section and large group creates the *Baroque echo effect,* which appealed to the baroque aesthetic and appears in many different kinds of baroque pieces (Figure 12.1).

Although any instrument could be the featured one in a concerto, the most common was the violin. It was in the baroque period that the craft of string-instrument making reached a level of perfection never surpassed, before or since. The best violins were made by the instrument builders in Cremona, Italy, which was the home of Antonio Stradivari (1648–1737), whose violins fetch more than a million dollars in today's market. Not uncoincidentally, it was in the baroque period that the first violin virtuosos appeared. The concerto was a vehicle to show off their skills.

The concerto is typically in three movements, usually with two fast movements surrounding a slow middle movement. (Note: for this *Standard Movement Outline* and those that follow, be aware that exceptions are about as common as the rules—composers often deviated from these plans in individual works.)

FIGURE 12.1: *The Baroque "Echo Effect," with Sudden Changes between Loud and Soft Passages.*

Opera

Oratorio
Baroque echo effect

Cantata

Prelude and fugue

Trio sonata

Concerto
Concerto grosso

STANDARD MOVEMENT OUTLINE: CONCERTO

MOVEMENT	TEMPO	USUAL FORM
First Movement:	Fast (*Allegro*)	*Ritornello* (see below)
Second Movement:	Slow (*Adagio, Andante*)	*Aria* (discussed in Chapter 15)
Third Movement:	Fast (*Allegro*)	*Rondo* (discussed later this chapter)

The term *ritornello* has two meanings: it is used as the name for the form of the first movements of concertos, and to refer to the most important feature of that form, a catchy theme played by the full orchestra that returns periodically throughout the movement. The Italian word *ritorno* means "return," and *ritornello* is the diminutive version of *ritorno*—thus, a *ritornello* is "a little thing that returns." The first-movement ritornello form is derived from the baroque echo effect mentioned above, an alternation between the loud, full orchestra playing the ritornello theme, and the quieter solo passages. Throughout the piece, even in most of the solo passages, the ubiquitous basso

continuo plays, like the rhythm section of a jazz ensemble keeping time during a jazz solo.

During the solo passages (called *episodes*), the key usually changes. This means that every time you hear the ritornello, it usually will be higher or lower than the last time. Sometimes, the mode will change, too (meaning if the ritornello was in major key, it will be changed to minor and vice-versa). In the end, the ritornello comes back to the original key and mode.

There are a few more aspects of ritornello form to take note of before we dive into the music. First, the number of ritornellos varies widely from piece to piece. Some might have just three or four

MUSICIAN BIOGRAPHY 12.1:

ANTONIO VIVALDI *(1678—1741)*

Vivaldi was born in the north Italian port city of Venice, a place so tied to the water that canals took the place of roads and boats called *gondolas* replaced horses and carriages. Vivaldi was trained for the priesthood and ordained in 1703, but soon stopped performing mass, supposedly due to his asthma. We do know, however, that Vivaldi also ran into trouble with Church authorities—trouble that eventually tarnished his career. Because of his ordination, red hair, and explosive temperament, he was known as the "Red Priest" during his lifetime.

Vivaldi was one of the leading violin virtuosos of his day, and soon after his ordination he began working as a professional musician. Although his fame took him all over Europe, his home base remained Venice for most of his career, where he served as violin teacher and music director at the Ospedale della Pietà, one of four girls' orphanages in the city. The 400 girls at the Pietà devoted almost all their time to music. They formed several separate orchestras and choirs, considered to be among the finest in all of Europe. Vivaldi wrote hundreds of concertos and concerto grossos for the girls, featuring several different instruments in solo parts, among them the bassoon, the lute, even the mandolin. But the majority (more than 230) feature the violin. Although Vivaldi also wrote beautiful vocal music for the orphanage and even some operas, he is best remembered for these concertos, with their appealing melodies and exciting virtuosity.

Vivaldi died in Vienna in 1741, and his music fell out of the public sphere for many years. Two hundred years later, Vivaldi's music was rediscovered, and now some of his concerto grossos rank among the most popular of all classical compositions.

LISTENING PREPARATION

Vivaldi, Violin Concerto in E Major, Op. 8, No. 1, "The Spring," I, *Allegro* (ca. 1725).

Around 1725 Vivaldi published a set of four concertos he called *The Four Seasons,* with one concerto for each season. He supplied a sonnet to accompany each of the concertos—which he probably wrote himself—meant to be read while listening to the music, and he placed these in each orchestra member's part to help with musical interpretation. *The Four Seasons* thus represent an early example of *program music,* music associated with a story, or something else written down. When you get a chance, you should listen to all four of the concertos in this set, which are all delightful and effectively capture the essence of their representative seasons.

Program music

Like all the concertos of *The Four Seasons,* "The Spring" features virtuosic violin solos, a catchy ritornello, and a form that is both relatively simple to follow, yet deviates somewhat from the standard alternation between orchestral and solo passages. The poem for this concerto is translated as follows:

> Spring has arrived, and festively
> The birds greet it with cheerful song
> And the brooks, caressed by soft breezes,
> Murmur sweetly as they flow.
>
> The sky is covered with a black mantle,
> Lightning and thunder announce a storm.
> When the storm dies away to silence, the birds
> Return with their melodious songs.

You can tell that this poem is not just presenting a still life, but rather captures a changing scene. Part of your task in the Listening Activity that follows will be to match up the lines of the poem with the changing musical landscape.

---

statements, while others may have a dozen or more. Second, the ritornello is usually abbreviated after the first statement, with perhaps just the first half of the ritornello played or even less. Often, the full ritornello comes back at the end. Third, the full orchestra is not limited to playing the ritornello; sometimes it might present a new theme in the middle of the movement, or it may even appear in the solo passages to provide supple support to the virtuoso's pyrotechnics.

Finally, toward the end of the movement, there often appears the highlight of the entire piece: the *cadenza.* This is a passage of free improvisation for the soloist, where even the basso continuo stops and the soloist shows off his or her virtuosity.

A simplified diagram of ritornello form might look like Figure 12.2 on the next page.

Cadenza

THE ORATORIO

*A*s noted above, the oratorio was another popular genre of the baroque period, similar in sound to opera, but a different experience for the audience. The most important difference was the setting: oratorios were performed in churches and concert halls, not opera houses. The show is a concert, not theater; thus, the singers and orchestra simply wear concert dress and sit together on stage or at the front of the church. Oratorios are religious in text, while operas almost never are. Oratorios also generally make greater use of choruses than operas do.

Oratorios first appeared in Italy at the beginning of the baroque period, gradually becoming longer and more dramatic over the course of the

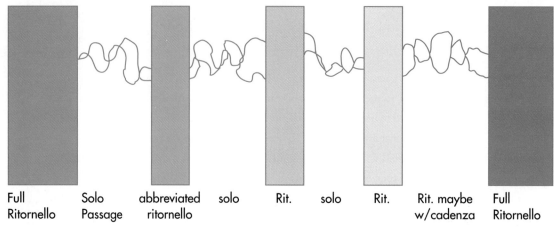

Full Ritornello   Solo Passage   abbreviated ritornello   solo   Rit.   solo   Rit.   Rit. maybe w/cadenza   Full Ritornello

FIGURE 12.2: *Generalized Diagram of Ritornello Form.*

Refer to the Appendix at the back of the book for this Listening Activity's complete worksheet. Use the following section to make notes for yourself

LISTENING ACTIVITY 12.1:

Vivaldi, Violin Concerto in E Major, Op. 8. No.1, "The Spring," I, Allegro (CD 1/13)

1. In this movement, Vivaldi uses *three* ritornellos rather than one, which we will label R1, R2, and R3. The first two can be heard at the beginning of the movement; the third appears later. The first ritornello (R1) is presented at the beginning, with the full orchestra. What happens at CD time 0:11?

2. At 0:18, the second ritornello (R2) is presented. How is this presentation similar to the presentation of R1?

3. What sort of mood is evoked by this initial orchestral section?

4. The first solo passage for the two violins plus basso continuo begins at 0:36. Which line of the poem's first stanza do you think this solo passage best represents?

5. When the orchestra comes in again at 1:10, is it playing R1, R2, or a new ritornello (R3)? _____ (If you are in doubt, go back to the beginning and listen again.)

6. After this ritornello, the orchestra plays new material. Which line of the poem's first stanza do you think this orchestral passage best represents?

7. At what CD time do you hear the next ritornello? _____ Is it (circle one): R1, R2, or R3?

8. After this ritornello, the orchestra plays another new section, but this time preparing us for a new solo section, one in which the orchestra and the soloists interact frequently. What part of the poem do you think this section best corresponds to?

9. At what time do you hear the next ritornello (R2)? _____

10. What is different about R2 this time?

11. After a rather languid solo by the two violins, we hear another ritornello. At what CD time does this occur? _____ Is it (circle one): R1, R2, or R3?

12. One last solo, and we arrive back in the home key and a final ritornello. At what CD time does this last ritornello begin? _____ Is it (circle one): R1, R2, or R3? How is this different from the previous ritornellos?

13. Fill in the following chart:

SONNET LINE(S)	CD TIME (BEGINNING)	SOLO OR ORCHESTRA?
Spring has arrived, and festively	0:00	Orchestra
The birds greet it with cheerful song		
And the brooks, caressed by soft breezes, Murmur sweetly as they flow.		
The sky is covered with a black mantel,		
Lightning and thunder announce a storm.		
When the storm dies away to silence, the birds		
Return with their melodious songs.		

seventeenth and early eighteenth centuries. The oratorio found an important function during the Christian season of Lent, between Ash Wednesday and Easter, when parishioners were supposed to give up worldly entertainment (such as opera) and focus on religious matters; oratorios proved to be a viable operatic substitute. George Frideric Handel (see Musician Biography 12.2) is probably the most famous composer of oratorios, but successful examples were also written by the classical composer Joseph Haydn (see Musician Biography 12.4) and the early romantic composers Robert Schumann (see Musician Biography 13.5) and Felix Mendelssohn (see Musician Biography 13.6). Although these eighteenth- and nineteenth-century oratorios remain popular to this day, very few twentieth-century composers wrote them.

Handel's contemporary J. S. Bach (see Musician Biography 12.3) favored a particular kind of oratorio called a *passion oratorio,* which tells the story of the betrayal, crucifixion, and resurrection of Jesus. Heard at Easter time, these *passions* were always drawn from just one of the four gospels; thus, Bach's *Passion*

According to St. Matthew (or *St. Matthew Passion*) is a different piece from his *St. John Passion.* The oratorios that Handel wrote were usually based on the Old Testament.

THE ORGAN

*K*nown as the "King of Instruments," the organ changed over the course of the baroque period from a squeaky

Passion

G. F. Handel (1685–1759)

MUSICIAN BIOGRAPHY 12.2:

GEORGE FRIDERIC HANDEL
(1685—1759)

*H*andel was born the son of a barber-surgeon (in the seventeenth century, a person with the skills to cut hair was also considered proficient at surgery) in northern Germany. His father hoped he would become a lawyer, but Handel's obsession with music was so pronounced his father finally relented and permitted lessons. By the time he was seventeen, Handel was the organist at a local church, but he dreamed of success in the most popular art form of the time, opera. Within a year he had moved to the opera capital of Germany—Hamburg, where he played violin and harpsichord in the opera house. Before long he was writing and producing his own operas—two by the age of twenty—and he was invited to Italy to write operas at the source of the genre.

His stay in Italy lasted three years, followed by a brief stint as a court composer back in Germany. Then, in 1712, he emigrated to London, where he took citizenship and stayed the rest of his life. His career there was a mixture of work for aristocratic or royal patrons and for private enterprise. Handel was a shrewd businessman and found considerable success promoting his Italian operas to the English audience. In the 1730s, however, a combination of increasing competition and the growing English disenchantment with the genre forced Handel to begin composing oratorios in English. After the stunning success of his oratorio *Messiah,* Handel never looked back, composing dozens of oratorios over the remainder of his life. He went blind in his last years, but lived comfortably. When he died in 1759 more than 3,000 people attended his funeral in Westminster Abbey, burial place of England's royalty and heroes.

Handel, "Hallelujah" Chorus from *Messiah* (1742).

Messiah may be the first piece of classical music to have remained in circulation ever since its premiere more than two and a half centuries ago. After its North American premiere in New York City in 1770, the oratorio has been equally popular on this side of the Atlantic. In Boston and other cities, "Handel Societies" sprang up, dedicated to performing his twenty-six English-language oratorios, and several of these societies still exist. To this day, at Christmas time in virtually every medium- or large-sized city in the United States and Canada, one can find a "sing-along" *Messiah* performance, where the audience gets the opportunity to sing all the choruses.

Handel wrote this monumental work in just twenty-four days, for a performance in Dublin. Unlike most of his oratorios this one does not tell a story; rather it just draws on texts from the Bible about Jesus. When King George II heard the famous "Hallelujah" Chorus, he stood up to honor the God the music evoked, and since then audiences around the world have stood up for this movement, too.

In these oratorios Handel displays both exquisite taste and a sure-fire instinct for box-office receipts. His music moves quickly between extremes, from soft, almost private prayers to grand, earth-shattering exaltations; from intricate and sophisticated polyphony to straight-forward homophonic and even monophonic textures. In this famous chorus, listen to how Handel alternates between these extremes to build up excitement and effectively express the content of the text.

Refer to the Appendix at the back of the book for this Listening Activity's complete worksheet. Use the following section to make notes for yourself.

LISTENING ACTIVITY 12.2:

Handel, "Hallelujah" Chorus from Messiah (CD 1/14)

This chorus features just five lines of text, repeated and tossed around in all sorts of combinations. For the purpose of analyzing this music, we will number the lines of text. Since Handel often splits up the last two lines, we will number these (a) and (b):

(1) Hallelujah!

(2) For the Lord God omnipotent reigneth

(3) The kingdom of this world is become the Kingdom of our Lord and of His Christ

(4a) And He shall reign

(4b) Forever and ever

(5a) King of Kings

(5b) And Lord of Lords!

Handel alternates setting the music in monophonic, homophonic, and polyphonic texture. Your job in the exercise below will be to analyze the entire movement for texture. In vocal music, monophonic texture occurs when everybody is singing the same melody together; homophonic texture is when everybody is singing the same words at the same time, in the same rhythm, but with different notes; and polyphonic texture is when two or more groups of singers are weaving together separate melodies (and often separate words). The underscored lines indicate the start of a new section. For each line of text, write in whether the texture is monophonic, homophonic, or polyphonic:

CD TIME	LINE NUMBER	TEXTURE?
0:00	Orchestral introduction	n/a
0:06	(1) "Hallelujah! Hallelujah . . ."	homophonic
0:24	(2) "For the Lord God omnipotent reigneth"	
0:30	(1) "Hallelujah! Hallelujah . . ."	
0:35	(2) "For the Lord God omnipotent reigneth"	
0:41	(1) "Hallelujah! Hallelujah . . ."	
0:46	(2 and 1 together)	
0:53	(2 and 1)	
1:02	(2 and 1)	
1:12	(3) "The kingdom of this world . . ."	
1:30	(4a and b) "And He shall reign forever and ever"	
1:35	(4a and b) "And He shall reign forever and ever"	
1:41	(4a and b) "And He shall reign forever and ever"	
1:46	(4a and b) "And He shall reign forever and ever"	
1:52	(5a) "King of Kings"	
1:54	(4b and 1) "Forever and ever, Hallelujah!"	
1:59	(5b) "And Lord of Lords"	
2:01	(4b and 1) "Forever and ever, Hallelujah!"	
2:06	(5a) "King of Kings"	
2:08	(4b and 1) "Forever and ever, Hallelujah!"	
2:12	(5b) "And Lord of Lords"	
2:14	(4b and 1) "Forever and ever, Hallelujah!"	
2:19	(5a) "King of Kings"	
2:21	(4b and 1) "Forever and ever, Hallelujah!"	
2:26	(5b) "And Lord of Lords"	
2:28	(5a and b) "King of Kings and Lord of Lords"	
2:33	(4a and b) "And He shall reign forever and ever"	
2:38	(4a and b) "And He shall reign forever and ever"	
2:44	(5a) "King of Kings"	
2:46	(4b) Forever and ever	
2:48	(5b) "And Lord of Lords"	
2:50	(1) "Hallelujah! Hallelujah . . ."	
2:53	(4a and b) "And He shall reign forever and ever"	homophonic
3:00	(5a and b) "King of Kings and Lord of Lords"	
3:04	(5a and b) "King of Kings and Lord of Lords"	
3:09	(4a and b) "And He shall reign forever and ever"	
3:15	(5a, 5b, 4b and 1)	
3:26	(1) "Hallelujah!"	

foot-pumped instrument to the massive machine whose sound could fill an entire cathedral with its huge pipes and multileveled keyboards (including one for the organist's feet—the pedals). Organ music was played as musical preparations for church services, as interludes, or as warm-ups to the anthems. Over time these developed into larger and larger-scale pieces—called simply *preludes* or *toccatas* (from the Italian "to touch"), both written manifestations of improvisatory practice. Toccatas were showier pieces, with fast passages and tricky footwork for the pedals. Toccatas and preludes were often followed by a *fugue,* a more disciplined genre that emphasizes *imitative polyphony,* that is, a polyphonic texture in which each of the separate musical lines is presenting the same melody, only set off in time. A simple example of imitative polyphony is a *round* such as the songs "Row, Row, Row Your Boat" and "Frère Jacques."

A fugue is considered among the most challenging kinds of classical pieces to write. The main melody of the fugue—called the *subject*—must be carefully crafted so that it can be played in imitative polyphony of three, four, or even more lines. These different lines of music are called *voices,* even though they have nothing to do with the human voice. Keeping all these independent voices going—and sounding good with all the other voices—is quite a juggling act (Figure 12.3).

Bringing all the fugue voices in is just the beginning of the work. After all the fugue voices have had a turn presenting the subject (the *exposition* of the fugue), the piece alternates between subject entries (sometimes abbreviated) and nonthematic *episodes* of new material. These episodes usually modulate (change key), so that each subject entry starts on a different pitch and may even change modes. The end of the fugue usually presents a final presentation of the subject. The following diagram will show that the fugue bears some resemblance to the ritornello form discussed under concerto grossos explained earlier (Figure 12.4).

Fugue subject

Fugue voices

Prelude
Toccata

Fugue
Imitative polyphony
Episodes

Round

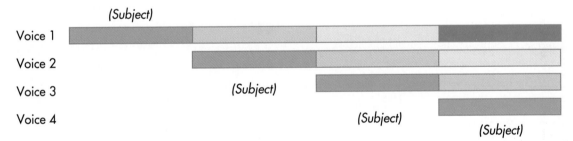

FIGURE 12.3: *The Exposition of a Four-Voice Fugue.*

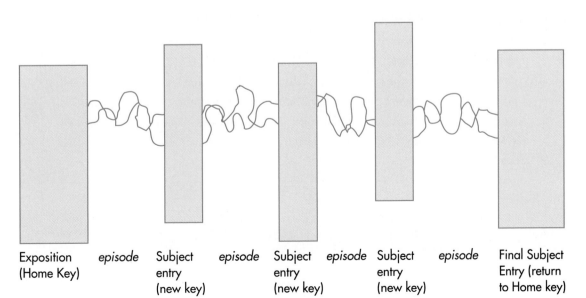

Exposition (Home Key)   *episode*   Subject entry (new key)   *episode*   Subject entry (new key)   *episode*   Subject entry (new key)   *episode*   Final Subject Entry (return to Home key)

FIGURE 12.4: *Generalized Diagram of Fugue Form.*

J. S. Bach
Source: CORBIS.

MUSICIAN BIOGRAPHY 12.3:

Johann Sebastian Bach
(1685—1750)

Johann Sebastian Bach was a member of a remarkable family of German musicians. Ancestors dating back to the sixteenth century and continuing into the nineteenth—more than seventy all together—were professional musicians, primarily for the Lutheran Church, passing down the craft from father to son or nephew, generation after generation. This particular Bach was born in a central German town called Eisenach, and studied music, like the Bachs before him, with his father. When his parents both died by 1695, he moved in with one of his brothers and continued his musical training.

Bach's specialty was the organ. By all accounts he was a brilliant player who could improvise better music than most others could compose. As a young man he worked as an organist in church, but his unprecedented musicianship soon led to an appointment composing entertainment music for a duke's court. Eventually he ended up in the large city of Leipzig in eastern Germany, where he directed the music at the four main churches and taught music and Latin to the choirboys who were in a boarding school at the largest of the churches. This was an important post, but in hindsight we wonder why he didn't achieve the kind of international acclamation his contemporary countryman Handel did.

Part of the answer may lie in Bach's personality. Although he was clearly proud of his talent, he was also a very devout man who thought music was best used in religious contexts. He never bothered to write an opera, then the most popular entertainment in Europe, but rather concentrated on honing his compositional craft to a peak of perfection as a product of his own personal devotion to God. He was also probably too busy to chase after fame. In addition to his taxing duties directing choirs, teaching, and composing new music for different services, he also put on concerts outside of church, earned a freelance living inspecting organs, was married, widowed and married again, and fathered some twenty children who required his attention as their primary music teacher.

Four of Bach's sons went on to greater wealth and fame as composers than Bach ever did. J. S. Bach was barely known outside a small region of Germany where he worked and lived. Seventy years after his death, however, a young Leipzig composer named Felix Mendelssohn (see Musician Biography 13.6) rekindled interest in Bach, and his music has been treasured around the world ever since.

LISTENING PREPARATION

Bach, Fugue in G Minor, "Little" (c. 1707).

The "Little" Fugue in G Minor is a four-voice fugue with a subject that becomes rhythmically compressed as is proceeds—starting with quarter notes, then moving to eighth and finally sixteenth notes.

Refer to the Appendix at the back of the book for this Listening Activity's complete worksheet. Use the following section to make notes for yourself

LISTENING ACTIVITY 12.3:

Bach, Fugue in G Minor, "Little" (CD 1/15)

Listen through the entire fugue once, paying close attention to the subject entries, then answer the following questions on your second pass through the piece.

1. Fill in the CD timer information for the subject entry of each voice. Note that after the second voice enters, there is a brief interlude (called a *codetta*) before the third voice enters.

Voice 1 <u>0:00</u>

     Voice 2 ___

          Voice 3 ___

               Voice 4 (Organ pedals) ___

2. At what CD time does the first episode begin? _____

3. The next subject entry is cut off, then continued by another voice. At what time does this begin? _____

4. The next subject entry occurs at 1:52, in Voice 3. What is different about this one?

5. When does the next subject entry begin? _____ And it is taken by which of the four voices? _____

6. In the middle of this subject entry, you can hear the upper voice trilling (alternating quickly between two notes). At what CD time do you hear this trill begin and end? _____ and _____.

7. Around the 2:54 mark, we hear the next subject entry, in the highest voice. Then follows the longest episode, followed by the final subject entry, in the lowest voice. At what CD time does this final subject entry begin? _____

8. Why do you think Bach made the episode before the final subject entry so much longer than previous episodes?

Checkpoint

We have looked at three genres of the late baroque: the concerto grosso, the oratorio, and the fugue. Although different in instrumentation, the three examples share several characteristics of the baroque style. Each one established a tempo at the outset and stuck to it with virtually no fluctuation. Bach's melody was probably the most exemplary of the baroque, with its long, winding phrases. In all three we can hear careful harmonic planning; in the Bach and the Vivaldi, we heard the main theme shifted into the opposite mode, then returned to the original. In all three we can hear the composers experiment with changing textures. Although different in character, all three have a certain regal quality: stately, elegant, and often intricate. The style that followed—the classical style—was in many ways a rejection of these very qualities that make baroque music so appealing. As we shall see, however, the music of the classical era was just as appealing in its own way.

THE CLASSICAL ERA

Enlightenment

*I*n many ways, the music of the classical era (1750–1815) was a product of the *Age of Reason,* or *Enlightenment.* This was a movement, led by the French philosophers Rousseau and Voltaire and the English philosopher John Locke, that emphasized the use of reason as the best means of discovering the truth. Enlightenment philosophers were *Empiricists,* meaning they believed that everything in the world could be understood through the use of the five senses and the application of reason. In the Middle Ages, the universe had seemed mysterious. Although there had always been a small group of intellectuals who liked to explore mathematics and science, for the most part God's universe was thought to be too awesome to be comprehended. Then, people like Sir Isaac Newton (1642–1727) began figuring out basic natural laws such as gravity, and insight into the nature of the world seemed to be unfolding like a flower. Voltaire saw God as a magnificent watchmaker, who created an elaborate mechanism and then stepped aside to let it run by itself. Enlightenment thinkers believed this great machine could be understood and harnessed as long as people eschewed superstition and used their brains in a rational manner.

Reason was thus considered the greatest human attribute, and all people were thought to have the potential for rational thought if only they were educated properly. But this was a natural attribute, something people possessed regardless of the wealth of their families. This led to the notion that "all men are created equal," and therefore that being born into royalty did not mean one was ordained by God to rule over others. These were radical ideas that would eventually blossom into a worldwide shift from monarchies to representative governments. The first two revolutions toward this end occurred during this period, first in the English colonies of North America (1775–1783) and then in France (1789–1794).

In many ways, however, the power of the aristocracy was already eroding by this time. The emerging middle class, made up in part by industrial capitalists and merchants, continued to grow in wealth, power, and size during this period. If a member of this middle class became wealthy enough, in some countries he could buy a title of nobility such as "count" or "marquis," but few ever did this. Meanwhile, the original landowning aristocrats, largely left out of this new market, frittered away their inherited wealth on fancy costumes for balls, new powdered wigs, estates in the country, and other such displays.

Music was one of these displays of wealth. Aristocrats with taste and breeding maintained private orchestras of considerable quality to accompany the dancing at their balls, to provide weekend entertainment, and even to help them digest food. Some

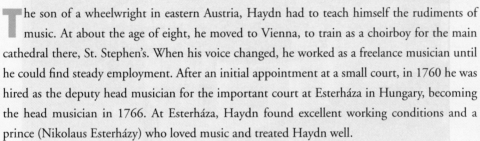

*Joseph Haydn.
Photo by Archivo
Iconografico, S.A.
Source: CORBIS.
© Archivo
Iconografico,
S.A./CORBIS.*

MUSICIAN BIOGRAPHY 12.4:

FRANZ JOSEPH HAYDN *(1732—1809)*

The son of a wheelwright in eastern Austria, Haydn had to teach himself the rudiments of music. At about the age of eight, he moved to Vienna, to train as a choirboy for the main cathedral there, St. Stephen's. When his voice changed, he worked as a freelance musician until he could find steady employment. After an initial appointment at a small court, in 1760 he was hired as the deputy head musician for the important court at Esterháza in Hungary, becoming the head musician in 1766. At Esterháza, Haydn found excellent working conditions and a prince (Nikolaus Esterházy) who loved music and treated Haydn well.

This is not to say his life was easy. The prince expected music to be played while he ate dinner; for the court's church services; for the big concerts twice a week; and he demanded a constant stream of new works for the prince himself to play on his peculiar string instrument called the baryton, now no longer made. In addition, Haydn had to compose and produce operas and put on other big productions, especially when distinguished visitors came to the palace (which was often). Despite the pressures to produce great quantities of music, the quality of Haydn's work rarely suffered, and some of these distinguished visitors helped spread his fame beyond the quiet countryside where he worked.

When Prince Nikolaus died in 1790 his successor disbanded the orchestra. Haydn bought a house in Vienna with the intention of retiring, but this last stage of his career proved to be even more exciting. He made two trips to faraway London (where his music received ecstatic praise), taught composition lessons (among his students was the temperamental young Ludwig van Beethoven), and wrote music for publishers and the growing audience for public concerts in Vienna. His death in 1809 was mourned internationally.

Haydn composed in many genres, including oratorios, of which he is considered the most significant composer after Handel. But his greatest contribution is to the string quartet and the symphony, both of which he helped develop into genres of great depth and richness. Despite his great success he remained a humble man, the last great composer to comfortably spend the majority of his career as a servant to an aristocrat.

courts also maintained dancers for ballets, actors for dramas, and singers for operas. Working for such a court or for the church was the primary mode of employment for a composer, but even this started to change during the classical era. The rising middle class, which did not yet have the means (nor, perhaps, the inclination) to maintain private orchestras, still had enough cash on hand to pay for entertainment, and by midcentury *public concert halls* were opening up across Europe. This was a new idea, rather egalitarian—that one could pay an admission fee and see a performance. As these grew in popularity, more

Public concert halls

THEME	CD TIME	COMMENTS
Closing Subsection		
Cla	1:20	Notes gradually rising
Clb	1:25	Relaxed ending statement
EXPOSITION (REPEATED)		
First Group of Themes		
1a	☐	
1b	☐	
1c	☐	
1c (repeat)	☐	
Bridge	☐	
Second Group of Themes		
2a, first half	☐	
2a, second half	☐	
2b	☐	
2c	☐	
2b (repeat)	☐	
2c (repeat)	☐	
Closing Subsection		
Cla	☐	
Clb	☐	
DEVELOPMENT	2:58	Altered at the end
First developed theme 1a	☐	
Second developed theme ☐	☐	(Find out which one!)
RECAPITULATION		
First Group of Themes		
1a	3:30	
1b	☐	
1c	☐	
1c (repeat)	☐	
Bridge	☐	Somewhat shortened
Second Group of Themes		
2a, first half	☐	(Now in original key)
2a, second half	☐	
2b	☐	
2c	☐	
2b (repeat)	☐	
2c (repeat)	☐	Altered at the end
CODA		
(New closing material, related to 1a)	5:02	

STANDARD MOVEMENT OUTLINE: SYMPHONY

MOVEMENT	TEMPO	USUAL FORM
First Movement:	Fast (*Allegro*)	Sonata
Second Movement:	Slow (*Adagio, Andante*)	Aria
Third Movement:	Moderate (*Moderato*)	Minuet and Trio
Fourth Movement:	Fast (*Allegro*)	Rondo

THE SYMPHONY

One of the most important genres developed during the classical era was the *symphony*, a piece for full orchestra in several movements, typically four. The term *sinfonia* was used as far back as the early baroque, but for a different sort of composition. The earliest version of the classical symphony emerged in Italy in the early eighteenth century, spreading throughout Europe by the middle of the century. The two great classical composers Joseph Haydn (see Musician Biography 12.4) and W. A. Mozart (see Musician Biography 12.5) took the genre to new heights, establishing it as the most versatile and compelling orchestral genre of the time. The symphony would maintain its central place in the orchestral repertoire well into the twentieth century.

Symphony

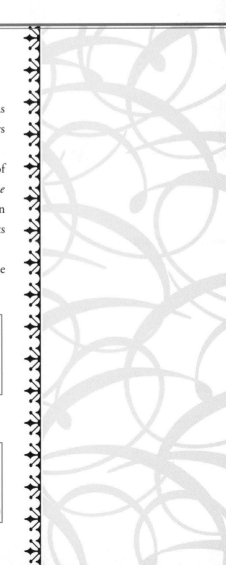

LISTENING PREPARATION

Mozart, Symphony No. 25 in G Minor, K. 183, I (1773).

Mozart wrote this compact symphony as a teenager living in Salzburg. It is sometimes referred to as the "Little" G Minor Symphony, in order to distinguish it from the longer work he wrote 15 years later in the same key, the famous Symphony No. 40, K. 550.

In this movement, as in other sonata form movements in the minor mode, the second theme of the exposition is in major, and thus strongly contrasted with the first theme in minor. The *first theme* of this symphony is famous for its exciting syncopation, played by the upper strings in unison. In the following diagram, the boxes represent measures and the dotted lines separate out the fours beats in each measure (Figure 12.10).

While the upper strings are playing this syncopated line, the two oboes are playing the same pitches as the strings, but held out for four whole beats each time (Figure 12.11).

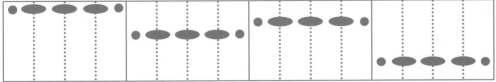

FIGURE 12.10: *First Theme of Mozart's Symphony No. 25 in G Minor, I.*

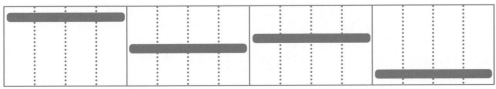

FIGURE 12.11: *Oboe Line at the Start of Mozart's Symphony No. 25, I.*

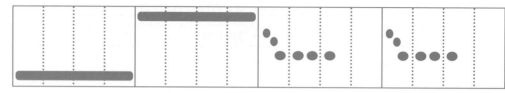

FIGURE 12.12: *The Second Theme of Mozart's Symphony No. 25, I.*

This four-note oboe melody is an important musical idea in this movement, coming back at several important points, most prominently in the bridge and the development section.

The *second theme* of the exposition is very striking, starting with two long notes played far apart, followed by two measures of the same set of short notes (Figure 12.12).

Like the first theme, the second theme is used in interesting ways throughout the movement.

Refer to the Appendix at the back of the book for this Listening Activity's complete worksheet. Use the following section to make notes for yourself

LISTENING ACTIVITY 12.8:

Mozart, Symphony No. 25 in G Minor, K. 183 I: Sonata form

*U*sing the following information as a guide, write a short essay about the form of this movement on a separate sheet of paper. Describe what happens in the movement, paying special attention to the sequence of events in the development section.

THEME	CD TIME	CHARACTERISTICS
EXPOSITION		
First Theme		
1a	0:00	Syncopated strings (see Figure 12.10)
1b	0:06	Fast rising figure
1a (repeat)	0:19	Softer
Bridge	0:25	Oboe theme takes over
Second Theme		
2a	0:46	See Figure 12.12
2b	0:58	Based on the second half of 2a
2c	1:16	Falling theme in strings
Closing Subsection		
Cla	1:31	Quieter; slowly rising up; Four measure.
Clb	1:37	Four-measure answer
Cla (repeat)	1:43	Louder this time
Clb (repeat)	1:49	
Clc	1:54	Rapid ascending line, then the lower strings go up and down.
Cld	2:05	Two-measure tag, leading to . . .
EXPOSITION (REPEAT)	2:07	
DEVELOPMENT	4:16	
RECAPITULATION	5:09	
CODA	7:18	

CI-9

The formal gardens in Villandry, France. Photo by Greg Meadors. Source: Stock Boston.

CI-10

Jacques Louis David (1748-1825), "The Oath of the Horatii," (c. 1784). Oil on canvas, 330 x 424 cm. Inv. # : 3692. Photo by G. Blot/C. Jean. Source: Art Resource/Reunio n des Musees Nationaux. © Reunion des Musees Nationaux/Art Resource, NY/Louvre, Paris, France.

CI-11

Franz Schubert rehearsing a musical serenade with his friends. Photo by Archivo Iconografico, S.A. Source: CORBIS. © Archivo Iconografico, S.A./CORBIS. Source: Stock Boston.

CI-12

Hector Berlioz. Source: The Granger Collection. the Granger Collection, New York.

◆CI-13◆

Claude Monet (1840-1926), "The Artist's Garden at Giverny." Oil on canvas. Photo by Herve Lewandowski. Source: Art Resource/Reunio n des Musees Nationaux. © Reunion des Musees Nationaux/Art Resource, NY/Musee d'Orsay, Paris, France.

◆CI-14◆

Barnett Newman (1905-1970), "Eve," (1950). Source: Art Resource, N.Y. © Artist Right's Society (ARS) NY © Tate Gallery, London/Art Resource, NY.

CI-15

Ballet performance of "Giselle." Source: Jack Vartoogian.

CI-16

Scene from the opera, "Falstaff." Source: Jack Vartoogian.

Alicia de Larrocha at the piano, with Pinchas Zukerman and the Mostly Mozart Orchestra.
Source: *Jack Vartoogian.*

THE SOLO CONCERTO

Over the course of the eighteenth century the solo concerto gradually replaced the baroque concerto grosso as the genre for orchestra and soloists. Like the symphony, the concerto was perfected by Haydn and Mozart during the classical period, then remained popular throughout the romantic era and into the modern period. Concertos can be written for any solo instrument (including,

part and conducted the orchestra at the premieres of his works.

A good many of today's concerts feature concertos of one kind or another, and it isn't hard to see why. In one piece, we get the power of the orchestra and the show-cased virtuosity of the soloist. Some listeners see the concerto as a titanic struggle between the individual and society, represented by the soloist and the rest of the group; others just enjoy the music.

Solo concerto

STANDARD MOVEMENT OUTLINE: SOLO CONCERTO

MOVEMENT	TEMPO	USUAL FORM
First Movement:	Fast (*Allegro*)	Double Exposition (see below)
Second Movement:	Slow (*Adagio, Andante*)	Aria
Third Movement:	Fast (*Allegro*)	Rondo

in the twentieth century, nonorchestral instruments such as the harmonica and electric guitar). In the classical era the violin concerto was still popular, but the piano gradually took over as the primary solo instrument. This was largely due to the brilliant piano concertos written by Mozart—who both played the solo

DOUBLE EXPOSITION FORM

The first movements of solo concertos in the classical period made use of a modified sonata form called the *double exposition form.* The basic outline is similar to the

Double exposition form

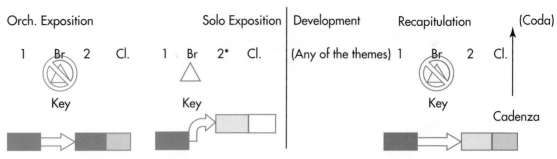

FIGURE 12.13: *Double Exposition Form.*

Orchestral exposition

Solo exposition

sonata form discussed above, but with two different expositions (thus the form's name) rather than one repeated exposition. The first exposition (called the *orchestral exposition*) features the orchestra without the soloist. The second (called the *solo exposition*) presents much of the same musical material as the orchestral exposition, but with both soloist and orchestra playing. After this follows the development and the recapitulation (recapitulating the solo exposition, not the orchestral) and the coda, just as in the standard sonata form. In between the recapitulation and the coda there is usually a cadenza, an improvisation based on the themes of the ex-positions. At the end of the cadenza the soloist

traditionally plays a *trill* to signal-the orchestra to come back in (Figure 12.13).

One of the things to listen for in a concerto is the subtle interplay between soloist and orchestra. Starting in the solo exposition, the soloist usually gets the first crack at a theme, but the orchestra either backs up the soloist or answers with its own version of the theme. There are places—such as the orchestral exposition and the coda—where the orchestra plays without the soloist, and there are other places where the soloists dominates (such as in the cadenza, played without the orchestra). For many listeners, the cadenza is a high-light of the movement, where all the themes come to-gether in the improvisational virtuosity of the soloist.

LISTENING PREPARATION

Haydn, Concerto in E-Flat Major for Trumpet and Orchestra, I, *Allegro* (1796).

This concerto was one of the first written for a keyed trumpet, capable of playing more notes than the old *natural trumpet,* for which all the changes in notes had to be done with the player's lips. We have already heard the last of the three movements; now we focus on the first movement, a blend of sonata form and baroque ritornello form.

The famous first theme of this movement is very *scalar* (that is, following along the notes of the scale). Haydn presents the first three notes of the scale, going up, then starts over and completes the scale before curling back down a bit. The dotted lines below represent the note E^b, the home pitch of the piece, both the first note of the scale and the *octave* above:

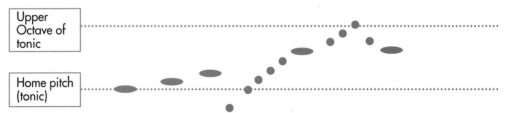

The cadenza in this performance was written by the soloist, the phenomenal jazz and classical trumpeter Wynton Marsalis (see Chapter 9).

LISTENING ACTIVITY 12.9:

Haydn, Concerto in E-Flat Major for Trumpet and Orchestra, I, Allegro (CD 1/20)

On a separate sheet of paper, write a short essay describing this movement. Follow the format for double exposition form (see Figure 12.13). Note that the solo exposition begins at CD time 1:05; the development at 2:46; the recapitulation at 3:46; the cadenza at 5:08; and the coda at 6:07. Use this information as a guide through this movement, pointing out highlights and interesting features. At what point is the trumpeter most virtuosic? What is your favorite part of the movement, and why?

Checkpoint

We have discussed five important forms of the classical era: minuet and trio, theme and variations, rondo, sonata, and the double exposition, along with the subsidiary form called rounded binary. We have also looked closely at two important genres, the symphony and the solo concerto, and listened to excerpts of two other Mozart compositions as examples of form. Some of the classical era elements present in these examples are tuneful, catchy melodies; the repetitions of phrases; and homophonic textures. There is also an increased attention to form. Much of the grandiosity of the baroque has been replaced by straightforward presentation of musical ideas in a cheerful, pleasing manner.

If you wish to explore the music of the baroque and classical eras further, you could hardly go wrong with any of the music of the five composers discussed in this chapter (Vivaldi, Handel, Bach, Haydn, and Mozart). All of them have enormous followings to this day because their music can offer a lifetime of listening pleasure.

KEY TERMS

Industrial Revolution	Prelude	Rondo
Ornaments	Toccata	Sonata
Recitative	Fugue	Exposition
Basso continuo	Imitative Polyphony	Development
Opera	Round	Recapitulation
Oratorio	Fugue subject	Slow Introduction
Cantata	Fugue voices	Coda
Prelude and fugue	Episodes	First Theme
Trio Sonata	Enlightenment	Bridge
Concerto	Public concert halls	Second Theme
Concerto Grosso	Solo Concerto	Closing Subsection
Baroque echo effect	String quartet	Symphony
Ritornello	Piano Sonata	Double exposition
Cadenza	Rounded Binary Form	form
Program Music	Minuet and trio	Orchestral exposition
Passion	Theme and variations	Solo exposition

Nineteenth-Century Music

A factory on the dockside at Canning Town, London, and a nearby ship under construction.
Source: Getty Images, Inc. Hulton Archive by Getty Images.

Classical music during the nineteenth century seemed to develop in several directions at the same time. Some composers wrote music of unprecedented length and scope, orchestral works requiring hundreds of players and hours of the audience's time. On the other hand, the nineteenth century was also a great time for quiet music, meant to be played by one person or a few friends just for their own enjoyment. In many ways, it was the age of the amateur, a time when more people made music for their own enjoyment than in any other era. On the other hand, it was also a time of increasing professionalism in music, a time of fascination with virtuosity, when performers of high ability attracted large crowds and cultlike followings. While some composers wrote music meant to embody the spirit of an entire nation, or even the entire world, others were concerned with expressing the intimate details of their own souls.

In the nineteenth century, classical music was widely enjoyed, and composers enjoyed a status and financial success far greater than in previous eras. The names of composers such as Beethoven, Berlioz, Chopin, Liszt, Wagner, Brahms, and others, were as familiar as the names of sports heroes today. More than in any other era of classical music, nineteenth-century composers wrote music that entranced a wide audience, and this music is enjoyed by a disproportionately large number of people even to this day.

ROMANTICISM

Like the music of the nineteenth century, the lives people led in Europe and North America at this time were full of contradictions and contrasts. The Industrial Revolution accelerated at the beginning of the century, with thousands of farm workers leaving their homes to work in the urban factories. The English novelist Charles Dickens (1812–1870), who himself worked as a child laborer in a "blacking" factory in London, putting labels on bottles, wrote elegantly of the plight of these workers in several popular works of the nineteenth century. Yet the same industrialization that caused so much suffering also improved the lives of many, with the invention of railroads (which reduced the time and perils of travel), of the telegraph, then the telephone, and electrical lights. The nineteenth century saw the construction of schools and hospitals, and both literacy and life expectancy rose during this century. Despite the continuing poverty in urban centers, the middle class grew rapidly, increasing its political muscle as it expanded.

These political gains did not come easily, however. The nineteenth century was also marked by political upheaval. In France, for example, after the revolution of 1789–1794, there were the revolutions of 1830, 1848, and 1870. And revolutions occurred in other nations of Europe during these same years. These political crises had a number of causes—voting rights, political autonomy from foreign rulers, even drought and famine—and were generally only partially successful. But gradually, rights were extended to more and more segments of society. Meanwhile, in Latin America, wars of independence from Spain were fought and won, and the bloody Civil War in the United States nearly tore the nation apart.

In the midst of all this upheaval came the birth of *romanticism*. Perhaps because of the squalid, smoky conditions of most big cities, more and more people became attracted to the countryside. A belief began to grow that all the hustle-bustle of the city, all the urgent scrambling after wealth, took away something *Transcendentalism* from the human soul. American *transcendentalists* such as Emerson and Thoreau advocated a return to nature. "Most of the luxuries, and many of the so-called comforts of life," wrote Thoreau in his famous book *Walden* (1854), "are not only not indispensable, but positive hindrances to the elevation of mankind." In reaction to the rationalism of the eighteenth century, romantics honored intuition above reason, feelings above logic, and, in the arts, expression over formalism.

All things spiritual fascinated the early romantic generation. In living rooms across America, mystics held seances to communicate with loved ones from beyond the grave. Gothic literature, such as Mary

Shelley's *Frankenstein* (1819), sent chills down the spines of thousands of readers. It was also a time of religious revivalism in the United States and in parts of Europe, a reemergence of evangelical Christianity.

Romantics became fascinated with all things remote in time and space. In part due to European colonialism—which reached its peak during the nineteenth century—there was a great interest in faraway countries. Romantics also sought escape from modern life through delving into the past, supposedly a more pure and innocent time. In Germany, the Grimm brothers scoured the countryside to collect myths and folktales from the nation's collective memory.

As always, the arts reflected and contributed to these social changes. Artists painted landscapes in great numbers, in response to the growing admiration of nature, and no matter what the subject matter there was a new sense of drama and sensuality to the art. Romantic literature often featured an outsider as protagonist, someone who, through defying the rules of modern society, redeems it. Novels were often set in the past, or in exotic locales. Poetry exalted great heroes and exhorted its readers to return to nature.

ROMANTICISM IN MUSIC

*I*n the nineteenth century, music was considered the highest of the arts, because it seemed to tap directly into the world of emotion, bypassing the rational structures required to read a text or comprehend the subject of a painting. Most romantic composers deliberately rejected the orderliness of the classical era for the sake of deeply expressive, unpredictable music with the greatest potential to move their audience. Romantic music makes distinctive use of several musical elements.

Rhythm: Starting with Beethoven (see Musician Biography 13.1), the pioneer of musical romanticism, rhythm took on a more prominent quality in art music. Beethoven was fond of syncopation, and his music in general featured great rhythmic drive and intensity. Later romantics spiced their music with rhythms from exotic countries. Perhaps the most characteristic feature of romantic rhythm, however, is *rubato,* the subtle push and pull of tempo for the sake of expression. Usually this feature was not written in the musical scores, but all performers used rubato to varying degrees.

Melody: In the previous classical era, melodies generally had been very tuneful and built on regular phrase structure. In the romantic era, melodies are less orderly and more emotional. They tend to be longer than classical melodies, and more oriented toward building up to emotional climaxes. Like other aspects of romantic music, the melodies often possess a great deal of yearning and could be colored by exotic effects.

Harmony: The harmonic language begins to deepen during the romantic era, with composers trying out new combinations of notes in order to achieve greater expression. Composers were more interested in experimenting with notes outside the standard scale, a feature called *chromaticism.* For some composers, in keeping with the gothic tastes in literature, there is an increased use of the minor mode, creating a glowering, spooky breed of music. Other romantic music is sunny and light.

Texture: Romantic composers were willing to try anything, it seems, for the sake of expression, but in the case of texture, homophony dominates.

Instrumentation: There was a continuing expansion of the orchestra during the nineteenth century, reaching its current size (about 100) and distribution of instruments at about midcentury. In the United States after the Civil War there developed a passionate interest in band music—large ensembles, originally military in origin, consisting of woodwind, brass, and percussion instruments that could be used in marching. Valves were invented for brass instruments, giving them increased flexibility and usefulness, and woodwind instruments received several critical improvements. The piano, too, became mechanically perfected during the romantic era and there was an enormous growth in the sales of pianos for middle-class homes. This, in turn, fueled the growth of the

sheet music industry and helped shape the kinds of genres composed (discussed below).

More important than the number of instruments in the orchestra was the *way* in which the music was written for these instruments. Composers, beginning with Berlioz (see Musician Biography 13.3), began to take increasing care in their *orchestration,* the art of writing for particular instruments. Composers seemed to relish in the sheer timbral quality of the instruments as a kind of sensual experience all its own, and wrote music that demanded a wide variety of tonal colors and effects from their musicians.

Form: As indicated above, form is important in the romantic era in the way composers stretched the boundaries established by the previous generations of musicians. Some composers loosely followed the structures handed down from the classical era, while others used stories to determine the sequence of musical events.

Genre: Many of the genres popular in the classical era continued throughout the nineteenth century, albeit in altered form, such as the symphony, the string quartet, the piano sonata, and the solo concerto. Opera remained among the most popular of all the arts, with several composers writing operas virtually exclusively. There were also new genres, such as the *symphonic poem* (or *tone poem*), a one-movement orchestral work that is based around a *program,* a story or a poem to be read while listening to the work. A related orchestral genre is the *concert overture,* again in one movement and programmatic. The nineteenth century in general saw an increase in the amount of program music and a decrease in its opposite, *absolute music,* or music that is not meant to tell a specific story.

Romantic genres grew both larger and smaller. Because composers could now earn a sizable proportion of their income from the sales of music to sheet music publishers, most composers spent at least some of their time writing music for amateurs. Some works were simple and short character pieces called *miniatures,* while other pieces were quite difficult, reflecting the wide variety of abilities in the amateur market. On the other hand, the growing size of

Rubato

Orchestration

Chromaticism

Program music

Absolute music

public concert halls during the nineteenth century brought about an expansion on the other end of the scale, with huge works for several orchestras plus chorus, creating a great deal of noise. In Tchaikovsky's famous *1812 Overture,* he even throws in the deafening roar of the cannon.

Other Elements: With the decline of classical forms as a governing principle, romantic composers relied more heavily on *thematic development,* the transformation of themes (the main melodies) over the course of the music. Sometimes these themes represented a character or some other element of the program they were following, and sometimes they were simply

Thematic development

musical ideas, but in any case melodies took on greater significance in the romantic era. Composers might put their themes through radical transformations over the course of their works—just as a character in a novel undergoes transformations through the events of the plot—sometimes having these themes emerge at the end in a form quite different from the original. Composers also brought back themes in subsequent movements, making a whole multimovement work into a unified artistic statement.

Virtually all these elements of romantic music were developed by a single composer, Ludwig van Beethoven, in some ways the archetypal music genius, whose influence can be felt in music to this day.

BEETHOVEN

*M*ore than any other classical composer Beethoven has become something of an icon, with his wild tousled hair and brooding expression. Most people know that Beethoven went deaf about halfway through his life. His career remains a source of inspiration to us all as he fought valiantly to triumph over his disability.

This triumph is all the more impressive when we place it in the context of his time. Before Beethoven, composing was seen as an adjunct activity. Musicians were generally considered to be performers first, composers second. They made their money through putting on concerts, or playing in them; their compositions appeared in those concerts primarily for the novelty of something new. To be sure, composers prior to Beethoven had made some income through their compositions, separate from performances, but this income was supplementary. When Beethoven realized, at the peak of his career, that he could no longer perform, this was tantamount to a death sentence for his life as a musician. By recreating his career so that he made a livable income from other people performing his works and through increased

publishing activity, Beethoven redefined the role of a composer. From now on, those who could compose generally considered composing their most important activity. Although there would be several significant composer-performers in the years to come, increasingly these two roles split into different specialties, so that today there are very few composers who would pass as professional performers, and vice-versa. Beethoven created the role of the composer as we now know it.

Impressive as this is, there is more to Beethoven's significance than this. Long before the first signs of deafness, Beethoven was changing the character of music. At first Beethoven was what we would now consider a classical composer in the mold of Mozart and Haydn, with light, pleasing melodies and a close adherence to standard forms. But even then, much of Beethoven's music had a different sound: more dramatic, stormy, and unpredictable. Soon, Beethoven began to break the rules of the forms. Contemporary critics were shocked at his experiments, but Beethoven ignored them and continued on his path. Beethoven's music takes listeners on an emotional journey, with

Ludwig van Beethoven Source: Getty Images, Inc. Hulton Archive by Getty Images.

MUSICIAN BIOGRAPHY 13.1:

LUDWIG VAN BEETHOVEN
(1770–1827)

Beethoven was born in the small German city of Bonn (later famous as the capital of the country of West Germany during the Cold War before German reunification in 1991). Beethoven was the oldest son of a town musician, whose father in turn was also a town musician. When Beethoven was a teenager the great composer Joseph Haydn heard him play while travelling through Bonn and urged him to come to Vienna. Beethoven's first trip to Vienna in 1787—in which he may have played for Mozart—was cut short by the death of Beethoven's mother. At twenty-one he set out for Vienna again and this time never came back.

Beethoven quickly established himself as the most dramatic and innovative musician in town. Although he took lessons from Haydn and others, he was soon publishing and performing with great success. The wealthiest members of Viennese society competed for his friendship and lavished him with praise and attention. Beethoven was a star.

Then this star fell to earth. All during his late twenties he noticed an intermittent ringing in his ears, and by the age of thirty it was incessant and blocking out other sounds. The hapless nineteenth-century doctors tried everything in their meager resources, but even to this day there is no cure for tinnitus. The best they could suggest was that he get away from the noise of the city for the solitude and quiet of the countryside. Beethoven, a true romantic at heart, took well to this suggestion, in part because he already loved nature and in part because, alone, he did not have to hide his deafness. His love of nature would play an important role in some of his music, such as the Sixth Symphony ("Pastoral").

Ultimately he could no longer hide the truth of his condition. He nearly committed suicide, saying that only his art held him back. Even as he underwent this crisis he produced some of his most popular and enduring music, music which seemed to describe his battle with what he called "fate," and his triumph over adversity.

He continued to compose even after all sounds were closed off to him, hearing the music in his head and writing it down. At the end of his life, he became isolated, and his compositions became more introspective. Some of his late works were so far ahead of their time they seemed to be more in line with the music at the end of the nineteenth century, not the beginning. Despite Beethoven's reclusiveness, 20,000 mourners lined the streets of Vienna at his funeral in 1827, acknowledging the passing of classical music's most influential composer.

highs and lows and an intensity of expression never heard before. Composers for at least a hundred years looked to Beethoven for inspiration.

Beethoven's iconoclasm perhaps is best explained by the circumstances of his employment. In many ways Beethoven succeeded where Mozart only found partial success: he lived the life of an independent musician, not employed by a single aristocrat. Beethoven had many friends among the aristocratic class, dedicating several of his famous works to princes, dukes, and archdukes, but he was never their employee. Part of the reason for this is simply a change in the society at the turn of the nineteenth century. With public concert halls and the increasing market for published works, composers now had options for independent living that did not exist before. But Beethoven, again, served as a particular model for composers who followed, with his shrewd sense of business and immense pride in his own worth. Being an artist, he seemed to believe, made him the natural equal of an aristocrat. Most aristocrats seem to have agreed with him.

LISTENING PREPARATION

Beethoven, Symphony No. 5 in C Minor, Op. 67, I, *Allegro con brio* (1808).

The first movement of Beethoven's Fifth Symphony, with its famous opening motive (short-short-short-LONG), has become almost a cliché in our culture, a parody of itself. The music, however, is intense and powerful, worth getting to know on its own terms.

Like other works emerging out of the classical era, the first movement of the Fifth Symphony follows sonata form, a three-part structure (discussed in more detail in Chapter 12) (see Figure 13.1).

Beethoven's genius in this movement is twofold. First, this movement is a model of thematic transformation. The main motive, with only four notes, not only spins out to create the whole first theme, but also underlies the entire movement and even generates the themes for the remaining three movements of the symphony (not included on your CD). Second, the music is extremely dramatic. In Mozart and Haydn's time, the unsettled development section was shorter in length than the exposition or recapitulation, but Beethoven—who seemed to relish the stormy turbulence of the development—makes it longer and more dangerous than it had ever been before. Developmental characteristics seem to seep into other parts of the movement, too, especially the long and intense coda, so that most of the music has an unsettled quality.

Beethoven once commented to a friend that the famous opening motive represented "fate knocking at the door." Although it is important to enjoy the music simply on its own terms and not read too much into it, something about this rings true. The music here seems to reflect a life-and-death struggle as it tosses the listener back and forth between the major and minor modes.

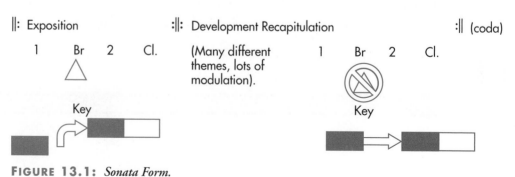

FIGURE 13.1: *Sonata Form.*

Refer to the Appendix at the back of the book for this Listening Activity's complete worksheet. Use the following section to make notes for yourself

LISTENING ACTIVITY 13.1:

Beethoven, Symphony No. 5 in C Minor, Op. 67, I, Allegro con Brio: Sonata Form (CD 2/1)

At the beginning of this movement we hear the famous motive, with the final note held longer. The motive then repeats at a lower pitch. An illustration of the beginning might look like this:

After that, Beethoven starts to stack up the motive, piling it up until it reaches a high note, then starting low and stacking it up again.

1. How many iterations of the motive are heard in each "stacking?" _____

2. After these two stackings, the motive gets repeated several times over a long *crescendo,* culminating in three loud chords with the violins holding out a single note. At what CD time does this final chord occur? _____

3. Now, we hear another presentation of the motive with the last note held, as in the beginning. After this, the motive gets stacked *downward* two times. How many iterations of the motive are heard in these reverse "stackings?" _____

4. Again, the motive gets repeated several times over a long *crescendo,* but now we are changing keys to major (the *bridge* of the exposition). You will know we have finished the modulation when the French horns play the motive in major, now expanded to six notes, rather than four:

   At what CD time does this occur? _____

5. We have now arrived at the second theme of the exposition, more lyrical and calm. Soon, however, the intensity starts to build again, leading to a more triumphant sounding subtheme (2b). At what CD time does this new idea occur? _____

6. At the end of the expositions of the sonata form there is usually a closing section. In this case, the closing material is drawn from the main motive. Where do you think the closing subsection begins? _____ (Hint: listen through until you hear the exposition repeating, then go back and try again.)

7. What instruments (or instrument families) start off the development section (at about CD time 2:54)? _____

8. What does Beethoven do after this initial musical statement in the development?

9. Describe what happens at about CD time 3:30:

10. After working with this idea for a while, Beethoven starts to disintegrate the motive, breaking it down to two-note segments that are tossed back and forth between the woodwinds and strings, then down to just one note. As this happens, there is a disconcerting *decrescendo*. Suddenly, the full six-note motive bursts forth. At what CD time does this occur? _____

11. What happens after this outburst?

12. The beginning of the recapitulation (around CD time 4:17) provides an example of Beethoven's breaking away from traditional form. There is something very different about the first theme here from the version in the exposition. What is it? (Hint: listen starting at about CD time 4:35.)

13. The second theme, too, breaks away from traditional form to some degree: it starts off in major (at around CD time 5:15), when it should be in minor. (Remember, in the recapitulation, there is supposed to be no key change between the first and second themes.) Is the second part of the second theme, 2b, in major or minor? (If you are uncertain which is theme 2b, go back to the exposition and listen again, following the answers at the beginning of this Listening Activity.) _____

14. After closing material similar to that of the exposition, we move directly into the coda (at about CD time 5:58). Here, Beethoven presents something interesting: after a long *crescendo* in the strings, the French horn gives us the motive *inverted* (upside-down). At what CD time do you hear this? _____

15. Describe what happens to finish off the movement.

16. How does the movement make you feel? How do you think Beethoven achieves this emotional response? Refer to specific sections of the movement in your response.

THE EARLY ROMANTICS

Between the years 1803 and 1813 a number of significant composers were born. All of them worked in the enormous shadow of Beethoven, who pointed the way forward for both musical expression and for how a composer should live and think of himself. This generation also moved away from Beethoven's legacy in several respects, however. One of the changes in this next generation was an increasing inclination to specialize in genres. While Beethoven had composed in virtually every genre enjoyed in the classical era, the early romantics often focused their energy on two or three genres, sometimes even just one, such as opera. Another change came with their conception of musical structure. While Beethoven pioneered the breaking of rules for the sake of expression, there is usually an underlying order to his works. Some members of the next generation, however, abandoned traditional form altogether. The early romantic era was also a time of great interaction between the arts, and so, more than Beethoven, these early romantic composers took a great interest in writing, painting, and other art forms, sometimes even practicing these themselves. Another difference between Beethoven and the early romantics has to do with geography. In Beethoven's time, Vienna was the musical capital of the world, but the early romantics were a more cosmopolitan set, working and touring in Paris, London, Italy, Switzerland, the various courts of Germany, even Russia.

In general it was a good time to be a composer. Now totally free from dependency on aristocrats, composers enjoyed more freedom and independence. This also meant they were less isolated, and several of the early romantic composers were close friends and helped each other out in their careers (and some, of course, were bitter enemies, too). The slow breakdown of social classes meant a composer could be born at any level and move up to socialize with princes and princesses, all based on the composer's talent. We even begin to see the crusty old doors of sexism open—just a crack—to let the first significant women composers in several generations begin to be heard.

Yes, it was a good time to be a composer. But almost without exception, the lives of the early romantic composers were marked by tragedy.

THE ART SONG

The art song is one of the oldest musical genres, traceable to the Middle Ages and probably to the beginning of music. Wandering minstrels wrote both words and melodies and accompanied themselves on various string instruments, and the genre appears periodically throughout music history—with examples by Mozart and Beethoven, among others. In the early nineteenth century, however, the art song became particularly popular and occupied most of the attention of our first important early romantic composer, Franz Schubert.

Romantic-era art song composers would usually not write the lyrics themselves, but rather use an existing poem. This has an effect on our understanding of the original poem, and sometimes poets were annoyed with musical settings of their poems. In the eras surrounding the romantic era—the classical and the twentieth century—composers would use poems in any language, but in the romantic era composers would almost always write for their own tongue. The music was usually for a single singer—man or woman, depending on the song—accompanied by piano.

On the surface, therefore, the art song seems to be a fairly simple genre, but under Schubert (who wrote over 600), the genre developed into something rich and complex. In Schubert's art songs (called *Lieder* in German), the piano is not simply accompanying the singer; rather, it serves a function similar to that of a

Lieder ("LEE-der")

movie score, adding drama, tension, even special effects. Schubert was also less interested than earlier art song composers in writing vocal parts to show off the skills of the singers. For Schubert, the singer's job was to communicate the drama and passion of the lyrics. Thus, the art song, under Schubert, becomes a three-way collaboration between singer, pianist, and the original poet.

THE PROGRAM SYMPHONY

The art song was just one of several romantic genres that sought to blend literary with musical art. Program music, which we've discussed before, became very popular during the nineteenth century, and whole genres cropped up that were dedicated to musical

Franz Schubert (1797–1828)

MUSICIAN BIOGRAPHY 13.2:

FRANZ SCHUBERT (1797–1828)

Schubert was one of the few great Viennese composers to have been born in that city. The son of a schoolteacher, Schubert planned to follow in his father's footsteps and even taught for a couple of years, but soon gave it up for composing. Unlike many composers, Schubert was a rather shy man with little interest in promoting himself. He admired Beethoven from afar, but could not work up the nerve to introduce himself. He found only middling success as an opera composer and concert-giver, and published only a fraction of his voluminous output. For his entire life, Schubert was unknown outside of Vienna—and barely known inside of it.

The one saving grace of this quiet life was companionship. Schubert was blessed with a large group of friends who loved his music and helped him out financially. They called themselves *Schubertians,* and met regularly in each others' living rooms for evenings of song and mirth they called *Schubertiads,* where Schubert would accompany one of them singing his latest song, or gather together instrumentalists to present his latest piece of chamber music. The Schubertians are important not just as they figure in Schubert's biography, but also for what they represent: the new sophisticated middle-class audience, literate in both music and literature, in many ways replacing the role of the aristocracy as consumers of music.

Schubert never married, and when he died at the age of 31, only his friends seemed to notice. Within a decade or so of his death, the musical world finally began to understand what sort of brilliance Schubert had possessed. His art songs—still enjoyed to this day—became the model for all art song composers who followed, and his symphonic and chamber works are important parts of the contemporary repertory.

LISTENING PREPARATION

Schubert, *Gretchen am Spinnrade* (1814).

Schubert was just seventeen when he composed "Gretchen at the Spinning Wheel," considered by some to be the first true nineteenth-century *lied*. He had just begun his unhappy stint as a junior teacher in his father's school, but still managed to find time in his schedule to compose every day.

This song, with words by the famous German poet Johann Wolfgang von Goethe (1749–1832), author of the romantic epic *Faust*, takes Gretchen's point of view as she laments a love lost. Notice the particular romantic elements—the power of love, so intense it becomes equated with death; and the sense of yearning which seems to cause the form to break down about halfway through. Notice also how Schubert's piano part imitates the rhythm of a spinning wheel, giving us the impression that this monologue is unfolding in real time, as she's spinning her thread.

Art songs speak for themselves, but only if you understand the language. Schubert is so careful with his word settings that he sometimes makes subtle shifts on particular words, so it is important to try to understand the translation on a word-for-word basis, as best you can.

Refer to the Appendix at the back of the book for this Listening Activity's complete worksheet. Use the following section to make notes for yourself

LISTENING ACTIVITY 13.2:

Schubert, Gretchen am Spinnrade *(CD 2/2)*

1. On your first listening, follow both the original German and the English translation closely, and mark the CD time for the start of each stanza. You will fill in the right-hand column in a moment.

CD TIME	GERMAN	ENGLISH	DYNAMIC LEVEL
	Meine Ruh ist hin	My heart is sad,	
	Mein Herz ist schwer	My peace is over;	
	Ich finde sie nimmer	I find it never,	
	Und nimmermehr.	And nevermore.	
	Wo ich ihn nicht hab'	When he is gone,	
	Ist mir das Grab,	The grave I see;	
	Die ganze Welt	The whole wide world	
	Ist mir vergällt.	Is soured for me.	
	Mein armer Kopf	Alas, my head	
	Ist mir verrückt,	Is well-nigh crazed;	
	Mein armer Sinn	My feeble mind	
	Ist mir zerstückt.	Is sore amazed.	

	Meine Ruh ist hin,	My heart is sad,	
	Mein Herz ist schwer,	My peace is over;	
	Ich finde sie nimmer	I find it never,	
	Und nimmermehr.	And nevermore.	
	Nach ihm nur schau ich	For him, from the window	
	Zum Fenster hinaus,	Alone I spy;	
	Nach ihm nur geh ich	For him alone	
	Aus dem Haus.	From home go I.	
	Sein hoher Gang,	His lofty step,	
	Sein' edle Gestalt,	His noble form,	
	Seines Mundes Lächeln,	His mouth's sweet smile,	
	Seiner Augen Gewalt,	His glances warm,	
	Und seiner Rede	His voice so fraught	
	Zauberfluß,	With magic bliss,	
	Sein Händedruck,	His hand's soft pressure,	
	Und ach, sein Kuß!	And, ah—his kiss!	
	Meine Ruh ist hin,	My heart is sad,	
	Mein Herz ist schwer,	My peace is over;	
	Ich finde sie nimmer	I find it never,	
	Und nimmermehr.	And nevermore.	
	Mein Busen drängt	My breast yearns	
	Sich nach ihm hin	For his form so fair;	
	Ach dürft ich fassen	Ah, could I clasp him	
	Und halten ihn,	and hold him there!	
	Und küssen ihn,	My kisses sweet	
	So wie ich wollt,	Should stop his breath,	
	An seine Küssen	And beneath his kisses	
	Vergehen sollt!	I'd sink in death!	
	(Meine Ruh ist hin,	(My heart is sad,	
	Mein Herz ist schwer . . .)	My peace is over . . .)	

2. On your next time through the song, listen for the dynamic level of the music. At any particular line in the stanzas, is the dynamic level the *same, increasing,* or *decreasing* compared to the previous line? Make note of this in the right-hand column next to each line of text (at least once per stanza, more if necessary).

3. Write a paragraph describing how Schubert illustrates and amplifies the meaning of the text through music, citing particular points in the song as examples.

storytelling. The tone poem and the concert overture were two such genres for orchestra, and even when writing a traditional symphony, many composers attached a story or some other literary clue to accompany the music. The first important *program symphony* was Beethoven's Sixth, subtitled the "Pastoral," which paints a music picture of experiences in the countryside—a different experience for each of the five movements. The program symphony took a quantum leap forward, however, with the *Symphonie Fantastique* of the French composer Hector Berlioz (see Musician Biography 13.3).

In this symphony—Berlioz's first—the composer tells a semiautobiographical tale which unfolds over five movements. The twenty-four-year-old Berlioz, like the rest of Parisian society, had been overwhelmed by the performances of a touring English Shakespearean company in 1827, and particularly by the beautiful Irish leading actress, Harriet Smithson (1800–1854). Berlioz, a man of extraordinary passions, became obsessed with Harriet, attending every performance of *Hamlet* and *Romeo and Juliet,* and watching her as she went to and from the theater. His love for her became a force of nature, consuming him. In one letter, he wrote to a friend of a "a rage, a madness which takes possession of all our faculties and makes us capable of anything," and in another letter to the same friend he spoke of his "unbearable agitation," which gave him a prolonged fever and continually erratic heartbeat. "I can't continue," he declared. He soon wrote letters to Smithson confessing his passion and asking for her hand in marriage. She, quite reasonably, thought he was crazy and ignored him. Two years later, he was still obsessed, writing to another friend that his heart "is the furnace of a raging fire. It's a virgin forest that lightning has set ablaze."

As if there were no other choice, Berlioz funneled this passionate energy into his first symphony, which premiered in 1830. The program, which he wrote himself, describes how a certain "young musician" sees "the woman of his dreams and falls hopelessly in love." In the second movement, "A Ball," Berlioz describes the artist "in the swirl of a party, but the beloved image appears before him and troubles his soul." In the third movement, "Scene in the Country," the musician flees from the city to escape this torment— but can't get her out of his mind. In the fourth movement, "March to the Scaffold," the musician attempts suicide by taking an overdose of opium—probably not the most effective method of taking one's life, but it provides the artist with suitably gothic hallucinations. He now thinks he has killed his Beloved, and is being taken to the town square to be guillotined. The fifth and final movement, "Dream of a Witches' Sabbath," presents a hellish scene in which the musician "sees himself in the midst of a frightful throng of ghosts, witches, monsters of every kind, who have assembled for his funeral." The Beloved is there too, transformed into a witch, and a wild dance ensues.

One can only imagine what Harriet thought of this tribute to her, but the *Symphonie Fantastique* was a watershed in the history of romantic music. Not only did Berlioz bring together storytelling and music as never before, the music itself was extraordinarily innovative. He experimented boldly with *orchestration,* writing for new instruments and for traditional instruments in new combinations, which makes his symphony awash in musical colors. Traditional musical form is not present, but Berlioz substitutes something new and powerful: a recurring theme that represents the Beloved, appearing in all five movements, in different guises. Berlioz called this an *idèe fixe* ("fixed idea"), and this musical device would play a role in much of the music that followed, even in film music of the twentieth century.

After the *Symphonie Fantastique* Berlioz wrote two more program symphonies (including one based on *Romeo and Juliet*), and most romantic composers followed in his footsteps. Some composers, such as Franz Liszt, were fond of adopting preexisting literary works; some, such as Mendelssohn, wrote symphonies describing a landscape. Still others, such as Tchaikovsky (see Musician Biography 15.1), wrote programs that were a secret, perhaps telling intimate details about the composer's life, but not meant to be uncovered by the public at large. The program symphony lost some of its popularity in the twentieth century, but still appeared occasionally, such as in the propaganda symphonies of Soviet composer Dmitri Shostakovich (1906–1975).

Program symphony

Idèe fixe

*Hector Berlioz
(1803–1869)*

MUSICIAN BIOGRAPHY 13.3:

HECTOR BERLIOZ *(1803–1869)*

Berlioz was the son of a provincial French doctor. A dreamy child, Berlioz loved literature and music, teaching himself guitar and the rudiments of harmony. When he came of age, he was sent to Paris to study medicine. The distractions of the big city took their toll on his studies, however, and he eventually dropped out of medical school. After this, there began a protracted battle with his parents, who, like parents of any age, were skeptical about their son abandoning a practical career to pursue his artistic passion. They threatened to cut off his allowance, and eventually did, but Berlioz still enrolled in the Paris Conservatory of Music and graduated in 1829.

Despite his parents' worries, Berlioz created a rather comfortable career for himself by combining three different musical activities: composing, writing reviews for the local newspapers and music magazines, and conducting. Berlioz became one of the first important conductors of his time, bringing out new music of his own and other contemporary composers, and organizing mammoth concerts that impressed the audience. He also wrote an important treatise on orchestration, which became a standard book of reference for many subsequent composers.

Berlioz ultimately broke down Harriet Smithson's resistance and married her in 1833. But Berlioz's life was ultimately an unhappy one. Despite his early success, the public never comprehended most of his music, and remained rather indifferent to his grandest schemes. He once haughtily declared that it would take a hundred years for his music to be understood. Unfortunately, he was right. He died in his mid-sixties a broken man, after the deaths of both Harriet, his second wife, most of his friends, and even his beloved son. And he died unaware of the full extent of his impact on the history of music.

LISTENING PREPARATION

Berlioz, *Symphonie Fantastique*, Op. 14, V, "Dream of a Witches' Sabbath" (1830).

This final movement of Berlioz's first symphony is the most romantic of the music we have discussed so far—passionate, full of rich orchestral color, morbid and supernatural in subject matter, and formally erratic and unpredictable. Fasten your safety belts and get ready for a wild ride.

LISTENING ACTIVITY 13.3:

Berlioz, Symphonie Fantastique, Op. 14, V, "Dream of a Witches' Sabbath" (CD 2/3)

1. Describe the first minute of this movement. What musical events occur? What effect does Berlioz seem to be after? Refer to CD times and instrumental families in your answer.

2. The *idèe fixe* appears at about 1:22, played by a squeaky clarinet. In previous movements it had been elegant and stately, but now it sounds shrill and crooked. What happens at the end of the first presentation of this melody?

3. Soon, the *idèe fixe* is presented again, this time with an intentionally crude woodwind accompaniment, complete with a bubbling bassoon underneath. Gradually the full orchestra joins in, leading us haltingly to the next section, marked by church bells. At what CD time do the church bells come in? _____

4. Next, we hear a medieval church chant called *dies irae,* which was sung at funerals and associated with death. It is played by the bassoons and an obscure brasslike instrument called the *ophecleide,* now no longer used, in stately long notes, starting at CD time 3:23. In what texture do these instruments play (circle one):   polyphonic   homophonic   monophonic?

5. Then, the rest of the brass section responds (at about CD time 3:45). In what texture do these instruments play (circle one):   polyphonic   homophonic   monophonic?

6. The high woodwinds and strings—playing *pizzicato*—now respond, leading into more of the *dies irae,* now accompanied by low strings *pizzicato.* When the *dies irae* continues, what CD time are we at? _____

7. These three elements (the solemn *dies irae,* the response by the brass section, and the carping woodwinds and *pizzicato* strings) alternate several times, building in intensity until we arrive at the next section, the "Witches' Round Dance," with a new theme we have only heard in fragmented form before, now played by the cellos and basses (starting at about 5:16). What kind of emotional effect do you think Berlioz was trying to achieve here?

8. After several minutes of this, the music changes. We hear four loud brass chords (at about CD time 6:20, played in a rhythm similar to the opening motive of Beethoven's Fifth Symphony—short-short-short-LONG), followed by a falling line in woodwinds and high strings. This repeats several times on different pitches, then the music seems to disintegrate.

We hear a hint of the *dies irae* theme played by the cellos (at about 7:01), then a moment later by the basses. Describe what follows, beginning at CD time 7:16 through about 7:45.

9. You should be hearing a buildup now to some big chords, then the *dies irae* and "Witches' Round Dance" themes get combined. At what CD time does this combination begin? _____

10. Soon, Berlioz introduces another of his famous orchestration effects: he asks the violins and violas to strike their strings with the wood part of the bow, rather than the hair part, creating a sound somewhat akin to dancing skeletons. At what CD time does this begin? _____

11. Describe the remainder of the movement:

12. What do you think Berlioz's goals were in this movement? Does he succeed? Refer to specific sections of the music in your answer.

THE PIANO

The piano had been the dominant keyboard instrument in Europe since the 1770s, but mechanical refinements had continued to improve the instrument well into the romantic era. With the change from a wooden to a cast-iron frame in the 1820s, the essentials of the modern piano were in place. It was now capable of supporting thicker, tighter strings which could produce a rich, ringing tone and a much wider range of dynamics. Later on in the nineteenth century, American piano manufacturers would invent upright pianos, and certain mass-production techniques that would help place pianos in living rooms across the country.

Beethoven was the first composer to take advantage of the particular qualities of the instrument, and his 32 piano sonatas remain to this day the central part of the piano repertory. Virtually all the early romantic composers played the piano—Berlioz was a notable exception—and wrote some of their most expressive music for the instrument. None of them, however, is as closely associated with the instrument as Fryderyk Chopin.

OTHER EARLY ROMANTICS

Chopin was one of several nineteenth-century composer-performers; among the other important figures were violinist Nicolo

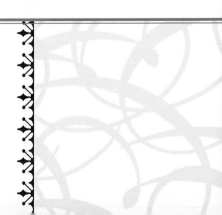

Frederic Chopin.
Photo by Archivo
Iconografico, S. A.
Source: CORBIS
© Archivo
Iconografico,
S.A./CORBIS.

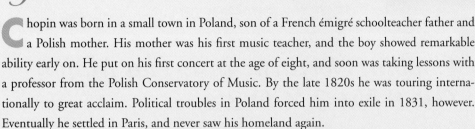

MUSICIAN BIOGRAPHY 13.4:

FREDERIC CHOPIN *(1810—1849)*

Chopin was born in a small town in Poland, son of a French émigré schoolteacher father and a Polish mother. His mother was his first music teacher, and the boy showed remarkable ability early on. He put on his first concert at the age of eight, and soon was taking lessons with a professor from the Polish Conservatory of Music. By the late 1820s he was touring internationally to great acclaim. Political troubles in Poland forced him into exile in 1831, however. Eventually he settled in Paris, and never saw his homeland again.

In Paris, Chopin did some concertizing, but like Schubert, he seemed to prefer performing in the small, intimate settings of Parisian living rooms. He made most of his money through publishing his works and through teaching piano, and by all accounts he was a patient and dedicated teacher. He continually battled ill health, however, and had shown symptoms of tuberculosis as a teenager, a disease which had already claimed the life of a beloved sister and which would soon claim his own.

Chopin had two great loves in his life: his homeland and Aurore Dudevant, a novelist who used the masculine pen name George Sand. They were lovers from 1837 to nearly the end of Chopin's life, a relationship that provided both with great artistic inspiration. Never, however, did Chopin stop pining for his native country. After he died in Paris at age 39, his heart was sent to be buried in Poland.

No other great composer devoted himself so exclusively to music for the piano, and his compositions showed great originality. Instead of sonatas, he favored genres with evocative titles such as *nocturne* (meant to suggest nighttime), or those that reflected his Polish heritage, such as the *polonaise,* a folk dance. While Chopin was an uncontested virtuoso of his instrument, his music was often notable for its restraint and delicacy. He made careful use of the piano's pedals—the sustaining and dampening pedals—to achieve unique colors on the instrument. The result was music of great variety, from stormy and impulsive to dreamy and serene.

LISTENING PREPARATION

Chopin, Nocturne in E-Flat Major, Op. 9, No. 2 (1831).

Chopin wrote this early nocturne during an eight-month stay in Vienna, before settling in Paris. In Vienna, Chopin was surprised at the waltz craze then current—"They call waltzes musical works here!" he wrote to a friend. And yet one can find the unmistakable imprint of the waltz on this and other Chopin works—the triple rhythm and regular *boom-chuck-chuck* in the left hand, with melody on top. In his nocturnes and other works, Chopin generally follows a rather simple outline: he makes a musical statement, repeats it with embellishments, departs from it, then returns to it at the end—a modified ABA form. In this nocturne, as we shall see, he makes some further modifications to this form. Notice also the use of *rubato,* the pushing and pulling of the tempo for expressive purposes.

Refer to the Appendix at the back of the book for this Listening Activity's complete worksheet. Use the following section to make notes for yourself

Refer to the Appendix at the back of the book for this Listening Activity's complete worksheet.

LISTENING ACTIVITY 13.4:

Chopin, Nocturne in E-Flat Major, Op. 9 No. 2 (CD 2/4)

1. On your first listening, map out the form of the nocturne, continuing the diagram below. Include CD time information for the start of each section, in the little boxes on top of the section boxes.

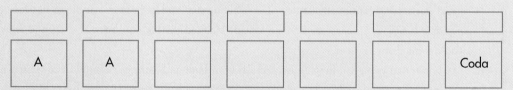

2. How is the "A" section modified on its repeat?

3. Where do you think the climax of this piece is? What happens then?

4. What kind of emotion do you think Chopin is trying to convey in this piece? What does he do to get this across?

Paganini (1782–1840) and pianist Franz Liszt (1811–1886), both of whom were so virtuosic on their instruments they were thought to possess supernatural powers. There were also several virtuosos who were not significant as composers, musicians who made their living as touring performers. The Norwegian violinist Ole Bull (1810–1880) and the Swedish singer Jenny Lind (1820–1887) were two of the most famous performers of the early nineteenth century, both of whom toured with great success as far away as the United States.

Despite the public's fascination with virtuosity, there were also composers (such as Schubert and Chopin) who avoided the public concert scene. In the nineteenth century there was far more opportunity than earlier for a composer to make money from publishing his or her works, and from related activities such as teaching, writing about music, and conducting.

Nicolo Paganini
(1782–1840)

Franz Liszt ("List")
(1811–1886)

MUSICIAN BIOGRAPHY 13.5:

ROBERT AND CLARA SCHUMANN
(1810—1856 and 1819—1896)

Robert Schumann, the son of a bookseller in northern Germany, like Berlioz, was supposed to pursue a practical career (in this case, law) and was sent away to the big city (in this case, Leipzig) to begin his studies. Like Berlioz, Schumann was distracted by the music and literary scene and soon drifted away from his parents' path. He began taking piano lessons from a teacher named Friedrich Wieck, eventually moving in with the family. In addition to music, the Wieck household had another attraction—a beautiful, talented daughter named Clara. Over time, Robert and Clara fell in love, and, against the wishes of Mr. Wieck, were married in 1840.

Robert Schumann and his wife, Clara Schumann.
Source: Getty Images, Inc. Hulton archive by Getty Images.

Robert had originally intended to become a virtuoso pianist, but an injury to one of his hands put an end to that dream. In many ways Clara lived that dream for him, travelling far and wide as a performer, playing works both she and Robert had composed, as well as other music. The biases of the time made it difficult for her to get works published—women were supposed to be wives and mothers, not artists. In fact, she was both a wife and a mother (of seven children!), but continued her career in spite of any prejudice she might have experienced.

The early days of their marriage were quite happy. Robert, unable to perform, poured his energy into two main activities: composing and writing about music. He had founded a magazine called *The New Journal for Music* in 1835, serving as lead writer and editor for many years, and in this magazine he not only reviewed concerts but also called attention to significant new performers, among them Chopin and Johannes Brahms (see Musician Biography 13.7). He also played a critical role in the revival of Schubert's music after that composer's death. His music, focussing on symphonies, art songs, and piano music, remains some of the finest examples of these genres in the nineteenth century.

Like other romantics, however, Schumann's life was ultimately tragic. To earn extra income he tried other ancillary careers such as teaching and conducting, and failed rather miserably at both. Like many other artists he suffered from periodic bouts with depression. In 1854, he attempted suicide by throwing himself into the Rhine River, and then had to be confined to a mental institution. He was attended to by his devoted wife and protégé, Brahms, until the very end.

Clara was deeply grieved by his death in 1856. Although she eventually started performing again, she gave up composing altogether, devoting her energy to the promotion of her late husband's works through performance and publication. Despite the romantic interest shown by the handsome young Brahms, Clara never remarried. In the last twenty years there has been a resurgence of interest in Clara's career, with a number of fine recordings and new biographies.

Felix Mendelssohn.
Source: Getty
Images, Inc. Hulton
Archive by Getty
Images.

MUSICIAN BIOGRAPHY 13.6:

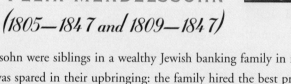

Fanny and Felix Mendelssohn
(1805—1847 and 1809—1847)

Fanny and Felix Mendelssohn were siblings in a wealthy Jewish banking family in northern Germany. No expense was spared in their upbringing: the family hired the best private tutors, gave the children lessons in literature and painting, and when they both showed immense musical talent, hired small orchestras to play their works after their Sunday dinners. It was a happy childhood—despite an episode when the family was compelled to convert to Christianity and take on the last name Bartholdy. The children resented this conversion and refused to use the Christian last name, but later on became devout Lutherans.

The two kids were equals in most respects, but when they became teenagers it was made clear that only Felix would be permitted to pursue a career in music. Their father wrote in a letter to Fanny, "Music will perhaps become [Felix's] profession, but for *you* it can and must only be an ornament. . . . It does you credit that you have always shown yourself good and sensible in these matters." Nineteenth-century women like Fanny were supposed to just get married and forego any dreams of a career. Fanny did indeed get married, to a good man, the painter Wilhelm Hensel, and had a child soon after. Secretly, however, she continued to compose, arranging with Felix to have some of her works published in his name.

Felix, meanwhile, quickly became an international figure in the music world. At the age of seventeen he wrote the *Overture to "A Midsummer Night's Dream,"* a work still enjoyed; and at twenty he put on a concert that brought attention to the music of Johann Sebastian Bach, master of the late baroque and then all but forgotten. Felix became a successful conductor and educator as well, founding the Leipzig Conservatory of Music in 1843. His travels took him all over Europe, as far away as London, and he composed musical portraits of various places he visited, such as his *Italian* and *Scottish* symphonies.

In all his travels and fame, however, he never forgot about his sister, writing to her continuously and intimately. When she died suddenly in 1847, he was devastated and followed her to the grave later that year.

THE LATE ROMANTICS

The great American writer Mark Twain (1835–1910) referred to the period after the American Civil War as the "Gilded Age," a term he used to satirize the pretentious culture of the *nouveau riches* in that period. Having made quick fortunes through industrialization, these newly wealthy Americans built showy mansions in imitation of European palaces, dressed in fashions imported from Paris, and attended European operatic performances and other such cultural events in an attempt to mimic the refinement and taste of the fading European aristocracy. Most Americans, however, found more enjoyment in their own homespun culture of circuses, fairs, dime-store novelettes, and baseball games. Nevertheless, the term *Gilded Age* has come to represent this entire era, both in North America and Europe—a time of grinding poverty and great fortunes, of political corruption, and of marvelous inventions, such as the typewriter (1867), the telephone (1876), the phonograph (1877), the electric light (1879), and the gasoline engine (1885).

The Gilded Age

Popular culture also had a branch in music, one which grew and prospered toward the end of the century. While opera remained the most popular form of music drama, new, more raucous variety shows emerged in the United States and Europe. Some of the popular songs of these shows were sold as sheet music, and the popular music industry was born. A craze for band music swept the United States, both in the form of rough-sounding amateur ensembles in towns and cities across the country and in professional groups, such as the one led by the "March King," bandleader and composer John Philip Sousa (1854–1932).

Despite the growth of popular music, classical music was still the dominant musical style in the last half of the nineteenth century. Composers of classical music, however, became divided by their musical philosophy. One group, which we might call the Nationalists, we will discuss below. The second group called itself the New German School, composers who advocated the complete abandonment of traditional rules for the sake of expression. This group was led by the dominant musical personality from midcentury on, the German opera composer Richard Wagner (1813–1883), a dedicated romantic in the mold of Berlioz who suspended traditional form and substituted theme-based organization and rich harmony

Nationalism

*John Philip Sousa
(1854–1932)*

*Richard Wagner
("REEK-hart
VAHG-ner")
(1813–1883)*

and orchestration (see Musician Biography 15.3). The third group of composers—a minority—was led by Johannes Brahms, who believed that Wagner had taken art music too far. He called for a return to some degree of restraint and order in musical expression.

NATIONALISM

The second half of the nineteenth century was a time when groups of people became increasingly conscious of their ethnic identities. For several centuries, more powerful nations had often claimed sovereignty over smaller ones. In the latter half of the nineteenth century, for example, the Austrian Empire controlled parts of what is now Italy, Belgium, Bosnia, the Czech Republic, Slovakia, Slovenia, Romania, and Hungary. But now these groups of people began to revolt, claiming independence from foreign domination. Most of these independence movements were thwarted by the powerful armies of the big European nations, but the desire for ethnic sovereignty could not be squelched. This desire continued throughout the twentieth century as well, sparking conflicts from World War I at the beginning of the century to the wars of the disintegrating nation of Yugoslavia at the end.

*Johannes Brahms.
Photo by Wiener
von Aufnahme.
Source: CORBIS.*

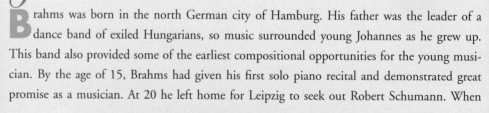

MUSICIAN BIOGRAPHY 13.7:

JOHANNES BRAHMS (1833–1897)

Brahms was born in the north German city of Hamburg. His father was the leader of a dance band of exiled Hungarians, so music surrounded young Johannes as he grew up. This band also provided some of the earliest compositional opportunities for the young musician. By the age of 15, Brahms had given his first solo piano recital and demonstrated great promise as a musician. At 20 he left home for Leipzig to seek out Robert Schumann. When

Schumann heard young Brahms play, he took him under his wing, wrote a laudatory article in his magazine about him, and invited him to live with his family. Brahms stayed with the Schumanns through Robert's declining days, forming an unreciprocated infatuation for Clara, which probably compelled him to move out after Robert's death. Nevertheless, they remained good friends until the end of their lives.

For the next twenty years he toured as a piano performer and took positions as a choral conductor in several cities. Ultimately he settled down in Vienna, city of his musical forebears, teaching piano, conducting choruses, publishing his compositions, and working as a music editor of the complete edition of the works of J. S. Bach. As his fame as a composer grew, he gradually trimmed away his other activities to devote more and more time to writing music. When he died at the age of 66 of cancer—shortly after Clara had died—he was the most well-respected composer of his time.

Brahms was reserved and formal in nature, with a sharp intellect and a sharper tongue. Against the trends of his time, he avoided program music (although some of his music seems to have contained secret programs, hidden meanings not printed in programs, known only to Brahms and his close friends). His music revived the spirit of Beethoven in many respects, using genre-based titles such as "Symphony No. 1," and employing a closer adherence to form than was then customary. On closer inspection, however, we find ample elements of progressive romanticism—wide ranges of emotions and plenty of broken rules for the sake of expression. The result is music that more effectively balances the head and the heart than most of the music of his contemporaries.

LISTENING PREPARATION

Brahms, Intermezzo in A Major Op. 118, No. 2, *Andante teneramente* (Moderately slow, tenderly) (1893).

In 1890 Brahms declared himself through with composing, wrote up his will, and thought about death. Even so, he still composed, although he told Clara in 1894 that now he only composed for himself. These scattered last works have often been described as "autumnal," with an element of resignation and introspection.

This intermezzo is one of a group of six piano pieces he wrote in this last stage. This is probably the most serene of the set, but it still has passages of storminess and a general mood of disconsolate yearning and melancholy. Typical features of Brahms include occasional rhythmic dislocation—such as when the left hand sounds like it is in triple meter and the right hand in duple—and somewhat irregular phrase structure, so that an initial phrase may be answered by a phrase a measure longer or shorter than the first one. See the Chapter 13 website for more help with this Listening Activity.

One result of this unrest is something we call Nationalism in music—when composers try to somehow express the character of their country or ethnicity through music. Composers achieved this through several means: using actual folk tunes from their people; writing story-based music with subjects from their peoples' mythology or history; and painting musical portraits of the landscape of their country. This was a very effective compositional trend; it aroused great enthusiasm at home and even abroad. Often these composers deliberately defied traditional rules of music composition, in part in defiance and in part in an attempt to forge a new national idiom.

Refer to the Appendix at the back of the book for this Listening Activity's complete worksheet. Use the following section to make notes for yourself

LISTENING ACTIVITY 13.5:

Brahms, Intermezzo in A Major, Op. 118, No. 2 (CD 2/5)

1. The main theme is based on a three note motive with the following shape:

    In the "a" subsection below, this motive is heard twice, followed by a "b" subsection that responds to it. Then both subsections are then repeated, with a change in the ending of the "b" subsection to bring closure:

    ## a b a b'

    We will call this group of subsections Section A. Then, the whole of Section A repeats. Is this an exact repeat of the first section? _____ If not, what has changed?

2. Now (at about CD time 0:39), we begin new material, which we will call Section B. Much of this music is continuous, meaning one subsection flows into the next without a cadence. The first time we take a "breath," so to speak, is about halfway through this section. Through this first half of Section B, Brahms takes us through several different stages. Describe what's happening in the music in the first part of Section B, until you hear it slow down and pause.

3. After the pause, we hear the main motive inverted—now taking the shape

and in fact continuing in an approximate inversion of the beginning of the piece, complete with a jagged response. At what CD time does this inversion occur? _____

4. Section C begins at around CD time 2:02. Describe the music for the next half minute or so:

5. What happens next, at around CD time 2:43?

6. At about CD time 3:14, the music changes again. What earlier part of the piece is this most similar to?

7. At what time do you hear a return to Section A? _____

8. What is different about Section A this time?

9. At what CD time do you hear a repeat of the inverted motive described in Question 3, above? _____

10. How does the piece end?

11. Fill in the CD timer information for the start of each section:

A	A	B	C	A	B	End

12. Using the above diagram as reference, write a paragraph describing the expressive landscape of this piece, what you think Brahms is intending the listener to feel in each section and how he achieves this.

Bedřich Smetana
(1824–1884)

MUSICIAN BIOGRAPHY 13.8:

*B*EDŘICH SMETANA *(1824—1884)*

Smetana was born the son of a brewmaster in rural Bohemia (the region now known as the Czech Republic). His father was a talented violinist and encouraged the boy's precocious musicianship, but, like other fathers, sent Bedř ich to school in Prague in the hopes of his taking a practical career. Smetana worked as a teacher for a while, then, like Schubert, abandoned this path for music. Most of his career was a struggle. After opening a new conservatory of music in Prague, which failed to generate any profit, he moved to Sweden to work in a court in Göteborg. It was abroad, ironically, that he first began to write music that might be termed nationalistic—perhaps out of homesickness. In 1861 he returned to Prague with the intention of creating a new music culture that focused on Czech ethnic identity.

Smetana himself hardly spoke the native Czech language at this point. German culture, through the political domination of the Austrian Empire, had completely overwhelmed the native folk traditions and customs. Only the German language was taught in school, and music composed by Germans was the primary fare in the concert halls. Smetana's decision to write and conduct operas in Czech was thus a form of political protest. Two of his operas, *The Brandenburgers in Bohemia* and *The Bartered Bride,* became hits in 1866 and finally put his career on a firmer financial footing. While he wrote other operas in the 1870s and early 1880s he gradually completed an epic six-part tone poem called *Má vlast* (My Fatherland), his greatest tribute to Bohemia.

Despite his growing success and the accomplishment of reviving Czech musical culture, Smetana's life was not a happy one. Three of his four daughters died between 1854 and 1856, and his first wife in 1859. Like many artists of his day, Smetana contracted syphilis, for which there was no cure, and this disease ultimately drove him insane. Syphilis also inflicted tinnitus on Smetana, so that by the early 1880s he was, like Beethoven, completely deaf. He died in a mental institution in 1884. Out of this mostly unhappy life came a reawakened Czech national musical identity, paving the way for the next generation of Bohemian composers, including Antonín Dvořák (1841–1901) and Leoš Janáček (1854–1928).

LISTENING PREPARATION

Smetana, "The Moldau" from *Má vlast* (1874).

Smetana's famous tone poem depicts the journey of Bohemia's main river from its source in the southern part of the country, down through the mountains, on through the farmlands, to the Rapids of St. John and into Prague. The beautiful main theme is actually derived from a Swedish

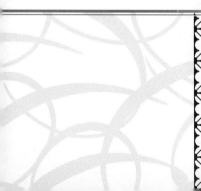

folk song, but right from the start the music struck Smetana's countrymen as a perfect evocation of their land, viewed, as it were, from the perspective of the river.

Here are the stages the river passes through:

1. In the mountains, we hear the springlike source of the river, several little streams coming together to create the Moldau.
2. The Moldau passes through a forest, and we hear the sounds of horns, associated with hunters.
3. Outside the forest, we pass by a peasant wedding, with the guests dancing to the sounds of a polka.
4. In the nighttime, *rusalkas,* the water nymphs of Czech mythology, play in the moonlight.
5. The river gathers momentum, eventually roaring through the Rapids of St. John above Prague.
6. At the climax of the piece, the Moldau flows through the city of Prague, then on to its confluence with the River Elbe north of Prague.

Refer to the Appendix at the back of the book for this Listening Activity's complete worksheet. Use the following section to make notes for yourself

LISTENING ACTIVITY 13.6:

Smetana, "The Moldau" from Má vlast (Symphonic poem) (CD 2/6)

1. At the beginning Stage 1, what instruments are used to depict the flowing of the rivulets?

2. What instruments present the main theme at CD time 1:07?

3. Map out the subsidiary form of the theme.

4. The end of the theme gets interrupted by the sounds of hunting horns. At what CD time does this begin? _____

5. What feeling is this section supposed to evoke?

6. At what CD time does Stage 3 begin? _____

7. How does Smetana create the feeling of a folk wedding?

8. What instruments dominate the moonlit scene in Stage 4?

9. Describe the feeling this section is supposed to evoke.

10. At what CD time do you hear the main theme return? _____

11. How does Smetana musically illustrate the river gathering momentum and passing through the rapids?

12. At what CD time do you think the Moldau has reached Prague? _____

13. How can you tell?

14. Describe the last minute or so of the piece.

THE END OF ROMANTICISM

*J*ust as the beginning of the romantic era emerged out of the shadow of Beethoven, composers at the end of the era were overwhelmed by the example of Richard Wagner. In his operas, Wagner had brought the various elements of romanticism to their fulfillment. His orchestration was both colorful and powerful, with beautiful effects and earth-shaking brass and percussion. He greatly expanded Berlioz's *idèe fixe* concept into a complex interlacing structure of the themes that help propel the drama of his operas. His harmony seemed to break all the rules, helping making the music extraordinarily rich. His operas were the most epic spectacles ever seen, each one lasting several hours and relying on some of the same deep myths that have helped make the *Star Wars* movie sagas a cultural phenomenon of our own time.

Ironically, Wagner's very success presented a problem to the next generation of composers. How could a composer "out-Wagner" Wagner? Many of the operas written immediately after Wagner's death were unsuccessful, possibly due to their seeming palidness when compared to the work of the master. One solution many composers pursued was to studiously avoid opera altogether. After 1890, the characteristics of Wagner's musical language most often appeared in orchestral form. Orchestral music soon began to surpass opera as the most popular and respected kind of classical music. Several world-class orchestras were founded in this era: the Boston Symphony in 1881;

the Berlin Philharmonic in 1882; and the Chicago Symphony in 1891. Many of the best musicians now became conductors instead of composers and a golden age of orchestras began, lasting about halfway through the twentieth century.

But even with these new virtuoso ensembles emerging in more and more cities, classical music was quickly coming to a crisis. Many composers— such as the last great *Lieder* composer, Hugo Wolf (1860–1903), and the last great symphonic poem composer, Richard Strauss (1864–1949), as well as Gustav Mahler (see Musician Biography 13.9)— found much to say in this late romantic idiom. Many others wrote music that sounded like warmed-over Wagner, and like a meal microwaved too many times, it began to taste rather stale. Romanticism would continue in various forms well into the twentieth century—in fact, much of our current film music still owes a great debt to Wagner and Beethoven—but in the second decade of the century a new music revolution would occur that was particularly antiromantic, completely transforming classical music. This revolution is discussed in Chapter 14.

The art music scene between about 1890 and 1910 was thus a kind of twilight time for romanticism. Thoughtful composers such as Mahler could tell that the style was reaching the end of its lifespan, yet they could not (or would not) throw it away. It is

Hugo Wolf ("Volf") (1860–1903)

Richard Strauss ("Shtrows") (1864–1949)

Richard Wagner.
Source: The Granger Collection, New York.

a tribute to their creative powers that they found so much to say at the end of the era.

Gustav Mahler (1860–1911)

MUSICIAN BIOGRAPHY 13.9:

GUSTAV MAHLER *(1860–1911)*

Mahler was born in Bohemia, but unlike Smetana did not become a Czech nationalist composer. He studied at the Vienna Conservatory of Music and at the age of twenty began a series of conducting posts in central Europe and Germany. Mahler quickly made a name for himself as a conductor: he demanded his musicians play with greater precision, and yet also managed to extract more expression from them. In his lifetime Mahler would be better known as a conductor than a composer.

As a conductor, Mahler focused on opera, but as a composer (an activity he pursued mostly during the off-season, in the summer), he dedicated himself to two genres, the symphony and the orchestral *lied*—an art song with orchestral accompaniment. His music is intensely personal and emotional, with inventive orchestration and riveting drama. He worked with a massive orchestra—in his Eighth Symphony, he calls for performing forces that number several hundred—and yet would usually use the full force of the ensemble sparingly, giving the listener a wide range of dynamics, color, and mood. A symphony, he once said, should be an entire world.

Mahler would be the last great composer for several years to see composing as a means of self-expression. Unfortunately, his life gave him ample material to work with. As a Jew in an anti-Semitic age, he was subject to all sorts of intrigues and challenges to his authority. Ultimately, in order to obtain the conductorship of the main opera house in Vienna, he was forced to accept Catholic baptism. Even with this concession, he suffered great hostility and eventually moved to New York to lead the Metropolitan Opera jointly with the great Italian conductor Arturo Toscanini (1867–1957). His personal life had more than its share of sorrow, too. Like many artists Mahler suffered from depression his whole life, and he even spent some afternoons on the couch of Vienna's Sigmund Freud, founder of psychotherapy. His marriage to the beautiful, independent Alma Schindler (1879–1964) was stormy and often unhappy. His brother committed suicide in 1895, and he lost his eldest daughter Maria to scarlet fever in 1907. Soon after, Mahler was diagnosed with the heart condition that would claim his life at age 50.

IMPRESSIONISM

Impressionism

There is some debate whether musical impressionism belongs with the romantic or twentieth-century style periods. The truth is that impressionism has elements of both styles and serves as a kind of bridge between the eras.

Like several other musical styles the term *impressionism* was first applied to the visual arts. The term was first used in 1874 and meant as an insult, to disparage the seemingly "fuzzy" artwork of French painters Claude Monet (1840–1926) and others. These paintings were a deliberate rejection of formalism, with a great attention to light and color and an avoidance of sharp outlines and precise rendering of the subject matter. Some historians have speculated that impressionism was a reaction to the increasing use of the camera at the end of the century—with mechanical means to accurately render an image, painting had to become something *else*, to distinguish itself from the crisp black-and-white images created by photographers.

In music, French composer Claude Debussy (see Musician Biography 13.10) launched what we now consider a musical corollary to artistic impressionism, although he himself rejected this term. Debussy and

Claude Debussy
("DE-byu-see")
(1862–1918)

MUSICIAN BIOGRAPHY 13.10:

CLAUDE DEBUSSY *(1862—1918)*

After studying piano and composition at the Paris Conservatoire as a teen, Debussy won the coveted Rome Prize, awarded for the outstanding composition of the year, in 1884. The winner was given an all-expense-paid trip to Rome for several months, where he or she was supposed to soak up the musical culture there and return to France refreshed. Debussy spent nearly two years in Italy, but found greater inspiration from the Asian music he heard at the Paris World's Fair of 1889. By the mid-1890s his compositions were decidedly impressionist no matter what the genre—ballet, opera, piano music, or symphonic poem. Influenced by the poetry, literature, and painting of his time, Debussy helped create the first post-Wagner musical language, one more concerned with aesthetic beauty than emotional expression. When he died of cancer in 1918, most of the important composers outside of Germany and Austria were in his artistic debt.

LISTENING PREPARATION

Debussy, "Nuages" ("Clouds") from *Trois Nocturnes* (1899).

"Nuages" is the first of a set of three symphonic poems known as the *Three Nocturnes,* a title evocative of Chopin's piano music; the other two are *"Fêtes"* ("Festivals") and *"Sirènes"* ("Sirens," the mythical female sea deities whose beautiful voices caused shipwrecks, depicted here by a female chorus singing without words). *"Nuages"* may have been the closest Debussy came to deliberately emulating the visual impressionists; he once said his depiction of clouds was "like a study in gray in painting."

Although Debussy uses a full orchestra for this piece, he never unleashes its full power, keeping its strength in check to produce a subtle, understated image. There is a six-note, falling theme:

This is repeated several times throughout the piece, but changes little. The net result is music that is rather static, like a tableau, rather than dramatic like most romantic works. This feeling is amplified by the shimmering quality of the string playing and the lack of a definite tonal center. See the Chapter 13 website for more help with this Listening Activity.

Maurice Ravel (1875–1937)

Whole-tone scale

his followers, such as Maurice Ravel (1875–1937), created music with a similarly blurred quality, and with greater attention to orchestral colors than had been heard before. One of the ways the impressionists made their music sound "blurry" was through the use of new scales such as the *whole-tone scale,* where all the notes are equal distance from one another. Both major and minor scales give the listener the feeling of *tonal center,* that one pitch is more important than the others and to which the music will always return. With the whole-tone scale there is no such feeling; all the notes seem to be equal. Without this sense of tonal gravity the music has a peculiar "floating" quality.

You can create a whole-tone scale by playing the following notes on the piano (Figure 13.2).

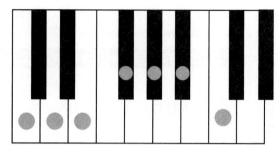

FIGURE 13.2: *Whole-tone Scale.*

Impressionism only lasted from the 1890s through the 1920s. But during this time, the music produced had a unique beauty, and its adventurousness pointed the way to more radical musical experiments of the next era.

Refer to the Appendix at the back of the book for this Listening Activity's complete worksheet. Use the following section to make notes for yourself

LISTENING ACTIVITY 13.7:

Debussy, "Nuages" *from* Trois Nocturnes *(Symphonic poem) (CD 2/7)*

1. How many times do you hear the six-note motive (Motive 1) played at the beginning? _____

2. After the first two runs through the motive, it changes slightly. What's different?

3. Next, we hear a new motive played by the English horn (Motive 2), rapidly going up then sinking back down more slowly. At what CD time does this begin? _____

4. At what CD time do the violins pick up Motive 1 again? _____

5. Now, Motive 1 leads into something new. Describe the music of the next minute or so, starting around CD time 1:00.

6. At what CD time does Motive 2 recur? _____

7. After Motive 2 repeats several times, we hear a buildup, climaxing in a falling violin line related to the main motive. After this, around CD time 2:10, the music changes more radically. What sort of feeling do you think this next section supposed to evoke?

8. Slowly, the music builds up again. What happens when it reaches a climax, around CD time 2:42?

9. Now, we hear the English horn motive again, slightly transformed and supported by soft *pizzicato* in the strings. At what CD time does this begin? _____

10. After Motive 2 repeats several times and changes, we hear Motive 1 as at the beginning, only accompanied by a solo instrument (at about CD time 3:39). What family does this solo instrument belong to? _____

11. We now hear a falling string line, followed by an orchestral swelling (at about 3:55), and these two ideas repeat. Then, another solo instrument plays a new musical idea, Motive 3, this time accompanied by single notes on the harp and a kind of watercolor wash in the strings (at about 4:13). What is this solo instrument? _____

12. Motive 3 is now taken up by two string instruments playing in octaves. At what CD time does this begin? _____

13. What happens after the strings repeat the new theme?

14. At what CD time does the English horn motive (Motive 2) come back? _____

15. Momentarily, the English horn continues (after about CD time 5:52), as if it had been trying to speak throughout the whole piece and only now has gotten the opportunity. Then, the piece seems to dissipate. We hear the main motive, lower and lower, then a fragment of the third motive, then several isolated *pizzicato* notes to wrap it up. Why do you think Debussy chose to end his piece this way?

16. Do you like this piece? Why or why not?

Checkpoint

In this chapter we have looked at several stages of nineteenth-century art music. Starting with Beethoven, the initiator of the style, we looked at the early romantic generation, the late romantics (including the nationalists), and finally the impressionists. We have looked closely at several genres: the symphony, the art song, the program symphony, the nocturne, the intermezzo, and the symphonic poem. We investigated the biographies of several musicians of the nineteenth century. The music we have heard has been, for the most part, concerned with the expression of emotion—often an autobiographical unveiling of the emotions of the composer. Nineteenth-century music became larger, both in length and in performing forces, and it defied many of the traditional rules of music composition for the sake of expression. Composers became more concerned with drama and color than with form.

Twentieth-century classical music would move in a very different direction, in many ways a repudiation of romanticism. Many listeners, however, have never left the romantic era, at least in their musical preferences, and the music of this century still dominates the repertoire of classical concert halls. On the World Wide Web you can find societies dedicated to most of the romantic composers discussed here, and several others not discussed, and if you like this music I encourage you to investigate these websites. Musical enjoyment is often a matter of personality, with different types of people enjoying different types of music. For those who enjoy music best when it takes the listener on an emotional journey, there was no better time for music than the nineteenth century.

KEY TERMS

Transcendentalism	Thematic development	Nationalism
Rubato	Lieder	Symphonic poem
Chromaticism	Program symphony	Impressionism
Orchestration	Idèe Fixe	Whole-tone Scale
Program music	Nocturne	
Absolute music	The Gilded Age	

Twentieth-Century Classical Music

A poor migrant mother and her children. Photo by Dorothea Lange.
Source: CORBIS.

The Great Depression

World War I

World War II

The twentieth century was a time of almost constant political upheaval, a century of revolutions and radical ideologies. In 1914, a Serbian nationalist assassinated the heir to the throne of the Austro-Hungarian Empire in protest against Austrian control over Serbia. Because of a series of interlocking treaties, before the year was over all the major nations of Europe were dividing into the Allies and the Central powers of World War I. They attacked each other with new, deadly weapons such as the machine gun and mustard gas. After three years of stalemate in which over a million young men died in the trenches of northern France, the entrance of the United States into the war tipped the balance in favor of the Allies. In the meantime, one of the important players, Russia, had backed out of the war due to domestic unrest. In 1917, Communists overthrew the Russian government, assassinated the royal family, and set up a new government, supposedly of the people. By the late 1920s, the new Soviet Union was run by a ruthless dictator named Joseph Stalin (1879–1953), one of several despots to mar the century.

After World War I, while the European nations licked their wounds, the United States emerged as the world's powerhouse economy. The following decade, the Roaring Twenties, was practically a nonstop party in America, a party which came to an abrupt halt when the stock market crashed in 1929. The Great Depression that followed touched every nation on Earth. As the lines for soup kitchens and unemployment services grew, so did serious doubts about traditional forms of government, giving rise to even more radical ideologies: Fascism in Italy and National Socialism in Germany. Franklin Delano Roosevelt (1882–1945), who became president of the United States in 1933, offered new hope through massive government relief programs. At almost exactly the same time, Adolf Hitler (1889–1945) rose to power in Germany, beginning one of the most notorious reigns of evil in the history of mankind. Millions of Jews, Gypsies, homosexuals, Slavs, liberals, and others considered dangerously different from Aryan Germans were deprived of property and freedom and, in many cases, their lives.

Hitler's hunger for worldwide domination eventually sparked World War II in 1939, a conflict that encircled the globe. By the time the United States ended the war with the atomic bombing of Hiroshima and

Nagasaki, the Axis powers—Germany, Italy, and Japan—as well as parts of Great Britain, Europe, and the Soviet Union lay in ruins. The Soviet Union quickly rebuilt, however, and before the smoke of battle cleared, fear of a third world war developed—this one a nuclear war between the United States and the Soviet Union, truly a war to end all wars. Because neither side ultimately had the stomach for Armageddon, what ensued was a tense standoff between the two superpowers that lasted for four decades. It was probably the neutral nations that suffered the most during the Cold War, as they were cajoled and bullied into supporting one side or the other of this ideological squabble. At the same time, many of these neutral countries were throwing off the last remnants of nineteenth-century colonialism and becoming independent nations. In many cases, as happened in India, what followed was a protracted and bloody internal struggle.

The Cold War finally ended in 1991 with the collapse of the Soviet Union. The political crises have continued since then, however, with revolutions and wars flaring up across the globe as various ethnic groups struggle to learn to live together. And despite its triumph in the Cold War, the United States has felt its own revolutionary tremors throughout the century, with presidential assassinations in 1901 and 1963; several other assassination attempts; one presidential resignation and one impeachment; and a near-revolution in the 1960s over the country's involvement in the Vietnam War and equal rights for African-Americans.

THE CLASSICAL MUSIC OF THE TWENTIETH CENTURY

*I*t was also a time of revolution and radical ideology for the classical music of the twentieth century. Many people considered the musical style of the nineteenth century spent by the start of the new century. Composers started experimenting with new directions in music composition, quite different from one another, but all reactions against romanticism. This new generation of

The Cold War

A Russian poster, "Worker Women." Photo by Swim Ink.
Source: CORBIS. © Swim Ink/CORBIS.

composers complained that romanticism's abandonment of rules for the sake of expression left music in a uncertain situation where "anything goes." They felt that romantic composers pandered too much to the common listener, creating music that may have been emotionally resonant but was rather superficial and trite. The new classical music would be less concerned with the expression of emotion and with appealing to a wide audience. The great composer Igor Stravinsky (see Musician Biography 14.1) said that his music had nothing to do with emotions. If a composition *did* cause a warm response from listeners, it was looked upon with suspicion by other composers. The most important American composer of the century, Aaron Copland (see Musician Biography 14.3), once wrote in a letter, "I can't get over the idea that if a thing is popular it can't be good." Later, he would change his mind about this, as we shall see.

This first, antiromantic stage of twentieth-century music coalesced after World War I and may loosely be referred to as the *atonal phase*. When we say a   *Atonal phase* piece of music is *atonal,* we mean it avoids a tonal center that serves as a kind of gravitational pull in tonal music (either major or minor). The leading composer of this period was Arnold Schoenberg (see Musician Biography 14.2). When people first hear this music, even today, their first reaction often is to recoil. With modern abstract visual art, people joked that it could have been painted by a chimpanzee with a paintbrush. Similarly, many listeners think that atonal music is random, making jokes about how the music could be composed by cats on a piano keyboard. Once you get to know this music, however, you will find that there is a highly refined system to it.

After the Depression began, many composers changed over to an opposite ideology, one we can call the *populist phase.* Atonal music was an elite taste, but with the collapse of the world economy in 1929, all forms of elitism were called into question. The moneyed elite were thought to have caused the crash due to financial overextension, and the refined tastes of the social elite (often the same group) were thought to be inappropriate while millions were starving. Composers started writing music for "the People," incorporating popular tunes and folksongs into their works, or they dedicated their efforts to writing music for amateurs to sing and play, rather than for just professionals. Aaron Copland was one populist composer during the 1930s and 1940s, but there were many others in Europe and the Americas.

The third stage of twentieth-century classical music came after World War II. In the United States, the so-called G.I. Bill enabled the thousands of discharged veterans to attend colleges and universities, leading to a tremendous expansion in postsecondary education. As demand for college education grew, many composers found attractive positions as professors, where composing became considered a research activity similar to the laboratory research conducted by professors in the sciences. Perhaps because of their new association with the intellectual activities of their colleagues in other fields, or perhaps because of the new emphasis on science and math emerging in the Cold War space race with the Soviet Union, the music of this time became highly mathematical and complicated. Atonality was revived, with even more

disciplined organization. The musical scores sometimes looked more like a schematic for an engineering project than a piece of music, and in general only those listeners with graduate training in music could begin to comprehend it. This music was generally referred to as *total serialization,* and we will call this substyle the *serialist phase.*

Typical of the twentieth century, this latest phase caused yet another reaction, which we will call *experimentalism.* There was a tradition of experimentation in American classical music that dated back to the start of the century with adventurous composers such as Charles Ives (1874–1954) and Henry Cowell (1897–1965)—who wrote piano pieces that required the performer to strum the insides of a piano like a harp, or play the keys with a block of wood. In the 1950s and 1960s, however, the American composer John Cage (see Musician Biography 14.4) took experimentalism to new heights, composing music in which some or all of the decisions about the structure of a composition were taken out of the hands of the composer. Other composers, including an important group in Europe, experimented with the emerging technology of synthesizers and computers, creating timbres never heard before and new approaches to composition as well. Emerging out of the experimentalist phase was another reaction against serialism called *minimalism.* This music, still being composed today, combines elements of popular music and non-Western music to create hypnotic sounds with lots of repeating elements.

Because most of these phases overlapped to some degree, and because the music in each of the phases was as often based on principles of composition rather than the actual sound of the music, the twentieth century has been marked by bitter rivalries and hostility. Serialist composers looked down upon music aimed, as one put it, at "the whistling repertory of the man in the street"; while the more populist composers accused the serialists of being stuck in ivory towers, writing painful music that scared listeners away from the concert hall. But since the fall of the Soviet Union, most of this overheated rhetoric has died down, just as much of the overheated political rhetoric of the Cold War has dissipated. At the turn of the twenty-first

Serialist phase

Experimentalist phase

Populist phase

century it seems that many different composers are working in many different styles, sometimes combining divergent trends into a single piece. This kind of freewheeling mixture of different styles—also found in other art forms and architecture—has been called *postmodernist,* a term we shall use for the final phase of twentieth-century art music, a phase that continues in use at the time of this writing.

OTHER CHALLENGES FOR CLASSICAL MUSIC

As suggested above, much of the classical music of the twentieth century was not very listener-friendly, and there is little doubt that this led to some of the loss of audience that classical music has experienced during this period. Other factors had a role, too, most of which were related to the rapid advance of technology.

The most significant of these factors was a new medium now considered rather innocuous: radio. Broadcasting emerged in the early 1920s in the United States and soon swept the nation, then the world. The radio became an indispensable household item. Poor people would purchase radio receivers rather than refrigerators, and by the end of the 1920s radio networks crisscrossed the continent. Early radio consisted of a lot of talking—advice shows, news programs, soap operas, and other forms of drama—but it was also a natural medium for music. And while many broadcasters emphasized classical music, it eventually became clear that a vast majority of American listeners preferred more folksy fare—music more associated with the barn dance than the ballroom. Radio also crossed geographic and cultural lines, so that north and south, rich and poor, black and white, all shared their musical fare. Today we wouldn't want it any other way, but in the first half of the century the arbiters of taste despaired at what they considered the cheapening of music culture.

Emerging hand-in-hand with radio was the phonograph. Thomas A. Edison (1847–1931) had invented the machine in 1877, but the widespread purchasing of disks and record players really began after World War I. Listeners, often first exposed to music over the radio, purchased records according to their tastes, and once again, this caused great concern. The proportion

Post-modernist phase

Radio Records

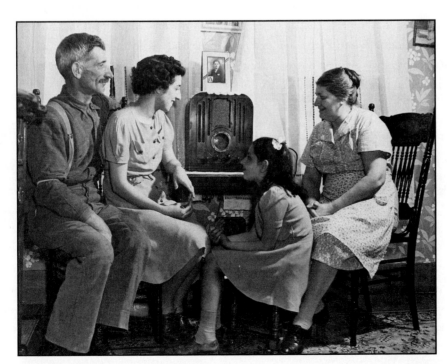

A family gathered around the radio.
Source: CORBIS.

of classical recordings compared to popular recordings generally declined over the course of the century, only increasing briefly with the advent of new technology such as the long-playing record in the late 1940s and the compact disc in the early 1980s.

As if this weren't enough, the twentieth century also saw the rise of new, more visual forms of entertainment: motion pictures and television. Although the finer theaters showing silent films usually had a house orchestra or at least an organ, movies were always primarily a visual form of entertainment, even after the advent of sound movies in the late 1920s. The same is true of television, which became ubiquitous in the early 1950s, superceding the old radio

Movies and television

networks. There has been some speculation that American society became a more visual one after the advent of these two forms of entertainment. This would probably be impossible to measure, but there is little doubt that they have taken away some of the audience for older forms of entertainment such as opera, ballet, theater, and the concert hall. At the end of the century the rise of personal computers and the internet provided yet another distraction.

All these challenges have led some observers to wonder if classical music will survive as a living art form in the twenty-first century. This question will be decided by the readers of this book, and those like them.

STRAVINSKY

One of the oldest games of speculation in the study of history is whether important events are determined by great people, or if the important events call on certain people to fulfill these roles. The answer, of course, is that both are true. The presidents of the United States we consider the greatest have generally served at times of great stress in the nation's history. But we still cannot say that their greatness was entirely due to the circumstances in which they served. In music history,

likewise, we can see times of great change that seem to have been inevitable in retrospect. And yet we could also argue that these changes were at least partly due to the forceful musicians who appeared at these junctures—musicians such as Ludwig van Beethoven and Louis Armstrong—who put their own personal imprint on the musical style of their time and deeply affected those who followed. Igor Stravinsky was one of these figures.

Igor Stravinsky.
Source: Getty
Images, Inc. Hulton
Archive by Getty
Images.

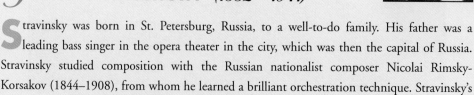

MUSICIAN BIOGRAPHY 14.1:

IGOR STRAVINSKY (1882–1971)

Stravinsky was born in St. Petersburg, Russia, to a well-to-do family. His father was a leading bass singer in the opera theater in the city, which was then the capital of Russia. Stravinsky studied composition with the Russian nationalist composer Nicolai Rimsky-Korsakov (1844–1908), from whom he learned a brilliant orchestration technique. Stravinsky's breakthrough piece was a ballet called *Firebird* (1910), a colorful piece written for a company called the Ballets Russes, working in Paris. Two more ballet commissions followed: *Petrushka* (1911) and *The Rite of Spring* (1913). The latter was boldly original, with much greater emphasis on rhythm than earlier music, and with sharp changes in dynamics and harsh dissonances—all elements which now entered the general music vocabulary. The choreography, depicting an ancient pagan ritual in which a young woman dances herself to death, was also radical departure from traditional ballet, emphasizing pantomime and primitivist gestures instead of graceful traditional dancing. At the first performance the shocked Parisian audience rioted.

Stravinsky had earned a name for himself, and stayed on in Paris to compose. World War I soon compelled him to move to neutral Switzerland, and the Russian Revolution made his exile a permanent one. Between the World Wars, he returned to France and led the way to a new musical direction, later called *neo-classicism*. Dissatisfied with both atonality and the vestiges of romanticism, Stravinsky and others looked to the more distant past for inspiration, reviving elements of the classical and baroque periods into their new, modernist musical language. Compared with atonality, neo-classicism enjoyed a reasonable popularity.

Neo-classicism

World War II forced Stravinsky into exile yet again, this time to the United States. He and his second wife, Vera, moved to Hollywood in 1940, where he taught at the University of Southern California. He was also in demand as a lecturer at other universities and as a conductor. After World War II Stravinsky's music changed yet again, moving toward the serialism then dominating the American compositional scene. No matter what style he wrote in, however, Stravinsky's own personal imprint remained evident. He remained active as a composer well into his late eighties.

LISTENING PREPARATION

Stravinsky, *Le Sacre du Printemps* (*The Rite of Spring*), excerpt (1913).

When Stravinsky was once asked, late in life, what he remembered most about his childhood, he replied, "The violent Russian spring that seemed to begin in an hour and was like the whole earth cracking. That was the most wonderful event of every year of my childhood." While working on another ballet in 1910, Stravinsky came up with the idea for *The Rite of Spring,* a solemn pagan ritual in which "wise elders, seated in a circle, [watch] a young girl dance herself to death. . . .

Bitonality

sacrificing her to propitiate the god of spring." He called on a friend who was an expert in ancient Slavic culture and together they wrote out a detailed sketch of the action. Although he began composing the work at this time, he set it aside to finish other projects before completing it in early 1913. The piece was choreographed—rather scandalously, it seems—by the famous ballet dancer Vaslav Nijinksy (1889–1950).

It was not just the choreography that shocked the audience of 1913; the music was different from anything else they had heard. Stravinsky used folklike melodies, but kept shifting notes around so that they never seem to repeat exactly. He changed the harmony between major and minor, and sometimes placed two chords right on top of each other—a technique which would be called *bitonality,* referring to two simultaneous tonal centers. The rhythm is also ambiguous at times. In some parts of the piece the meter changes every single measure, making the listener uncertain where the next downbeat will fall. Even when the meter is regular, there are often

Vaslav Nijinsky in "Afternoon of a Faun."
Source: CORBIS.

accents in strange places—*syncopation*—which unsettle the situation. Stravinsky also directed the orchestra to play in new ways. For example, the opening bassoon melody is played so high that most bassoonists of that time could not play it when the piece was written. Stravinsky expanded the percussion section so much that afterwards it became seen as a section unto itself, on a par with strings, woodwinds, and brass.

After the fateful premiere of *The Rite of Spring,* the ballet was presented only a few more times before it was withdrawn. There have been several revivals since then, usually with new choreography, but the music has found more success as a concert piece for orchestra. In 1940, an altered version of the *Rite* was included in the Walt Disney film *Fantasia* to accompany scenes of dinosaur battles, earthquakes, and volcanic eruptions. Stravinsky objected to this treatment of his music, but the movie probably did more than anything else to familiarize the public with both the music and the modern musical idiom. Since then, the piece has come to be considered one of the masterworks of the twentieth century.

On your CD there are two excerpts drawn from the beginning of the piece: the "Adoration of the Earth" and the "Auguries of Spring (Dances of the Young Girls)." The entire piece is about 35 minutes long.

Refer to the Appendix at the back of the book for this Listening Activity's complete worksheet. Use the following section to make notes for yourself

LISTENING ACTIVITY 14.1:

Stravinsky, The Rite of Spring *(ballet) (CD 2/8)*

1. At the beginning of *The Rite of Spring* we hear the famous opening bassoon line, alone at first then accompanied by French horn and clarinets. Using proper musical terms, describe the rhythm of the bassoon line.

2. After a moment or two, the bassoon repeats the opening line, now somewhat varied, and then the English horn takes over. Now, very gradually, the texture starts to thicken, with more and more instruments added. How would you characterize the music from about CD time 1:13 to 3:00?

3. At what CD time do you hear a repeat of the original bassoon melody? _____

4. We begin the next section, "Auguries of Spring (Dances of the Young Girls)" at about CD time 3:35. Describe the rhythm and the harmony at this point.

5. What kind of effect do you think Stravinsky was after here?

6. After a brief break, the music from the beginning of this section returns. Then there is a longer break, before it comes back again. At what CD time does this occur? _____

7. Soon, we hear the bassoons present a rather disjointed melody in a clear duple meter, traded back and forth with the trombone. Then, at about CD time 4:54, we hear a loud chord, followed by a resumption of the steady duple meter. At about CD time 5:18, we hear a new melody. What instrument family is this from? _____

8. What instrument takes the next solo? _____

9. Describe the ending of this selection, first from this point to about CD time 6:10, then from that point to the end:

10. Do you like this piece? Why or why not? Use musical terms in your answer.

MODERNISM

Modernism

The early twentieth century was a time of similar revolutions in all the arts. In 1907 a group of painters in Paris, most notably Georges Braque (1882–1963) and the Spaniard Pablo Picasso (1881–1973), developed a new style called *cubism,* which presented severe distortion of the subject matter. Instead of using the traditional tools of perspective to replicate the images in the eye, cubists sought to paint what the *mind perceived* of the object—all sides at once. Like Stravinsky, cubists were influenced by the art of non-industrial cultures, in this case the beautifully carved masks used in African rituals. But cubism was not about beauty; it was a decided intellectual movement, meant to challenge the viewer to reassess his or her sense of perception. Cubism flickered out after World War I, but the next stages of modernism in art were even more abstract and antiromantic. The Russian painter Wassily Kandinsky (1866–1944) was probably the first to dispose of a subject in painting altogether; his works are simply about the theory of shapes and color. The Dutch painter Piet Mondrian (1872–1944) took this even further, eliminating all curved lines from his art. His works feature straight lines at 90-degree angles almost exclusively, with the

Cubism
Bauhaus
architecture

Modern dance

resulting boxes filled in with just two or three colors, usually the primary colors (yellow, red, or blue). Modern art was meant to be cool and crisp, erased of any emotional qualities, pure and uncluttered.

The same principles were at play in the creation of modern architecture. In 1919, Walter Gropius (1883–1969) founded the Bauhaus School of Architecture in Weimar, Germany, launching what would eventually be called the International Style of architecture. These modernist architects rejected the decoration found on buildings of the nineteenth century in favor of a simpler, straightforward design. Like the paintings of Mondrian, modern architecture emphasized geometric buildings made of reinforced concrete and glass, with little or no attempt to hide the structural elements of the building, as previous architectural styles had done. Many of the tall buildings found in American cities and universities are remnants of the International Style—clean, unadorned "glass boxes."

Modern dance was born about this time, and it, too, involved a sharp break with the past, as we have seen in our discussion of *The Rite of Spring.* One of the great figures of modern dance, Martha Graham (1895–1991), made it clear that these changes were very much related to the changes occurring in other

The exterior of the Bauhaus School at Dessau, Germany (1926).
Source: Getty Images, Inc. Hulton archive by Getty Images.

arts. "Like the modern painters and architects, we have stripped our medium of decorative unessentials," she said in 1930. "Just as fancy trimmings are no longer seen on buildings, so dancing is no longer padded. It is not pretty, but it is much more real."

The atonal phase of twentieth-century music emerged from the same antiromantic impulses as modern art, architecture, and dance—a move away from prettiness and emotional excess toward a clean, cool intellectualism. The result was perhaps the most radically new compositional style in the history of music.

THE ATONAL PHASE

*A*tonality—the lack of tonal center—had been creeping into music for a long time, at least since the middle of the nineteenth century. In the music of Richard Wagner (1813–1883), for example, there are long stretches where it is uncertain which pitch is the tonal center. Only in the first two decades of the twentieth century, however, was atonality completely embraced. Similar to modern art's rejection of a subject matter, modern music abandoned tonality, allowing no single note to serve as a "center of gravity." Indeed, a sense of tonal gravity was now rigorously avoided.

This abandonment of tonality was liberating for many composers, but it also presented a new set of problems. Tonality is not just a "gravitational" pull toward a single pitch; it also involves a complex harmonic system where certain kinds of chords usually follow other kinds of chords. Without the governing system of tonality, composers risked anarchy.

Eventually, the Viennese composer Arnold Schoenberg (see Musician Biography 14.2) created a substitute for tonality called the *twelve-tone method,* or *serialism.* In it, the twelve pitches within an octave are assigned a number, starting with zero and going through 11 (Figure 14.1).

And a *tone-row,* or series, is established with these numbers (Figure 14.2).

Twelve-tone method

Tone-row

Atonality

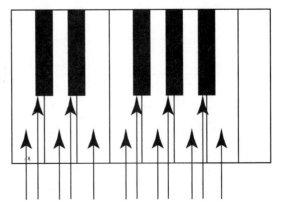

0 1 2 3 4 5 6 7 8 9 10 11

FIGURE 14.1: *The Twelve Pitches in an Octave, Assigned a Number.*

Numbers:	2	10	3	9	4	1	11	8	6	7	5	0
Pitches:	D	A#	D#	A	E	C#	B	G#	F#	G	F	C

FIGURE 14.2: *The Twelve Pitches Organized into a Row.*

This row becomes the basis for the composition. Composers can present the row in a linear fashion (creating a melody) or horizontally (creating harmony) or both. After presenting the row, composers can alter it in certain ways—transposing it up or down, playing it backwards (called a *retrograde row*) or upside-down (an *inverted row*), or some combination of these (Figure 14.3).

Note that this system, at least at this point, does not determine any other elements of the music, such as rhythm. This is the substructure of the composition, not the composition itself.

Retrograde Inverted

This serial system proved very intriguing to many composers. The fact that a pitch is not returned to until all other eleven pitches have been played makes them all sound equal in importance. This helps prevent listeners from expecting tonality. And the system's mathematical principles appealed to the logical and scientific orientation of the times.

Serialism slowly grew in popularity among composers, but never among listeners. After World War II it became the dominant compositional style for a generation (see "Serialist Phase," below), but only a

Original Form:

2	10	3	9	4	1	11	8	6	7	5	0
D	A#	D#	A	E	C#	B	G#	F#	G	F	C

Transposed:

4	0	5	11	6	3	1	10	8	9	7	2
E	C	F	B	F#	D#	C#	A#	G#	A	G	D

Retrograde:

0	5	7	6	8	11	1	4	9	3	10	2
C	F	G	F#	G#	B	C#	E	A	D#	A#	D

Inversion:

2	6	1	7	0	3	5	8	10	9	11	4
D	F#	C#	G	C	D#	F	G#	A#	A	B	E

Retrograde–Inversion:

4	11	9	10	8	5	3	0	7	1	6	2
E	B	A	A#	G#	F	D#	C	G	C#	F#	D

FIGURE 14.3: *The Row Used by Schoenberg in His String Trio, Op. 45, in Its Original Form, Then Transposed a step, Then the Original Row in Retrograde, Inversion, and Retrograde-Inversion.*

specialized taste for the audience, which never seemed to accept this system as a substitute for tonality. All during the atonal and serialist phases, other composers continued to write in a modified tonal system, creating music much gentler to the ear and much more warmly embraced by the audiences of the time. But for a time, the composers considered the most serious were all serialists.

Arnold Schoenberg. Photo by Sylvia Salmi. Source: CORBIS.

The Second Viennese School

MUSICIAN BIOGRAPHY 14.2:

ARNOLD SCHOENBERG *(1874—1951)*

Schoenberg, born in Vienna, was composing from early childhood, but only began formal music training as a teenager. His first works hewed to a late romantic idiom, but gradually became more removed from traditional tonality. He spent some of his early years as a cabaret musician in Berlin, then returned to Vienna in 1903 and began to teach composition. With his two most famous pupils, Alban Berg (1885–1935) and Anton Webern (1883–1945), he established what he called the *Second Viennese School* (Haydn, Mozart, and Beethoven had constituted the First Viennese School). They established a society for private performances to promote their atonal music and to ensure the music was played properly. Schoenberg developed the Twelve-tone Method only after 1920, and would continue to tinker with it for the rest of his life. His students Berg and Webern adopted very different versions of the Method.

Schoenberg was working in Berlin again when the Nazis came to power in 1933. Schoenberg, a Jew who had converted to Lutheranism back in 1898, was nonetheless compelled to leave Germany that year. He moved to Paris, where he converted back to Judaism, then settled in Los Angeles. From 1936 to 1945 he was a professor of music at the University of California, Los Angeles. In 1945 he suffered a heart attack, then retired and spent his final years composing.

LISTENING PREPARATION

Schoenberg, *Five Pieces for Orchestra*, Op. 16, No. 1, "Premonitions" (1909, rev. 1949).

Schoenberg's *Five Pieces for Orchestra* were written long before he devised the serial system. These were in-between years for Schoenberg, having abandoned tonality but not yet having found a permanent substitute. In these pieces, the binding force is often rhythmic, with a motive repeated and changed throughout. In this piece listen for a figure of four fast, equal notes, first heard in the low strings about a half a minute in:

If you have never heard atonal music before, listen through the entire piece at least two times before passing judgment. Atonality usually requires several listenings before understanding starts to settle in.

Refer to the Appendix at the back of the book for this Listening Activity's complete worksheet. Use the following section to make notes for yourself

LISTENING ACTIVITY 14.2:

Schoenberg, Five Pieces for Orchestra, *Op. 16, No. 1, "Premonitions" (CD 2/9)*

1. In the graph below, make an analysis of this piece in terms of tension, including CD timer information for at least three points of interest.

Tension Level ⟶

CD Time:

2. Describe what happens at these points of interest.

3. What do you think Schoenberg's intentions are with this music? Does he succeed?

POPULISM

Populism

Socialist realism

The atonal music of the Second Viennese School was only one of several concurrent trends in classical music in the early twentieth century. The French composer Maurice Ravel (1875–1937) and others continued to compose impressionist music in the style of Claude Debussy well into the 1920s (see Musician Biography 13.10). Ravel, along with Stravinsky, the Russian composer Sergei Prokofiev (1891–1953), and others also experimented with neo-classicism, using forms, genres, and other elements borrowed from the late baroque and classical periods intertwined with contemporary elements. Some composers, such as the Russian-born pianist-composer Sergei Rachmaninov (1873–1943), even continued to compose in a late romantic idiom, writing music of great virtuosity and emotional resonance.

The term *populism* in music can be applied to some or all of these divergent musical styles; what unifies them is an interest in composing music for ordinary people. For composers working in the Soviet Union, such as Dmitri Shostakovich (1906–1975), there was a kind of forced populism through what was called *socialist realism.* Stalin had declared in

1932 that all artwork should be relatively conformist and paint a happy picture of life in the Soviet Union, and that artists ignored this edict at their peril. But populism was naturally emerging across Europe and America, appearing in several different guises. The German composer Paul Hindemith (1895–1963) wrote operas and symphonic works, but also advocated *Gebrauchsmusik* ("music for use"), meaning works for amateurs and children to sing and perform, as well as music for film and radio. In the United States Ruth Crawford Seeger (1901–1953) began her career as a composer of atonal music, then turned her energies toward teaching music to children and collecting and arranging American folk songs.

TWENTIETH-CENTURY NATIONALISM

The collecting and arranging of folk songs is an activity closely related to another musical trend, *nationalism,* also described in Chapter 13. And in truth, there was usually a great deal of overlap between nationalism and populism; if a composer is interested in writing music for his or her people, he or she is often also interested in writing music that celebrates their nation. Indeed, nationalism was probably just as prominent in the twentieth century as it had been in the nineteenth, although the nations may have been different. Some of the twentieth-century composers who explored nationalism in music included Jean Sibelius (1865–1957; Finland); Ralph Vaughan Williams (1872–1958; Great Britain); Manuel de Falla (1876–1946; Spain); Bèla Bartòk (1881–1945; Hungary); Heitor Villa-Lobos (1887–1959; Brazil); Benjamin Britten (1913–1976; Great Britain); and Alberto Ginastera (1916–1983; Argentina).

Nationalism hit the United States in the 1930s. Although the United States had produced excellent composers since its founding, only in the twentieth century did they begin to make an international mark. One of the reasons for this may have been the international popularity of jazz at this time

Gebrauchsmusik

Nationalism

Aaron Copland ("COPE-land") (1900–1990)

MUSICIAN BIOGRAPHY 14.3:

AARON COPLAND *(1900—1990)*

Copland was the son of a Jewish department store owner from Brooklyn, a member of a large, happy extended family. Copland started piano lessons at age eleven, first from his sister, then three years later from a local teacher. At sixteen he moved on to a composition teacher and decided to dedicate his life to music. Soon, he was composing adventurous modern music beyond the comprehension of his instructor—music combining atonality with elements of jazz. In 1921 he began a three-year course of study with one of the greatest music teachers of the twentieth century, Nadia Boulanger (see Sidenote, on the next page) and by the late 1920s his music was being performed by major orchestras on two continents.

Copland's musical style shifted from atonal to populist with his orchestral piece *El salón México* (1936), depicting a bar in Mexico. His most famous works are three ballets written on American themes, *Billy the Kid* (1940), *Rodeo* (1942), and *Appalachian Spring* (1944). He also wrote several other popular works at this time, including *Lincoln Portrait* (1942) and *Fanfare for the Common Man* (1942), as well as film scores and two operas.

In the 1950s his music turned atonal again, and he experimented with serialism. He also increased his activity as a conductor—he was usually a guest conductor, brought in to lead his own works, but an effective one. He also worked as a teacher, a lecturer, and an author of several books about listening to music.

Copland was the first American composer to achieve a great amount of acknowledgment, and his greatest achievement may have been how he conducted himself in light of this success. He remained dedicated to his fellow American composers, directing many of them to study with his beloved teacher in France, and helping them out at home by organizing concerts of new music and using his connections to promote their careers. Almost every important American composer of his generation and the next came in contact with Copland and benefited from his kindness and generosity.

SIDENOTE: THE FRENCH CONNECTION

Nadia Boulanger (1887–1979) was a gifted composer as a young woman, but when her sister Lili was born (1893–1918) she took it on herself to train her. When Lili died young, Nadia felt a sacred trust to continue teaching in Lili's memory, and gave up composing forever. She studied at the Paris Conservatory, then taught at the American Conservatory at Fontainebleau (starting in 1921), where Aaron Copland studied, becoming its director in 1950. Later she became professor of composition at the Paris Conservatory (1945). The list of her students after Copland is a veritable who's-who of American composers, among them Virgil Thomson, Roy Harris, and Philip Glass. Boulanger was ruthless and demanding of her students, but also had an uncanny ability to understand her students' particular genius, always pushing them to find their own voice as composers rather than replicate another. Her students universally credit her with their most important musical education.

Nadia Boulanger at Southern Illinois University as a guest instructor advising an individual musician. Photo by Al Fenn.
Source: TimePix.

LISTENING PREPARATION

Copland, *Appalachian Spring*, excerpt, Section 7 (1944).

Appalachian Spring is the most famous of Copland's three American ballets. The great philanthropist Elizabeth Sprague Coolidge (1864–1953) commissioned the score for Martha Graham (1895–1991), then the most experimental and significant choreographer alive. She was unafraid of doing abstract things, both musically and choreographically. The theme of *Appalachian Spring* is pioneer America, depicting a celebration surrounding the building of a farmhouse in rural Pennsylvania in the late 1800s, and featuring a young farmer and his wife. In the following excerpt, Copland makes use of an old shaker tune called "Simple Gifts," which we have heard in the Elements section of this text. The words of the original hymn are:

> *'Tis a gift to be simple, 'tis a gift to be free,*
> *'Tis a gift to come down where we ought to be.*
> *And when you find yourself in a place just right,*
> *'Twill be in the valley of love and delight.*
>
> *When true simplicity is gained,*
> *To bow and to bend we shan't be ashamed.*
> *But to turn, turn, 'twill be our delight,*
> *And by turning, turning, we come 'round right.*

The ballet was originally scored for a string quartet plus bass, three woodwinds, and a piano; what we hear in this excerpt is a version expanded to be played by a full symphony orchestra in concert.

Copland's score earned him a Pulitzer Prize in 1944.

Martha Graham in the ballet, "Appalachian Spring." Photo by Jerry Cooke.
Source: CORBIS.

Refer to the Appendix at the back of the book for this Listening Activity's complete worksheet. Use the following section to make notes for yourself

Copland, Appalachian Spring, Section 7 (ballet) (CD 2/10)

1. What instrument leads in the presentation of the melody at the beginning? _____
2. What instrument dominates the melody in the second presentation? _____
3. Describe what happens when the tune is presented a third time.

4. After this, we hear a short interlude, with a change of key and a slight increase in tempo, then the tune appears again. What family of instruments presents it this time? _____
5. At what CD time does this begin? _____
6. During this presentation of the tune, we occasionally hear rapid runs going up and down, in the background. What instruments play this figure? _____
7. The second half of the tune is now repeated at a slower tempo. What family of instruments takes over at this point? _____
8. Describe how Copland presents the tune for the final time.

9. Fill in the following table, outlining this whole section.

TUNE PRESENTATIONS	CD TIME	INSTRUMENT FAMILY	DYNAMIC LEVEL	TEMPO
First	0:00			
Second				
Third				
Brief interlude				
Fourth				
(Second Half Repeat)				
Fifth and final				

(see Chapter 8), which prepared European ears to take American music seriously for the first time. It was also only in the 1930s that most American composers attempted to find their own voice rather than just imitating the music of European composers. Whatever the reason, American composers burst onto the international scene in the 1930s and 1940s, led by Aaron Copland.

SERIALISM

*J*ust as in the other arts, the end of World War II in 1945 marked the end of one era in music and launched another. Typical of the ideological extremes of the century, many composers now reacted strongly against the principles of populism. The American composer Milton Babbitt (b. 1916), in his famous magazine article "Who Cares If You Listen?," first printed in the magazine *High Fidelity* in 1958, advocated that composers withdraw from the "public world" to the universities, where they could enjoy the "complete elimination of the public and social aspects of musical composition." Composers, now mostly university professors at American research institutions, began writing for each other rather than the public, just as their colleagues in other university departments were writing articles only understood by a handful of specialists around the globe.

Composers of this generation expanded Schoenberg's twelve-tone method in their music. No longer did a series of twelve numbers simply provide the pitch material for a piece; the same row, or ones related to it mathematically, could be used to determine pitch duration, dynamics, form, instrumentation, and other elements of the music. This all-encompassing mathematical system has been called *total serialism,* since it can determine the basis for all aspects of a composition. It is important to understand that composers were rarely slavish about adhering to this system. Indeed, every composer of merit during this period devised his or her own version of serialism, and so to the trained ear subtle differences between various composers can be discerned. Some serialist composers used early versions of synthesizers, while others wrote for traditional instruments, and still others wrote for a combination of electronic and traditional instruments or alternated between these two kinds of performing forces—so this provides another distinction between serialist composers.

While serialism dominated the North American and European compositional scene from about 1950 through the 1970s, it is important to realize that there were many composers who never went that route, such as the famous composer-conductor Leonard Bernstein (see Musician Biography 15.6) and Samuel Barber (1910–1981). And during the heyday of serialism, mischievous experimentalists such as John Cage (see Musician Biography 14.4) were following a wildly different, rather irreverent approach to music composition.

Total serialism

Milton Babbitt (b. 1916)

EXPERIMENTALISM

*E*xperimental composers usually bear very little similarity to one another, except in their commitment to compose in new ways. New England composer Charles Ives (1874–1954), who worked for most of his life as an insurance salesman and composed as a hobby, was one of the first composers to use *bitonality,* two different tonal centers at the same time. The French-born American composer

4. Describe the other two vocal parts in this section.

5. At what CD time do you hear even more voices enter in this section? _____
6. What are they doing?

7. How does this section end?

8. Listen to the selection again (all three CD tracks), and write a paragraph describing how the music unfolds and what sorts of feelings it evokes.

late 1960s that rejected, to some degree, the stark modernist structures then so dominant. American Architects such as Philip Johnson (b. 1906), originally a modernist, and Robert Venturi (b. 1925) began to revive architectural elements from the past, such as columns and cornices, in their skyscraper designs. The movement really took hold in the 1980s and 1990s and spread to other art forms, including the visual arts and literature. In all the arts, postmodernism is characterized by the use of parody and pastiche, and by the playful interaction between "high" and "low" art and contemporary and historical styles. Postmodernism has been criticized as shallow and undisciplined, but the artists who have embraced it enjoy what they call the messy vitality of this style, and argue that interaction with popular culture is inevitable in our age.

There are enough parallels between art and architecture and current trends in art music to argue that we are now in a postmodernist phase in classical music history. Just as architects rejected the cool functionalism of the "glass box," with its heavy philosophical baggage, so too have many composers abandoned both atonality and serialism, returning to tonality just as architects returned to decorativeness and ornamentation. When atonality *does* appear in contemporary music it is often used as part of a pastiche, just one of several historical styles blended together, often whimsically. Granted, art-music composers have used pastiche all throughout music history, but never with such fervor as today. World music and popular music, too, show up in recent classical compositions, and in some cases the line between popular and art music is starting to blur.

Some of the minimalist composers of the 1960s and 1970s, such as Steve Reich and John Adams, have moved decisively toward postmodernism, as have other composers such as David del Tredici (b. 1937) and the Estonian composer Arvo Pärt (b. 1935). It has also been arguably the best time in music history for women composers, who have finally gotten the acknowledgment they have long deserved, innovative artists such as Pauline Oliveros (b. 1932) and Ellen Taaffe Zwilich (b. 1939), the first woman to win the Pulitzer Prize in music (for her First Symphony, 1983).

Checkpoint

The twentieth-century was a time of great upheaval for classical music. Not only was it challenged by the rise of popular culture and new technology, but also within classical music itself there were a series of upheavals that pushed the music in radically different directions over the course of the century. This chapter grouped these into five phases—*atonal, populist, serialist, experimentalist,* and *postmodernist*—but many of these phases were simultaneous, at least to some degree. To a large extent these trends in classical music paralleled trends in architecture and other arts. We also looked at the lives of four composers, starting with Stravinsky, the dominant figure of classical music in the first part of the century.

Now that the century has ended, we are compelled to look forward as well as back. The twentieth century produced music of great extremes; will the twenty-first century be similar? Or will we begin new trends in music as yet unimagined? Whatever the case, I urge you to take a stand in the inevitable cultural debate that will transpire, and let your tastes and wishes be known. Only through active participation can we make our culture the best it can be.

KEY TERMS

World War I
The Great Depression
World War II
The Cold War
Atonal phase
Populist phase
Serialist phase
Experimentalist phase
Post-modernist phase
Radio
Records
Movies and television
Neo-classicism
Bitonality

Modernism
Cubism
Bauhaus architecture
Modern dance
Atonality
Twelve-tone Method
Tone-row
Retrograde
Inverted
The Second Viennese School
Populism
Socialist Realism
Gebrauchsmusik
Nationalism

Total Serialism
Dada
Surrealism
Aleatoric music
Electronic Music
Synthesizer
Recording technology
Magnetic Tape
Tape Loops
Electronic music concerts
Minimalism
Postmodernism

Music Combined with Other Arts

Music is a temporal art, one which unfolds over time. The visual arts, in contrast, are spatial, making use of a canvas or the three-dimensional space of sculpture. Literary art forms may involve time, but still allow the reader to enjoy the material at his or her own pace. In music, time is ordered and controlled, and because of this a natural affinity exists between music and other temporal arts such as theater and dance. This affinity stretches back to the dramas of Ancient Greece and beyond—perhaps to the very beginnings of these three art forms. In this chapter we will explore some of the ways in which music interacts with its sister art forms: dance, theater, and a relative newcomer, film.

When these art forms come together the result is usually a hybrid between the two original parent forms, a hybrid from which neither parent can be removed. Ballet without either music or dance would no longer be the art form we call ballet. The same is true of the marriages of music and theater known as operas and musicals. This is *not* true, however, of film. Although music has been an important part of films even in the days of silent movies, when the "soundtrack" was performed live in the theaters, we cannot say that movies without music are no longer movies. There have been experimental films that have dispensed with music altogether or used it minimally. Nevertheless, the role of music in film is an important one.

Just as one cannot understand music without listening to it, one cannot understand the following genres without truly experiencing them. Most of what we will talk about is amply represented in the home video and DVD market, but these are but pale shadows compared to the live experience. Again, this is less true in the case of films, but even here we must acknowledge that movie music is usually written with the sound systems of movie theaters in mind, not the speakers on a television—to say nothing of the importance of the visual impact of the big screen. In the case of opera, musicals, and dance, the splendor and excitement of a live performance is an integral part of each genre's essence, something that cannot be fully replicated through videorecording.

MUSIC AND DANCE

*I*t has been said that the dance is the oldest art form, that primitive men and women moved their bodies in imitation of the animals of their world, perhaps telling the story of a hunt or perhaps just trying to access the divine spirit of the wild. If this is true, it must also be the case that music appeared soon after, for dancing gravitates to regular rhythms, beats which may have been simply supplied by the clapping hands of the onlookers. This is not to say that dance *requires* music, for it does not; just that from its beginning dance *probably* had some form of musical accompaniment. Likewise, prehistoric music was probably associated regularly with some kind of movement. If we look at nonindustrial societies, in fact, we find that there are often no clear divisions between music and dance; the music is supplied by the jangles worn around the ankles of the dancers, or by the dancers' singing. This music/dance art form is usually associated with some kind of religious ceremony.

Over time around the world these intertwined elements gradually separated out: dance and music have taken on an existence separate from ritual (although ceremonies still involve movement and music), and a separation between musician and dancer started to emerge, with musicians holding their instruments around the periphery of the dance. In many cultures, too, there eventually developed a distinction between *social dance* and *theatrical dance*. The social dance is the dance of the people, more or less unschooled and spontaneous, while theatrical dance involves professional dancers presenting carefully planned movements before an audience.

Social dance and theatrical dance

Plenty o' Nuttin'," "It Ain't Necessarily So," and "Bess, You Is My Woman Now." The opera, featuring an all-black cast, found only middling success on Broadway until after Gershwin's death.

Gershwin struggled throughout his career with what might be called an inferiority complex. He longed to be taken seriously as a composer, even taking lessons with great European composers such as Maurice Ravel and Arnold Schoenberg to fill in the gaps in his knowledge. His music, which lay at the nexus of classical music and jazz, was never fully accepted by either camp. Today, however, his willingness to break out of the confines of style categories is broadly admired, as are his remarkable gifts as a melody writer.

In 1936 Gershwin moved to Hollywood to write songs for movies and to enjoy the rowdy lifestyle of the rich and famous. He was at the peak of his abilities when he suddenly died of a brain hemorrhage at the age of 38.

Breakthrough Musicals: At the end of the Roaring Twenties musical theater began to change. The first breakthrough musical, *Show Boat,* with music by Jerome Kern (1885–1945) and words by Oscar Hammerstein II (1895–1960), premiered in 1927. Instead of witty commentary on contemporary life, *Show Boat* was set in the nineteenth century. Instead of a silly plot stringing together precomposed songs, *Show Boat* featured songs integrated into a thoughtful, more serious storyline, one which dared to take on the touchy theme of interracial relations. A second breakthrough musical, also with words by Hammerstein, and with music by Richard Rodgers (1902–1979), was *Oklahoma!* of 1943. This musical extended the principals of *Show Boat,* featuring a nostalgic look at bygone America, songs even more integrated with the plot, and a story which substituted earnestness and homey values for the cleverness of early musicals. Most of the successful musicals of the 1940s and 1950s followed in this mold.

"Oklahoma!" Photo by Michael Le Poer Trench.
Source: The Image Works.

MUSICIAN BIOGRAPHY 15.6:

*L*EONARD BERNSTEIN *(1918—1990)*

Bernstein, one of the great figures of twentieth-century American musical life, was a multi-talented musician who, like Gershwin, was interested in the intersections between classical music and popular culture. Born in Lawrence, Massachusetts, Bernstein studied at Harvard University, then at the Curtis Institute, focusing his attention at first on classical piano performance, then orchestral conducting. He made a spectacular debut with the Boston Symphony Orchestra in 1943, stepping in at the last minute when the scheduled guest conductor was ill. Bernstein went on to become the first American-born music director of the prestigious New York Philharmonic (from 1958–1969), by which time he was the dominant orchestral conductor of his generation.

Leonard Bernstein conducting the Boston Symphony Orchestra.
Source: CORBIS.

Meanwhile, Bernstein was also making a name for himself as a composer of both serious and more popular music. He wrote piano music, symphonies, choral music, and other works in the classical style, and also wrote Broadway musicals and light operas, starting with *On the Town* (1944). His greatest success as a composer came with the epic musical *West Side Story* (1957), a retelling of Shakespeare's *Romeo and Juliet* set in modern New York, created in close collaboration with choreographer Jerome Robbins and lyricist Stephen Sondheim.

Bernstein also believed strongly in music education, developing a popular show on television in the 1950s to help the public understand classical music, and writing popular books on music. Bernstein died of lung disease in his early seventies.

NAME_____

LISTENING ACTIVITY 5.1:

Identifying Instruments

*I*n the list below are several excerpts from your recordings. Listen to the specified segment on the CD track, then determine the *predominant instrument* in the excerpt (usually the one carrying the melody). List the instrument's *family* (voice, woodwinds, brass, etc.) and the *range*—whether it's a *high, medium,* or *low* member of that family. (If none of the choices applies, write in *n/a*.)

EXCERPT	FAMILY	RANGE
1. Smetana, "The Moldau," (CD 2/6) 0:00–0:30		
2. Smetana, "The Moldau," (CD 2/6) 1:00–1:30		
3. Puccini, *Che Gelida Manina,* (CD 2/15) 0:00–0:30		
4. Copland, *Appalachian Spring,* (CD 2/10) 1:53–2:15		
5. Meyer, Listening Activity 2.2, track 2		
6. Parker, "Mohawk," (CD 1/8) 0:40–1:40		
7. Puente, *Mambo Guzon,* (CD 1/11) 1:56–2:00		
8. Berry, "Johnny B. Goode," (CD 1/10) 0:00–0:15		
9. Vivaldi, "Spring," I, (CD 1/13) 0:30–1:00		
10. Brahms, Intermezzo, (CD 2/5) 0:00–0:30		

271

Stanza 4:

3. Based on what you wrote above, construct a narrative of the events Robert Johnson describes.

4. How does the music—both the guitar work and the vocal delivery—correspond to the meaning of the words? Refer to specific lines of the text in your answer.

LISTENING ACTIVITY 7.2:

Bessie Smith, "Poor Man's Blues" (CD 1/2)

1. On your first listening, mark the CD times for the start of each line:

0.00   Introduction

0.12   Mister rich man, rich man, open up your heart and mind,

_____ Mister rich man, rich man, open up your heart and mind,

_____ Give the poor man a chance, help stop these hard, hard times.

_____ While you're living in your mansion, you don't know what hard times mean.

_____ While you're living in your mansion, you don't know what hard times mean.

_____ Poor working man's wife is starving; your wife is living like a queen.

_____ Please listen to my pleadin', 'cause I can't stand these hard times long.

_____ Aw, listen to my pleadin', 'cause I can't stand these hard times long.

_____ They'll make an honest man do things that you know is wrong.

_____ Poor man fought all the battles, he'd fight again today.

_____ Poor man fought all the battles, he'd fight again today.

_____ He would do anything you ask him in the name of the U.S.A.

_____ Now the war is over; poor man must live the same as you.

_____ Now the war is over; poor man must live the same as you.

_____ If it wasn't for the poor man, mister rich man, what would you do?

2. Does Smith sing the same notes in each verse? If not, where does she change the melody?

7. The next solo is divided between the pianist and the bass player. Describe Thelonious Monk's piano solo.

8. The final solo is by Russell on the bass. What other instrument(s) do you hear during the bass solo?

9. How is the piece ended?

10. Make a diagram of the entire piece, as you have done before, indicating which instrument takes the solos.

LISTENING ACTIVITY 8.6:

Miles Davis, "Flamenco Sketches"

1. On your first listening, record the CD timer information for the start of each solo:

   Muted Trumpet: _____

   Tenor Saxophone: _____

   Alto Saxophone: _____

   Piano: _____

   Muted Trumpet: _____

2. Each of these players does a different thing with this raw material. How is each solo different in melodic contour, mood, and other musical characteristics?

   First Trumpet Solo:

   Tenor Sax Solo:

   Alto Sax Solo:

LISTENING ACTIVITY 10.2:

Little Joe & La Familia, "Margarita" (CD 1/12)

1. What is the meter of this song? _____

2. Is the tempo closest to (circle one): 50 BPM 100 BPM or 150 BPM?

3. What family of instruments dominates at the beginning of the song? _____

4. Name an aspect of this song that connects it with Anglo-country music.

5. At what CD time do you hear the tejano accordion come in? _____

6. What is the general mood of this song? _____

7. How is this achieved?

7. At what CD time do you hear the next ritornello? _____ Is it (circle one): R1, R2, or R3?

8. After this ritornello, the orchestra plays another new section, but this time preparing us for a new solo section, one in which the orchestra and the soloists interact frequently. What part of the poem do you think this section best corresponds to?

9. At what time do you hear the next ritornello (R2)? _____

10. What is different about R2 this time?

11. After a rather languid solo by the two violins, we hear another ritornello. At what CD time does this occur? _____ Is it (circle one): R1, R2, or R3?

12. One last solo, and we arrive back in the home key and a final ritornello. At what CD time does this last ritornello begin? _____ Is it (circle one): R1, R2, or R3? How is this different from the previous ritornellos?

13. Fill in the following chart:

SONNET LINE(S)	CD TIME (BEGINNING)	SOLO OR ORCHESTRA?
Spring has arrived, and festively	0:00	Orchestra
The birds greet it with cheerful song		
And the brooks, caressed by soft breezes, Murmur sweetly as they flow.		
The sky is covered with a black mantel, Lightning and thunder announce a storm.		
When the storm dies away to silence, the birds		
Return with their melodious songs.		

LISTENING ACTIVITY 12.2:

Handel, "Hallelujah" Chorus from Messiah (CD 1/14)

This chorus features just five lines of text, repeated and tossed around in all sorts of combinations. For the purpose of analyzing this music, we will number the lines of text. Since Handel often splits up the last two lines, we will number these (a) and (b):

(1) Hallelujah!

(2) For the Lord God omnipotent reigneth

(3) The kingdom of this world is become the Kingdom of our Lord and of His Christ

(4a) And He shall reign

(4b) Forever and ever

(5a) King of Kings

(5b) And Lord of Lords!

Handel alternates setting the music in monophonic, homophonic, and polyphonic texture. Your job in the exercise below will be to analyze the entire movement for texture. In vocal music, monophonic texture occurs when everybody is singing the same melody together; homophonic texture is when everybody is singing the same words at the same time, in the same rhythm, but with different notes; and polyphonic texture is when two or more groups of singers are weaving together separate melodies (and often separate words). The underscored lines indicate the start of a new section. For each line of text, write in whether the texture is monophonic, homophonic, or polyphonic:

CD TIME	LINE NUMBER	TEXTURE?
0:00	Orchestral introduction	n/a
0:06	(1) "Hallelujah! Hallelujah . . ."	homophonic
0:24	(2) "For the Lord God omnipotent reigneth"	
0:30	(1) "Hallelujah! Hallelujah . . ."	
0:35	(2) "For the Lord God omnipotent reigneth"	
0:41	(1) "Hallelujah! Hallelujah . . ."	
0:46	(2 and 1 together)	
0:53	(2 and 1)	
1:02	(2 and 1)	

CD TIME	LINE NUMBER	TEXTURE?
1:12	(3) "The kingdom of this world . . ."	
1:30	(4a and b) "And He shall reign forever and ever"	
1:35	(4a and b) "And He shall reign forever and ever"	
1:41	(4a and b) "And He shall reign forever and ever"	
1:46	(4a and b) "And He shall reign forever and ever"	
1:52	(5a) "King of Kings"	
1:54	(4b and 1) "Forever and ever, Hallelujah!"	
1:59	(5b) "And Lord of Lords"	
2:01	(4b and 1) "Forever and ever, Hallelujah!"	
2:06	(5a) "King of Kings"	
2:08	(4b and 1) "Forever and ever, Hallelujah!"	
2:12	(5b) "And Lord of Lords"	
2:14	(4b and 1) "Forever and ever, Hallelujah!"	
2:19	(5a) "King of Kings"	
2:21	(4b and 1) "Forever and ever, Hallelujah!"	
2:26	(5b) "And Lord of Lords"	
2:28	(5a and b) "King of Kings and Lord of Lords"	
2:33	(4a and b) "And He shall reign forever and ever"	
2:38	(4a and b) "And He shall reign forever and ever"	
2:44	(5a) "King of Kings"	
2:46	(4b) Forever and ever	
2:48	(5b) "And Lord of Lords"	
2:50	(1) "Hallelujah! Hallelujah . . ."	
2:53	(4a and b) "And He shall reign forever and ever"	homophonic
3:00	(5a and b) "King of Kings and Lord of Lords"	
3:04	(5a and b) "King of Kings and Lord of Lords"	
3:09	(4a and b) "And He shall reign forever and ever"	
3:15	(5a, 5b, 4b and 1)	
3:26	(1) "Hallelujah!"	

LISTENING ACTIVITY 12.3:

Bach, Fugue in G Minor, "Little" (CD 1/15)

Listen through the entire fugue once, paying close attention to the subject entries, then answer the following questions on your second pass through the piece.

1. Fill in the CD timer information for the subject entry of each voice. Note that after the second voice enters, there is a brief interlude (called a *codetta*) before the third voice enters.

Voice 1 <u>0:00</u>

  Voice 2 ____

    Voice 3 ____

      Voice 4 (Organ pedals) ____

2. At what CD time does the first episode begin? _____

3. The next subject entry is cut off, then continued by another voice. At what time does this begin? _____

4. The next subject entry occurs at 1:52, in Voice 3. What is different about this one?

5. When does the next subject entry begin? _____ And it is taken by which of the four voices? _____

6. In the middle of this subject entry, you can hear the upper voice trilling (alternating quickly between two notes). At what CD time do you hear this trill begin and end? _____ and _____.

7. Around the 2:54 mark, we hear the next subject entry, in the highest voice. Then follows the longest episode, followed by the final subject entry, in the lowest voice. At what CD time does this final subject entry begin? _____

8. Why do you think Bach made the episode before the final subject entry so much longer than previous episodes?

LISTENING ACTIVITY 12.4:

Mozart, Eine kleine Nachtmusik, *K. 525, III: Minuet and Trio (CD 1/16)*

1. How many measures long is the "a" section of this minuet? Remember that minuets are generally in a moderate tempo triple meter. Note that it begins with a pick-up, so when you hear the first note, say "three," then begin counting the first measure ("One-two-three, One-two-three," etc.) _____

2. At the end of the "a" section it's easy to get lost in the counting, because different beats of the measure (other than the downbeat) keep getting emphasized. What is the term used to describe this shifting emphasis? _____

3. Next, you hear a repeat of the "a" section. Is it an exact repeat? _____

4. Now, we move on to the second part of the rounded-binary structure, the "b" section then the "a'" section. How many measures long is the "b" section? You will know you have reached the end of the "b" section when you hear a repeat of the "a" material. Here again, start counting the "b" section with the pick-up. _____

5. How many measures long is the "a'" section? _____

6. After the repeat of the second half of the minuet, we hear the start of the trio. How many measures long is the "c" section? _____ Again, we start with a pick-up.

7. How many measures long is the "d" section? _____ And the "c'" section? _____

8. After the trio, we hear the repeat of the minuet. Does this minuet and trio follow the standard form described above? _____

LISTENING ACTIVITY 12.5:

Mozart, Variations on "Ah vous dirais-je, Maman" (excerpt): Theme and Variations form (CD 1/17)

1. We begin with the theme. How many measures long is the "a" section of the rounded binary form? _____

2. At what CD time do we begin the "b" section of the rounded binary form ("Up above the world so high")? _____

3. How many measures long is the "b" section? You will know you have reached the end of the "b" section when you hear the first variation begin. _____

4. At what CD time does the *first variation* begin? _____

5. What is the most striking difference between this variation and the theme?

6. After the pianist plays a variation on the "b, a′" section, we begin the *second variation*. At what CD time does this new variation begin? _____

7. In this variation, the left hand of the pianist is playing fast notes. What is the *right hand* doing?

8. The *third variation* begins at about CD time 1:25. Describe the differences between this variation and the ones that preceded it.

9. The *fourth variation* begins at what CD time? _____

10. The *fifth variation* begins at about CD time 2:20. Describe the cluster of this variation.

11. When does the *sixth variation* start on the CD time? _____

12. Describe this variation.

LISTENING ACTIVITY 12.6:

Haydn, Concerto in E-Flat Major for Trumpet and Orchestra, III: Rondo form (CD 1/21)

1. In this rondo, the orchestra presents the rondo theme first, then the solo trumpet. At what CD time does the trumpet present the "A" theme? _____

2. The "B" section begins around CD time 1:09. How would you describe the trumpet part in this section?

3. At what CD time do we hear the next reiteration of the "A" theme? _____

4. After the trumpet presents the "A" theme, the orchestra takes over, then changes the tonal center and moves into a "C" section, starting as a variation of the "A" theme (at about 2:07). How would you describe the "C" section?

5. At what CD time do we hear the next reiteration of the "A" theme? _____

LISTENING ACTIVITY 13.1:

Beethoven, Symphony No. 5 in C Minor, Op. 67, I, Allegro con Brio: Sonata Form (CD 2/1)

At the beginning of this movement we hear the famous motive, with the final note held longer. The motive then repeats at a lower pitch. An illustration of the beginning might look like this:

After that, Beethoven starts to stack up the motive, piling it up until it reaches a high note, then starting low and stacking it up again.

1. How many iterations of the motive are heard in each "stacking?" _____

2. After these two stackings, the motive gets repeated several times over a long *crescendo,* culminating in three loud chords with the violins holding out a single note. At what CD time does this final chord occur? _____

3. Now, we hear another presentation of the motive with the last note held, as in the beginning. After this, the motive gets stacked *downward* two times. How many iterations of the motive are heard in these reverse "stackings?" _____

4. Again, the motive gets repeated several times over a long *crescendo,* but now we are changing keys to major (the *bridge* of the exposition). You will know we have finished the modulation when the French horns play the motive in major, now expanded to six notes, rather than four:

   At what CD time does this occur? _____

5. We have now arrived at the second theme of the exposition, more lyrical and calm. Soon, however, the intensity starts to build again, leading to a more triumphant sounding subtheme (2b). At what CD time does this new idea occur? _____

6. At the end of the expositions of the sonata form there is usually a closing section. In this case, the closing material is drawn from the main motive. Where do you think the closing subsection begins? _____ (Hint: listen through until you hear the exposition repeating, then go back and try again.)

16. How does the movement make you feel? How do you think Beethoven achieves this emotional response? Refer to specific sections of the movement in your response.

LISTENING ACTIVITY 13.2:

Schubert, Gretchen am Spinnrade *(CD 2/2)*

1. On your first listening, follow both the original German and the English translation closely, and mark the CD time for the start of each stanza. You will fill in the right-hand column in a moment.

CD TIME	GERMAN	ENGLISH	DYNAMIC LEVEL
	Meine Ruh ist hin Mein Herz ist schwer Ich finde sie nimmer Und nimmermehr.	My heart is sad, My peace is over; I find it never, And nevermore.	
	Wo ich ihn nicht hab' Ist mir das Grab, Die ganze Welt Ist mir vergällt.	When he is gone, The grave I see; The whole wide world Is soured for me.	
	Mein armer Kopf Ist mir verrückt, Mein armer Sinn Ist mir zerstückt.	Alas, my head Is well-nigh crazed; My feeble mind Is sore amazed.	
	Meine Ruh ist hin, Mein Herz ist schwer, Ich finde sie nimmer Und nimmermehr.	My heart is sad, My peace is over; I find it never, And nevermore.	
	Nach ihm nur schau ich Zum Fenster hinaus, Nach ihm nur geh ich Aus dem Haus.	For him, from the window Alone I spy; For him alone From home go I.	
	Sein hoher Gang, Sein' edle Gestalt, Seines Mundes Lächeln, Seiner Augen Gewalt,	His lofty step, His noble form, His mouth's sweet smile, His glances warm,	
	Und seiner Rede Zauberfluß, Sein Händedruck, Und ach, sein Kuß!	His voice so fraught With magic bliss, His hand's soft pressure, And, ah—his kiss!	

CD TIME	GERMAN	ENGLISH	DYNAMIC LEVEL
	Meine Ruh ist hin,	My heart is sad,	
	Mein Herz ist schwer,	My peace is over;	
	Ich finde sie nimmer	I find it never,	
	Und nimmermehr.	And nevermore.	
	Mein Busen drängt	My breast yearns	
	Sich nach ihm hin	For his form so fair;	
	Ach dürft ich fassen	Ah, could I clasp him	
	Und halten ihn,	and hold him there!	
	Und küssen ihn,	My kisses sweet	
	So wie ich wollt,	Should stop his breath,	
	An seine Küssen	And beneath his kisses	
	Vergehen sollt!	I'd sink in death!	
	(Meine Ruh ist hin,	(My heart is sad,	
	Mein Herz ist schwer . . .)	My peace is over . . .)	

2. On your next time through the song, listen for the dynamic level of the music. At any particular line in the stanzas, is the dynamic level the *same, increasing,* or *decreasing* compared to the previous line? Make note of this in the right-hand column next to each line of text (at least once per stanza, more if necessary).

3. Write a paragraph describing how Schubert illustrates and amplifies the meaning of the text through music, citing particular points in the song as examples.

LISTENING ACTIVITY 13.3:

Berlioz, Symphonie Fantastique, *Op. 14, V, "Dream of a Witches' Sabbath" (CD 2/3)*

1. Describe the first minute of this movement. What musical events occur? What effect does Berlioz seem to be after? Refer to CD times and instrumental families in your answer.

2. The *idèe fixe* appears at about 1:22, played by a squeaky clarinet. In previous movements it had been elegant and stately, but now it sounds shrill and crooked. What happens at the end of the first presentation of this melody?

3. Soon, the *idèe fixe* is presented again, this time with an intentionally crude woodwind accompaniment, complete with a bubbling bassoon underneath. Gradually the full orchestra joins in, leading us haltingly to the next section, marked by church bells. At what CD time do the church bells come in? _____

4. Next, we hear a medieval church chant called *dies irae,* which was sung at funerals and associated with death. It is played by the bassoons and an obscure brasslike instrument called the *ophecleide,* now no longer used, in stately long notes, starting at CD time 3:23. In what texture do these instruments play (circle one): polyphonic   homophonic   monophonic?

5. Then, the rest of the brass section responds (at about CD time 3:45). In what texture do these instruments play (circle one): polyphonic   homophonic   monophonic?

6. The high woodwinds and strings—playing *pizzicato*—now respond, leading into more of the *dies irae,* now accompanied by low strings *pizzicato.* When the *dies irae* continues, what CD time are we at? _____

7. These three elements (the solemn *dies irae*, the response by the brass section, and the carping woodwinds and *pizzicato* strings) alternate several times, building in intensity until we arrive at the next section, the "Witches' Round Dance," with a new theme we have only heard in fragmented form before, now played by the cellos and basses (starting at about 5:16). What kind of emotional effect do you think Berlioz was trying to achieve here?

8. After several minutes of this, the music changes. We hear four loud brass chords (at about CD time 6:20, played in a rhythm similar to the opening motive of Beethoven's Fifth Symphony—short-short-short-LONG), followed by a falling line in woodwinds and high strings. This repeats several times on different pitches, then the music seems to disintegrate. We hear a hint of the *dies irae* theme played by the cellos (at about 7:01), then a moment later by the basses. Describe what follows, beginning at CD time 7:16 through about 7:45.

9. You should be hearing a buildup now to some big chords, then the *dies irae* and "Witches' Round Dance" themes get combined. At what CD time does this combination begin? _____

10. Soon, Berlioz introduces another of his famous orchestration effects: he asks the violins and violas to strike their strings with the wood part of the bow, rather than the hair part, creating a sound somewhat akin to dancing skeletons. At what CD time does this begin? _____

11. Describe the remainder of the movement:

12. What do you think Berlioz's goals were in this movement? Does he succeed? Refer to specific sections of the music in your answer.

LISTENING ACTIVITY 13.4:

Chopin, Nocturne in E-Flat Major, Op. 9 No. 2 (CD 2/4)

1. On your first listening, map out the form of the nocturne, continuing the diagram below. Include CD time information for the start of each section, in the little boxes on top of the section boxes.

A	A					Coda

2. How is the "A" section modified on its repeat?

3. Where do you think the climax of this piece is? What happens then?

4. What kind of emotion do you think Chopin is trying to convey in this piece? What does he do to get this across?

4. Section C begins at around CD time 2:02. Describe the music for the next half minute or so:

5. What happens next, at around CD time 2:43?

6. At about CD time 3:14, the music changes again. What earlier part of the piece is this most similar to?

7. At what time do you hear a return to Section A? _____

8. What is different about Section A this time?

9. At what CD time do you hear a repeat of the inverted motive described in Question 3, above? _____

10. How does the piece end?

11. Fill in the CD timer information for the start of each section:

A	A	B	C	A	B	End

12. Using the above diagram as reference, write a paragraph describing the expressive landscape of this piece, what you think Brahms is intending the listener to feel in each section and how he achieves this.

LISTENING ACTIVITY 13.6:

Smetana, "The Moldau" from Má vlast (Symphonic poem) (CD 2/6)

1. At the beginning Stage 1, what instruments are used to depict the flowing of the rivulets?

2. What instruments present the main theme at CD time 1:07?

3. Map out the subsidiary form of the theme.

4. The end of the theme gets interrupted by the sounds of hunting horns. At what CD time does this begin? _____

5. What feeling is this section supposed to evoke?

6. At what CD time does Stage 3 begin? _____

7. How does Smetana create the feeling of a folk wedding?

8. What instruments dominate the moonlit scene in Stage 4?

10. After Motive 2 repeats several times and changes, we hear Motive 1 as at the beginning, only accompanied by a solo instrument (at about CD time 3:39). What family does this solo instrument belong to? _____

11. We now hear a falling string line, followed by an orchestral swelling (at about 3:55), and these two ideas repeat. Then, another solo instrument plays a new musical idea, Motive 3, this time accompanied by single notes on the harp and a kind of watercolor wash in the strings (at about 4:13). What is this solo instrument? _____

12. Motive 3 is now taken up by two string instruments playing in octaves. At what CD time does this begin? _____

13. What happens after the strings repeat the new theme?

14. At what CD time does the English horn motive (Motive 2) come back? _____

15. Momentarily, the English horn continues (after about CD time 5:52), as if it had been trying to speak throughout the whole piece and only now has gotten the opportunity. Then, the piece seems to dissipate. We hear the main motive, lower and lower, then a fragment of the third motive, then several isolated *pizzicato* notes to wrap it up. Why do you think Debussy chose to end his piece this way?

16. Do you like this piece? Why or why not?

LISTENING ACTIVITY 14.1:

Stravinsky, The Rite of Spring *(ballet) (CD 2/8)*

1. At the beginning of *The Rite of Spring* we hear the famous opening bassoon line, alone at first then accompanied by French horn and clarinets. Using proper musical terms, describe the rhythm of the bassoon line.

2. After a moment or two, the bassoon repeats the opening line, now somewhat varied, and then the English horn takes over. Now, very gradually, the texture starts to thicken, with more and more instruments added. How would you characterize the music from about CD time 1:13 to 3:00?

3. At what CD time do you hear a repeat of the original bassoon melody? _____

4. We begin the next section, "Auguries of Spring (Dances of the Young Girls)" at about CD time 3:35. Describe the rhythm and the harmony at this point.

5. What kind of effect do you think Stravinsky was after here?

8. Is there any time when you think the music is meant to be subconscious—present, but beneath the level of audience awareness? Describe these scenes.

9. When is the music *meant* to be noticed in these films? (If you find any examples of diagetic music, make note.)

10. Overall, do you think this is a successful film score? Use examples from the film to explain your answer.

PHOTO/TEXT CREDITS

Captions/Source Lines for Meyer, Perspectives on Music

CHAPTER 1:   Photo by Nancy Richmond. Source: The Image Works, 1

CHAPTER 2:   Photo by Neal Preston. Source: CORBIS, 7

CHAPTER 3:   Photo by James L. Amos. Source: CORBIS, 14

CHAPTER 4:   Photo by David H. Wells. Source: CORBIS, 23

CHAPTER 5:   Photo by Rune Hellestad. Source: CORBIS, 29

CHAPTER 6:   Photo by Lynn Goldsmith. Source: CORBIS, 38

CHAPTER 7:   Photo by Ray Flerlage. Source: Chansley Entertainment Archives, 47

CHAPTER 8:   Source: AP/Wide World Photos, 67

CHAPTER 9:   Source: AP/Wide World Photos, 96

CHAPTER 10:   Photo by Joe Sohm. Source: The Image Works, 127

CHAPTER 11:   Source: CORBIS, 140

CHAPTER 12:   Photo by Donald Dietz. Source: Stock Boston, 150

CHAPTER 13:   Source: Getty Images, Inc. Hulton Archive by Getty Images, 182

CHAPTER 14:   Source: Corbis, 217

CHAPTER 15:   Source: Jack Vartoogian, 242

Meyer Perspectives on Music 1/e – Copyright Credits

CHAPTER 1–6:
[No copyrighted material, no credits.]

CHAPTER 7:   Listening Activity 7.1: Robert Johnson (1911–1938), "Cross Road Blues." © 1990 Lehsem II, LLC/Claud L. Johnson. Used by permission.

Listening Activity 7.2: Bessie Smith (1894?–1937), "Poor Man's Blues." © 1930 (renewed), 1974 FRANK MUSIC CORP. All rights reserved. Used by permission of Hal Leonard Corp.

Listening Activity 7.3: Willie Dixon, "Hoochie Coochie Man," recorded by Muddy Waters. © 1957 (renewed) HOOCHIE COOCHIE MUSIC (BMI)/Administered by BUG. All rights Reserved. Used By Permission. For additional information on the style of the blues please contact: The Blues Heaven Foundation (founded by Willie Dixon in 1981), 2120 S. Michigan Avenue, Chicago, IL 60616 USA. Phone (312) 808-1286 www.bluesheaven.com

Listening Activity 7.4: Kevin Moore (Keb' Mo'), "Am I Wrong," from the album "Keb' Mo'," released (p) 1994. Rights controlled by Warner-Tamerlane Publishing Corp., Miami, Florida.

CHAPTER 8:
[No copyrighted material, no credits.]

CHAPTER 9:   Listening Activity 9.1: Chuck Berry (b. 1926), "Johnny B. Goode." Copyright © 1958 by Arc Music Corporation (BMI), copyright renewed by Isalee Music. All Rights Reserved. International Copyright Secured. Used by Permission of Isalee Music Co. and Arc Music Corporation.

Listening Activity 9.3: Peter Brown & Robert Rans, "Material Girl," 1984. Rights controlled by Warner-Tamerlane Publishing Corp., Miami, Florida, A/C Frederick De Man DBA Candy Castle Music.

CHAPTER 10:   Listening Preparation 10.1: Tito Puente (1923–2000), "Mambo Gozón." Copyright © 1957 by Peer International Corporation. Copyright renewed. Used by permission.

Listening Preparation 10.2: H. Santiago Jiménez, lyrics to "Margarita," from the album "Little Joe: 20 de Colección" (Sony–Discos). SAMP © 1993. Used by permission of San Antonio Music Publishers, Inc.